GENDER SEGREGATION
AT WORK

GENDER SEGREGATION AT WORK

edited by
Sylvia Walby

Open University Press
Milton Keynes · Philadelphia

Open University Press
Open University Educational Enterprises Limited
12 Cofferidge Close
Stony Stratford
Milton Keynes MK11 1BY

and
242 Cherry Street
Philadelphia, PA 19106, USA

First Published 1988

British Library Cataloguing in Publication Data

Gender segregation at work.
   1. Women. Employment. Sex discrimination
   I. Walby, Sylvia
   331.4'133

   ISBN 0–335–15563–4
   ISBN 0–335–15562–6 Pbk

Library of Congress Cataloging-in-Publication Data

Gender segregation at work/ [edited by] Sylvia Walby.
   p. cm.
  Bibliography: p.
  Includes index.
  1. Pay equity—Great Britain. 2. Sex discrimination against
women—Great Britain. 3. Sexual harassment of women—Great Britain.
  I. Walby, Sylvia.
  HD6061.2.G7G46 1988 331.4'133'094—dc19
  ISBN 0–335–15563–4   ISBN 0–335–15562–6 (pbk.)

Typeset by Burns & Smith
Printed in Great Britain by Biddles Limited, Guildford and Kings Lynn

Contents

Tables and figures

Tables

Figures

Contributors

Cynthia Cockburn is a Senior Research Fellow in Sociology at the Department of Social Science and Humanities, The City University, London. She is author, among other books, of *Brothers: Male Dominance and Technological Change* (Pluto, 1983), *Machinery of Dominance: Women, Men and Technical Know-How* (Pluto, 1985) and *Two-Track Training: Sex Inequalities and the Youth Training Scheme* (Macmillan, 1987).

Sally Dench is a Senior Research Associate at the Department of Sociology, University of Liverpool. She is co-author of *The Changing Structure of Youth Labour Markets* (Department of Employment, 1987).

Valerie Ellis was formerly Lecturer in Industrial Sociology and Personnel Management at the University of Manchester Institute of Science and Technology (UMIST) and Research Associate at Templeton College, Oxford, and is now Assistant General Secretary of the Institution of Professional Civil Servants. Her publications include (as joint author) *Social Stratification and Trade Unionism* (Heinemann 1973), *A Professional Union* (Allen & Unwin, 1980), *Change in Trade Unions* (Hutchinson, 1981) and (author of) *The Role of Trade Unions in the Promotion of Equal Opportunities* (Equal Opportunities Commission/Social Science Research Council 1981).

Jane Mark-Lawson is a Senior Research Officer at the Manpower Services Commission. She was previously a researcher and lecturer at the University of Lancaster. Her publications include joint authorship of *Localities, Class and Gender* (Pion, 1985).

Chris Middleton is Lecturer in the Department of Sociological Studies, University of Sheffield. He is writing a book analysing the impact of capitalism on the sexual division of labour and patriarchal relations.

Annie Phizacklea is a Lecturer in the Department of Sociology, University of Warwick. She was previously a researcher with the Race Relations Research Unit. She is editor of *One Way Ticket: Migration and Female Labour* (Routledge, 1983) and joint author of *Labour and Racism* (Routledge, 1980).

Deborah Richardson is a Research Assistant in the Department of Sociology, University of Liverpool. She is co-author of *The Changing Structure of Youth Labour Markets* (Department of Employment, 1987).

Ken Roberts is Professor of Sociology, and Head of Department at the University of Liverpool. He is author of *School Leavers and Their Prospects* (Open University Press, 1983) and co-author of *The Changing Structure of Youth Labour Markets* (Department of Employment, 1987).

Olive Robinson is a Reader in the School of Management, University of Bath. She has researched and published extensively in the field of employment and pay structure, part-time employment and sex discrimination in labour markets.

Elizabeth Stanko is an Associate Professor of Sociology at Clark University, Worcester, Mass. She is author of *Intimate Intrusions: Women's Experience of Male Violence* (Routledge, 1985).

Sylvia Walby is Lecturer in Sociology and Director of the Women's Studies Research Centre, University of Lancaster. She is author of *Patriarchy at Work* (Polity, 1986) and joint author of *Localities, Class and Gender* (Pion, 1985) and *Contemporary British Society* (Cambridge, Polity Press, 1988).

Anne Witz is a Lecturer in Sociology at the University of Exeter and was previously a graduate student and lecturered in Sociology at the University of Lancaster. She has researched and published in the area of gender and professionalisation in the medical division of labour.

Acknowledgements

We would like to thank Basil Blackwell Ltd for permission to publish the paper by Chris Middleton, a longer version of which is appearing in Ray Pahl (ed.) *On Work* (Blackwell, 1988).

1: Introduction

Sylvia Walby

Gender segregation at work is the most important cause of the wages gap between men and women in Western economies. Its existence defies conventional theories of gender relations in employment since it is inexplicable in terms of women's position in the family.

This book is based on papers presented at conference, financed by the Economic and Social Research Council, to discuss segregation in employment, organized under the auspices of the Social Stratification Group. The volume addresses the explanation of gender segregation at work, the changing forms of segregation, whether it is increasing or decreasing and deliberate attempts to reduce it.

These debates have implications for wider questions of social theory. The positioning of the genders in the occupational order is central to issues of social stratification. It is vital to questions of the place of women in the class structure, and hence of the nature of the class structure itself, as most sociologists would now agree. Indeed, the previous symposium organized by the Social Stratification Group addressed precisely these issues of gender and stratification (Crompton and Mann 1986). The nature and extent of the differential barriers to the social mobility of men and women affect the working of the class structure in important ways. Understanding the maintenance of gender segregation at work is, then, central to explaining the sexual division of paid work and, indeed, of the division of labour more generally.

In the USA occupational segregation has recently become a major issue of intellectual debate because it is at the basis of the hot political topic of comparable worth. This is beginning to occur in Britain with the recent amendment to the Equal Pay Act which makes it possible to argue for equal pay for work of equal value, not merely if women and men are doing similar work. Potentially this legislation provides a solution to the problem of occupational segregation for women's pay, since it enables comparisons of economic worth across occupations. This places on the political and intellectual agenda the question of whether occupational segregation can be justified as a rational economic practice (as conservative economists argue) or whether it is a patriarchal protection racket which interferes with the efficient working of labour markets and firms, as well as denying women social justice. In the USA there has been a plethora of work, with several authoritative volumes being generated by research funded through the National Academy of Science (Reskin 1984; Reskin and Hartmann 1986; Treiman 1979; Treiman and Hartmann 1981). As yet British research has no comparable funding.

Segregation and the wages gap

Gender segregation at work is the key to the paradox that, while women's paid employment has increased dramatically since the Second World War, there has been little improvement in their pay and conditions relative to men. Conventional economic theory would have predicted a convergence between men's and women's remuneration as women's labour market experience increased relative to that of men, and as the gap in the educational qualifications between men and women narrowed. Yet there has been little reduction in the wages gap. It is the separation of women's from men's work which is the key to the solution to the paradox.

This is because the wages gap between men and women is not caused primarily by differences in education and skills (or human capital). Instead this inequality is largely due to women being more often in low-paid occupations than men, while the differences in the wage rates between the occupations is not explicable in terms of skill or training. This interpretation is also the view of the US National Academy of Science, in its official report *Women, Work and Wages* (Treiman and Hartmann 1981). Drawing on econometric analysis, the authors demonstrate that differences in human capital explain less than half of the gap between men's and women's wage rates.

The explanation of occupational segregating, then, becomes the crux of an explanation of wage inequality between men and women. Conventionally women's position in paid work has been considered to be a consequence of their position in the family. This challenge to human capital theory is thus also a challenge to a presumption which is widely held through a range of social sciences. No longer can women's position in paid work be read off from the family; no longer must women 'wait for their liberation from the family' (Giddens 1973: 288) before their significance for the class or occupational structure can be realised. Causal forces other than the family must be addressed if an explanation for women's disadvantaged position in employment is to be found.

Patterns of segregation

Segregation has both horizontal and vertical components (Hakim 1979). Women both do jobs which are simply different from those that men do (horizontal segregation) and also work at lower levels in the occupational hierarchy (vertical segregation). The degree of segregation is greater the more detailed the level of analysis. A survey of jobs sampled at the level of the establishment showed that 45 per cent contained no women at all, while 21 per cent employed no men (McIntosh 1980). The Department of Employment/Office of Population Censuses and Surveys survey of 6,000 women showed that 63 per cent of women worked only with other women, while among the husbands of these women 81 per cent worked only with other men (Martin and Roberts 1984: 27–8). The intensity of segregation varies by occupation, being highest in semi-skilled domestic and factory occupations and lowest in the higher occupational categories, especially professionals (Martin and Roberts 1984: 27).

The segregation of the contemporary British workforce by sex can be seen from data in Table 1.1. In almost all of the occupational groupings women are significantly either over- or under-represented. A similar picture emerges if an industrial classification is used. Dex (1987) suggests that a distinctive set of labour market barriers and segments exists for women.

Chapter 3 in this volume, by Cockburn, includes a description of some of these features of contemporary sex segregation. In 1986 men held 89 per cent of general managerial jobs and 91 per cent of professional jobs in science, engineering and technology. In mechanical engineering men are employed in 86 per cent of the jobs; while in retail distribution women are 67 per cent of the workforce. Part-time women workers are employed in an even narrower range of jobs than full-time women workers; all bar 8 per cent are to be found in selling, clerical, education, health and welfare, cleaning, catering and hairdressing.

Segregation by sex is not confined to Britain, nor even to the capitalist world, since it is to be found in pre-capitalist Britain (as Middleton shows in Chapter 5) and in the post-capitalist USSR (Lapidus 1976). However, it does vary a little by country, both in which jobs are allocated to women (the majority of doctors are women in the USSR) and in intensity. In a comparison of Britain, Sweden, the USA and West Germany, Jonung (1983) finds that Sweden has the highest rate of segregation and West Germany the lowest.

Segregation in employment is by ethnicity as well as by gender, with complex patterns as these intersect. Black women are subject to greater restrictions in their access to good employment conditions and pay than any other group, and we need to be careful not to overgeneralise from the experience of white women. Chapter 4 by Phizacklea details the nature of this additional layer of segregation. She argues that the historical legacy of colonialism has been important in the construction of racism in contemporary Britain, with disadvantages for all black people. The employment niches available to black women are usually in the most vulnerable parts of the economy, making efforts to improve

Table 1.1   Occupation by gender, Great Britain, 1986.

Occupational grouping	*Percent female*
Managerial (general management)	11
Professional and related supporting management and administration	20
Professional and related in education, welfare and health	69
Literary, artistic and sports	32
Professional and related in science, engineering, technology and similar fields	9
Managerial (excluding general management)	16
Clerical and related	74
Selling	57
Security and protective service	11
Catering, cleaning, hairdressing and other personal services	76
Farming, fishing and related	10
Materials processing (excluding metal)	24
Making and repairing (excluding metal and electrical)	35
Processing, making, repairing and related (metal and electrical)	5
Painting, repetitive assembling, product packaging and related	45
Construction, mining and related not identified elsewhere	0.4
Transport operating, materials moving and storing and related	4
Miscellaneous	5
Total	42

Source: adapted from Equal Opportunities Commission (EOC) 1987b: figure 3.4; ultimate data source: *New Earnings Survey*.

their position especially difficult. Some of the most exploited workers, such as Asian homeworkers, are relatively hidden from view, often even outside official records.

Progress or regress?

Distinctions in the employment of different social groups, such as genders or ethnic groups, have been predicted to wither away with the development of capitalism or with the full development of an industrialised economy. Marx suggested that the working class would become more homogeneous. Likewise, human capital theory suggests that increases in women's educational qualifications relative to those of men might lead to a decrease in segregation, and the increase in women's labour-market experience to an increase in women's employment opportunities. Thus both these Marxist and conservative theories would predict a decrease in segregation.

However, Edwards, Gordon and Reich argue that there has been an increase in segmentation of the labour market with the development of capitalism, as a result of the advantages which accrue to capital from a divided workforce; while Hartmann considers that there has been little change in the extent of segregation since pre-capitalist times.

It is primarily theories which focus on the causal power of capital or the market which predict the reduction of differentiation between workers. Theories which have paid more attention to the political level tend not to suggest such an evolutionary development. It is those writers who examine general economic laws, such as Marx and the human capital theorists, who see the withering away of worker differentiation or segregation. Feminist writers such as Hartmann who see the organisation of men around their own interests as an important part of patriarchy do not predict an elimination of segregation with the development of capitalism. Neither do Marxists such as Edwards, Gordon and Reich, who emphasize the importance of struggle between capital and labour in the development of particular forms of capitalist social relations.

Early empirical studies, such as those of Hakim (1979, 1981), found very little change in the segregation of men and women. In the period between 1901 and 1971 she found only small reductions and only marginal decreases in the mid-1970s (which she suggested were rather a result of men moving into women's occupations than vice versa).

Hakim's evidence does not address changes in the 1980s, and it might be thought that more recent developments would facilitate a reduction in segregation by sex in employment. There has been a significant reduction in the gap between the qualifications of young men and women leaving school over the last couple of decades. Girls now gain more O-levels than boys, and the gap in A-levels and degrees is closing (EOC 1986). Further, in so far as there have been cultural changes in the expectations relating to work for men and women, we might expect that they would have greatest impact on the young, rather than on those more set in their ways. This would be expected to lead to a lesser degree of segregation by sex within youth labour markets than among those for adults.

Roberts, Richardson and Dench in Chapter 8 examine patterns of segregation among young workers who have just entered the labour force. These researchers examined recruitment policies and the structure of youth labour markets in 308 firms in the mid-1980s. They find that there is little change and that youth labour markets are still highly segregated. The changing gap in levels of educational qualification appears to have made little impact among these workers. Neither have the considerable changes in the business environments of these firms, and their shape and size, had much impact. They find quite blatant sexism among managers, despite the 1975 Sex Discrimination Act. Female entrants are denied the same training as boys, so are likely to do worse in the future. They suggest that firms focus on the short run in their recruitment decisions and fail to consider longer-run changes if the present is satisfactory. While outside factors such as the different qualifications of young men and women and an uneven domestic division of labour are seen to play a part, so too are short-sighted managerial decisions.

Few British writers have yet addressed the question as to whether segregation might be on the increase. Resegregation is, however, a possibility. The development of part-time work can be considered just such an eventuality, as Robinson argues in Chapter 9. The definition and conceptualisation of segregation are important here both in order to identify accurately the processes at work, but also in order to measure the extent of the segregation. Robinson argues that the division between part-time and full-time work is itself a form of segmentation of the labour market. This division entails different conditions of employment, different access to legal protection and *de facto* different levels of pay. Almost all part-time workers are female, so this form of segmentation of the labour market is also a form of gender segregation. The increase in the extent of part-time working is thus an increase in gender segregation at work. Robinson convincingly argues that these changes cannot be seen simply in terms of the changing technical requirements of employers, but must be analysed in terms of the social relations, especially gender relations, in employment.

Crompton and Sanderson (1986), in a paper originally given at the same conference, suggested that some women were entering traditional male areas of employment. These were especially those women who gained professional qualifications which gave them access to a range of top jobs. However, this is a very small proportion of total jobs.

There has not been the general reduction in segregation which some theories predicted would occur with the development of capitalism, industrialisation and increasing periods of time being spent by women in paid work. The overall picture suggests a widening differentiation of the occupational positions between women, with women at the top doing better and women at the bottom doing worse. While there does seem to have been some increase in the number of women gaining access to qualifications and jobs in previously heavily male professions, this does not appear to be a process which extends to lower levels of occupations. Youth labour markets appear as segregated as ever, while the expansion of badly paid, low-level, part-time work, which is a segment of the labour market almost entirely confined to women, adds to the segregation of men and women in employment.

Explanations

The explanation of segregation is contested in several different directions. On the one hand, the conventional view holds that women's position in the labour force can be explained in terms of their performance of domestic work; on the other, the structured labour market theorists focus on the processes within the labour market itself, rather than on processes prior to it. The conventional view is held both by orthodox economists and by some Marxists, though for different reasons: the former because of a belief in the market as accurately transmitting the pressures for the demand and supply of labour, the latter because of the theoretical priority given to production rather than the market. These positions have come under extensive criticism by writers in the field of labour market segmentation for their failure to deal with the structuring of the labour market itself.

Those who focus on labour market structures are not unanimous in how these might be explained, and this volume contains some of these debates. On the one hand, Witz (Chapter 6) and Cockburn (Chapter 3) argue for the importance of theorising patriarchal forces in the construction of gender segregation at work. On the other, Middleton (Chapter 5) argues that other social relations, in his period feudal ones, should be given theoretical priority. Witz and Middleton argue this issue using historical data, while Cockburn focuses on the contemporary period. Cockburn argues that we cannot see the gendering of jobs as an isolated phenomenon, but that it is related to the gendering of many aspects of social relations. In a society where items from clothes to colours (pink and blue), from notions of rationality to toilets, are gendered, it is unsurprising that jobs are gendered too. Cockburn goes on to examine the role of cultural work in maintaining sex-segregated employment, of the identification of certain aspects of jobs with the cultural attributes of one sex or the other (e.g. hard and soft).

Stanko (Chapter 7) also addresses the significance of non-economic issues in the maintenance of sex segregation in her analysis of sexual harassment at work. Women more often report sexual harassment if they are working in non-traditional areas. She asks whether this is because sexual harassment is intensified if women enter male occupations and acts to deter women from crossing such employment boundaries. Stanko suggests that harassment is endemic rather than unusual and that the difference may be more of willingness to report harassment than actual differences in occurrence. In female occupations, such as waitressing and secretarial work, sexual harassment may be recognised as an occupational hazard, but women entering non-traditional areas may have expectations of full equality with their male colleagues and be more shocked by unwanted sexual advances, which they are more prepared to report as harassment.

Middleton demonstrates the historical continuity in segregation in employment by sex by looking at wage labour among the English peasantry of the feudal period, thus substantiating his argument that segregation is not to be explained in terms of the new entry of women into the capitalist economy. While disagreeing with the uses of the concept of patriarchy on theoretical grounds he argues that gender inequality cannot be seen as an exogenous variable, since these social relations are too deeply entwined in the wider matrix of historically specific social relations.

Witz, unlike Middleton, argues that the concept of patriarchy is a necessary theoretical tool in the analysis of gender segregation at work. She considers instances of sex segregation to be historically constituted as patriarchal structures, as the outcome of processes of gendered occupational closure. She argues that we can write of patriarchal modes of occupational closure when male power is utilised to sustain gender-specific forms of closure. Witz differentiates between various forms of closure, developing the distinctions made by theorists such as Parkin for ungendered forms of occupational closure. She uses an analysis of the historical development of different forms of gender segregation within medical occupations in the nineteenth and twentieth centuries to substantiate her argument. Medicine, midwifery and radiography show different forms of closure against women. In particular Witz distinguishes between exclusionary closure in which men control their own occupation and demarcationary closure in which there is an attempt to control the boundary with adjacent occupations. Finally Witz turns to wider issues of the key location of patriarchal power in contemporary society, suggesting that her analyses of occupational closure demonstrate the greater significance of patriarchal power in civil society as compared to the state.

A common feature of both human capital theory and cultural theories is their implication that women actively choose their areas of employment themselves. In human capital theory women make rational choices using economic criteria, usually as part of a household work strategy, while in cultural theories the choice is based on adherence to particular values associated with femininity. For both approaches there is no implication of unfairness or discrimination involved, and hence no need for public policy intervention. Indeed, in a legal case in the USA the defendant in a case of sex discrimination, Sears, a large department store, called as an expert witness in its defence a historian who held the cultural values position. The court room became a battle between feminist historians with different theoretical positions on the causes of segregation (Kessler-Harris 1987).

The significance of gender segregation for class theory

The conventional analysis of gender and employment was that women's position was to be explained in terms of the family, which enabled theorists to treat the determination of gender as a variable exogenous to the determination of employment and class structures. The current analyses of gender segregation at work challenge such an explanation of women's position in the occupational structure and hence the treatment of gender as an exogenous variable in class analysis. Rather gender relations in employment are critically structured by processes within production, within the firm, and also by political forces, such as state policy. Women are not peripheral to class theory 'until they receive their liberation from the family'; the family is not the only social structure of relevance in determining the position of women in the class structure.

The relationship between occupational structure and the state is gendered. There have been major changes in state policy as a result of gendered political struggle, which have affected the position of women in the occupational and class structure. It is inappropriate to see the state only in class terms. State power was used in patriarchal interests to exclude women from the skilled manual trades at the end of the wars; it is now being used to undercut forms of patriarchal closure against women. This change in policy has a significant impact on the location of women in the class structure.

Occupational closure has both a class and a gender dimension. The closure of an occupation against others is a strategy frequently employed by men against women. This is always in a class context, but is not theoretically reducible to that. In terms of the debate on segregation, what is of especial significance is the greater restriction of the upward mobility of women through clerical to managerial grades than is the case for men. The upward mobility of male clerks has been used by Stewart, Prandy and Blackburn (1980) to argue that clerks are inappropriately designated proletarian, and indeed to argue for a reformulation of the link between occupation and class to take account of typical occupational trajectories. The failure of this situation to apply to the majority of clerks, who are women, who remain confined to the lower grades for their occupational lives, must cast some doubt on the general application of this theory. That is, occupational segregation which restricts women's mobility has significant implications here for class theory.

The most important change in the occupational structure of post-war Britain has been the enormous increase in the proportion of women in it. Women are not randomly distributed across this system, but concentrated in two areas in the middle and lower levels. Their distribution is shaped by the pattern of occupational segregation, and their mobility through it is severely curtailed by it.

Politics and legislation

Gender segregation at work is now set to become a major legal and political issue, since there has been recent legislation which enables women to claim 'equal pay for work of equal value', not merely 'equal pay for the same work'. In the USA this has already become a large campaign around the issue of 'comparable worth'; there is every reason to believe that the same may happen in the UK.

Legislation to tackle discrimination against women in employment has been operative in Britain since 1975 when the Equal Pay Act of 1970 came into force and the Sex Discrimination Act was passed by Parliament. This latter Act was designed to tackle the issue of occupational segregation which confined women to the lower-paid jobs by making discrimination against women in recruitment and promotion illegal. The impact of this legislation is subject to a variety of interpretations. Some have argued that it was responsible for the closing of the wages gap between men and women from 62 per cent in 1970 to 74 per cent in 1978 (Weir and McIntosh 1982). However, this gap has now remained roughly constant over the last ten years. The lack of continuing effectiveness of the legislation has been attributed to a variety of causes. The inadequacy of the machinery to assess claims, which built in a bias for patriarchal forces, is a serious problem (Gregory 1987). Further, this legislation can have an impact only in so far as women are changing jobs and considering moving into better areas of paid employment. It is thus a very slow route to change, since major changes in career trajectory are rare and usually confined to the early stages of a person's occupational history. Essentially, this is significant for new entrants and for women seeking promotion. It cannot tackle the massive sectoral segregation which underpins much occupational segregation.

Comparable worth campaigns in the USA have been addressing this issue for some time and are beginning to arise in the UK as a result of the equal value amendment to the equal opportunity legislation at the end of 1983. This is an attempt to revalue the work that large numbers of women do, rather than get women in higher-paying jobs or having to prove discrimination in individual cases. It entails the systematic evaluation of women's work and its comparison with an evaluation of male jobs. It uses techniques of job evaluation which establish a number of dimensions of comparison and allocate points for each job along each of these, finally summing these points for the weighted dimensions, to give a total job score. This is the value of the job which is used to establish its pay. It can lead to significant increases in the pay of women workers, whose jobs typically involve more skill, responsibility and effort than the previous methods of pay determination suggested. Rather than attempting to eradicate occupational segregation, this strategy tries to deal with its consequences for women, involving changes in the rates of pay between occupations, rather than moving women between occupations.

The comparable worth campaign is now of major proportions in the USA, with thousands of women having received significant pay rises as a consequence. This is even though there is no national legislation establishing the case for 'equal pay for work of equal value'. Rather the campaigns have been fought at the level of the states, in their role as major employers, and against large employers, typically public sector ones. The Pay Equity League is a national federation of dozens of bodies interested in this issue on behalf of women.

In Britain comparable worth came on the political agenda after the European Community decreed that the UK legislation for equal opportunities did not meet the standards of the Treaty of Rome (the UK was not alone in this). The 'equal pay for work of equal value' amendment was reluctantly introduced on to the British statute book by the Conservative government in response to this European legal intervention. Many cases are now pending under this legislation. At the time of writing, in 1988, few cases have been finally resolved, because of appeals against early rulings. Some of the early cases were victories for working women, for example the case of the woman cook who won equal pay with a welder in a shipyard. The British legislation is complex and with loopholes. Nevertheless this could be a major initiative on equal pay with far reaching consequences. It sidesteps the problem of occupational segregation as a barrier to equal pay for women, since individual women no longer have to be doing the same work as men in order to have their claims assessed. In short, if the machinery of the law sustains the spirit of the law, one of the major causes of the wages gap between men and women, occupational segregation, will have been short-circuited. However, whether this will occur remains to be seen.

Trade unions and worker organisation

Legislation is not the only route to change in segregation in employment. Recently British trade unions have begun to make efforts to change the situation. This is in striking contrast to the majority of previous trade union policies towards women. As the historical papers by Witz (Chapter 6) and Mark-Lawson (Chapter 11) demonstrate, organised workers have not always been supportive to women's opportunities for paid work. Ellis (Chapter 10) describes the turn-around in practices by the Trade Union Congress and major unions since the mid-1970s (although of course the specialist women's unions have always represented the interests of their members). Partly as a consequence of the increasing representation of women within these trade union bodies, partly because of the growing proportion of women in the labour market and partly as a result of issues such as employer initiatives on 'flexibility' trade unions have paid more attention to the needs of women members. These efforts range from conference resolutions and the issuing of policy statements, to setting up women's or equal opportunities committees and working groups, to joint committees with employers and negotiation of policy changes with employers, to campaigns for better child-care facilities. Ellis provides a comprehensive, up-to-the-minute guide to the equal opportunities policies at the forefront of British trade unions today.

Mark-Lawson argues that the relationship between occupational segregation and political action is two-way. Not only do male workers organise to create and maintain segregation, but these forms of segregation significantly affect the propensity of women to engage in political action around their own interests.

Flexibility and segregation

Recent developments in the organisation of the firm have been characterised as 'flexible' working. The increase in part-time working has been identified elsewhere (Atkinson 1986; Beechey and Perkins 1987; Hakim 1987b; Walby 1988) as part of the process of the creation of greater 'flexibility' among the workforce. Employers, in their drive to increase their room for manoeuvre in terms of the amount of labour that they employ, increasingly employ part-time women workers, whose conditions of employment make them easier to shed in times of contraction, and whose hours of work are easily varied without the need to pay overtime bonuses. In so far as the increase in part-time work is to be seen as an increase in segregation, then segregation and flexibility would appear to be part of the same process. This might seem contradictory given that flexibility is ostensibly being introduced to break down labour market rigidities, and it might appear that segregation constituted just such a instance of labour market inflexibility. The answer to this paradox is that part-time work increases an employer's numerical flexibility in that it makes it easier to vary the level of labour inputs at short notice; but it also increases divisions and distinctions within the workforce which cut across functional flexibility or the ability of the employer to break down traditional distinctions between jobs.

Conclusion

Gender segregation at work underlies the wages gap between men and women. Despite the increase of women in employment, this has diminished little since the turn of the century. It is widely deplored today as a restriction on economic efficiency and inconsistent with social justice for women. Yet gender segregation tenaciously persists.

As part of an international political economy it is not surprising if attempts to reduce segregation pioneered in the USA are applied to the British situation. The equal value amendment paves the way for comparable worth cases to be taken through the British as well as US courts. However, the peculiarities of the English mean that this will take a different form here. On the one hand, the absence of the ability to take collective cases or class actions through the British courts restricts the use of the legislation as compared to the USA, where, curiously given the liberal individualist ideology, this solidaristic legal form is allowed. On the other hand, the greater extent of unionisation in Britain means that there is greater potential for collective action in the workplace to support equal value claims. However, the success of this latter route depends at least partially on how far the unions have been transformed by the new feminist pressure away from their patriarchal heritage.

The solution to the problem of gender segregation depends upon its causes; on this the theorists are far from agreed, as we shall see in the next chapter.

2: Segregation in employment in social and economic theory

Sylvia Walby

Introduction

The analysis of segregation in employment is not only important in its own right but also has challenging implications for existing social and economic theory. Segregation in employment is the key to the explanation of the wages gap between men and women and the general question of the occupational location of women. Thus it is also a key to the analysis of social class, which is generally seen to be closely if not directly related to occupational position.

The fundamental debate is between those who theorise segregation as a result of rational, freely made choices and those who argue that it is a result of structural constraints on women. The latter subdivided between those who theorise these constraints as a result, ultimately, of capitalism or of patriarchy.

There are three further themes which run throughout the debates on segregation in employment. Firstly, there is the issue as to whether the family is the basis of women's position in paid employment. Traditionally, explanations of the disadvantages women face in paid work have focused upon their position in the family. This position is commonly found among both neo-classical economists and Marxist writers. In contrast, the significance of organisational and political forces in the structuring of labour markets has been argued by a variety of writers whose common position is that labour markets are not pure markets. These include institutional labour market economists and radical economists as well as dual systems theorists. Most of the contributors to this volume have argued for the greater importance of labour market processes than has traditionally been the case.

A second line of differences is that between those who stress material factors and those who emphasise cultural processes. This draws upon more general debates as to the determination of gender divisions and cuts across the first debate. It raises the question of how far inequalities within the workplace are determined by processes of socialisation prior to it.

A third and more specialised debate is over whether a concept and theory of patriarchy are necessary for an understanding of segregation (and indeed women's position in society more generally). This again raises broader issues as to the understanding of gender relations and their interconnection with other social relations, especially those of class and race.

These foci of debate cut across more traditional differences in the social sciences, between schools of thought such as the neo-classical economists, institutional labour market theorists, Marxists and feminists. Nevertheless they will keep re-emerging during the ensuing discussion of theories of segregation in social and economic theory.

Human capital theory

Neo-classical economists have typically explained the position of women in paid work in terms of their lesser human capital, arguing that women have acquired fewer skills and qualifications and less labour market experience than men (Mincer 1962, 1966). They suggest that this is due to the domestic division of labour in which women spend more time than men looking after children and performing other household tasks. Men are considered to spend more time in paid work. This division of labour is supposed to be part of a household work strategy in which the interests of the family unit as a whole are best served by this form of specialisation, and in which the individuals rationally and voluntarily engage.

Polachek (1976, 1981) argues that human capital theory can explain occupational segregation, in that women choose those occupations for which their lesser skills will give the best rewards, and in which they are least penalised for their intermittent work patterns. Women's occupations are considered to require fewer skills than are men's and to attach fewer penalties to interrupted work histories. Human capital is considered to decline during a period out of the labour market, resulting in lower wages on re-entry after childbirth. Women are predicted to choose those occupations where this decline is least steep.

However, Polachek's account has empirical problems. England (1982, 1984) found that the decline in women's earnings consequent on a period out of the labour force was not significantly different between male and female occupations. That is, it could not be argued that they chose women's occupations because it would penalise them less harshly for a period out of the labour market for child rearing.

Human capital theory also has more general problems in its overall presumption that workers get paid wages proportionate to their human capital: that is, that there is a perfect labour market. It is further problematic in its constitution of the household rather than the individual as the unit of decision-making which represents the interests of all its members equally.

The issue of whether there has been an increase or decrease in the extent of occupational segregation in recent years constitutes a further test of human capital theory. This theory would predict that occupational segregation should decline as women's possessions of human capital rises towards that of men. The decrease in the gap in the educational qualifications of boys and girls and the decrease in the number of years women take out of the labour market to have children, hence increasing their work experience, might be considered to be closing the human capital gap between men and women. Yet there is little evidence that this is leading to a decline in segregation, except in restricted areas of the professions. Hakim (1979, 1981) found only very small decreases in occupational segregation between the turn of the century and the mid-1970s, while Roberts, Richardson and Dench argue later in this volume that youth labour markets, which might be expected to reflect the latest changes, are not significantly less segregated than adult ones. Crompton and Sanderson (1986) have noted that there is some movement of women into the professions consequent upon their gaining high-level qualifications; however, this is a very small part of the labour market. Overall, then, human capital theory is contradicted by the lack of significant decline in occupational segregation to be found in the data available.

Cultural theories

Human capital theory is based on the assumption that people act as a consequence of rational calculations of economic benefit. It is thus quite different from explanations in terms of culture. This latter approach usually focuses upon the socialisation of women into different social and cultural values from men. It suggests that people choose jobs which are in line with their beliefs as to appropriate masculine or feminine behaviour. An implication of this is that the major causal determinants of gender segregation lie outside the workplace.

Many accounts of gender divisions in employment do not develop a theory of segregation, but make passing reference to 'tradition' as its basis. Culture and ideology are often heavily implicated in this notion of tradition. For instance, Oppenheimer (1970), in her pioneering analysis of the significance of gender segregation in changes in women's employment, uses a concept of 'sex-typing' which is heavily cultural. Similarly Rubery and Tarling (1982), in their otherwise powerful account of the relationship between women's employment and the recession, largely fall back on the concept of 'tradition' to explain gender segregation (with some additional reference to the family). We shall see below that even some versions of dual labour market theory draw heavily upon notions of ideology in their work (Barron and Norris 1976). However, these accounts do not make a strong case for an explanation of gender segregation in terms of culture; the point is rather that many writers on women's employment use this argument implicitly.

One of the more developed versions of this approach is presented by Matthaei in her economic history of women and men in the USA. Matthaei (1982) argues that the sex-typing of occupations is adhered to by both sexes in order to sustain their conceptions of their own masculinity and femininity. Each new job is constructed as suitable for either men or women. The sex-typing of occupations is maintained because individuals have a strong interest in maintaining their identity as either masculine or feminine and thus would not only try to stop members of the other sex from entering their area of employment, and contaminating it with inappropriate gender values, but also hesitate to enter the terrain of the other sex themselves for the same reason. Matthaei provides an economic history of the USA in terms of these issues. She concludes by suggesting that there is currently a breakdown in the sexual division of labour.

Matthaei's work provides a much needed historical dimension to the development of sex segregation and is interesting in its explanation of the links between different aspects of gender relations in society. However, her work is problematic for several reasons. Firstly, her historical accounts omit the struggles which took place over the sex-typing of the various occupations that she describes; these processes were less consensual than she suggests. For instance, male clerks fought the entry of women into this occupation; it was not an issue settled by some smoothly functioning market (see Walby 1986). This is related to a second problem: the relations between individual and collective action in the development and maintenance of the sex-typing of occupations. Matthaei treats the issue of boundary maintenance in individual terms; it is an individual who decides not to try to break with the prevailing gender ethos of a job. But this only addresses one small part of the questions around the development and maintenance of sex-typed occupations. It omits the collective social struggles both over the definition of occupations as men's or women's and over the location of the occupation as a whole in the hierarchy of occupations. This lack of analysis of collective struggle is related to a third problem in Matthaei's work: the refusal to conceptualise, let alone theorise, gender inequality.

Segmented labour market theory

Segregation and segmentation

There is sometimes some confusion as to the distinction between the concepts of segregation and segmentation. Segregation is the concentration of persons by ascriptive criteria such as sex and race in particular sectors (here of employment), while segmentation is the differentiation of the labour market into distinctive types of employment, which may or may not be filled disproportionately by members of different gender or ethnic groups. Thus theories of a segmented labour market are one type of approach to the question of the explanation of the segregation of genders and ethnic groups into different types of occupations.

Dual labour market theory

Barron and Norris (1976) explicitly apply segmented labour market theory to sexual divisions and explore the specifically gendered aspects of dual labour markets. They try to explain why it is women who tend to fill the secondary slots. Secondary sector jobs are characterised by low pay and instability; there is little mobility across the boundary between primary and secondary sector jobs (Barron and Norris 1976: 49). Barron and Norris suggest that the structure of the labour market is a consequence both of attempts by employers to retain workers whose skills they need and also of an attempt by employers to buy off the best-organised workers.

Barron and Norris suggest that women are primarily secondary workers because of five characteristics: dispensability, clearly visible social differences, little interest in acquiring training, low economism and lack of solidarity. These characteristics are partially the result of the individual's labour market experience and partly the result of aspects of the social structure outside the labour market. It would appear that employers hold unsubstantiated beliefs that women possess these five characteristics of secondary workers. Employers perceive women as conventionally set apart from men and with less commitment to advancement at work because of women's orientation to their domestic situation and their socialisation. Women are seen as reluctant to struggle to obtain, or even seek, high monetary reward. Thus the characteristics of women at work are seen to fit with those required from secondary rather than primary workers.

However, despite Barron and Norris's emphasis on the importance of the labour market, much of their article is taken up with merely a description of the characteristics that women bring, or are believed by employers to bring, to the labour market. They describe the structuring of the labour market into two sectors in non-gender-specific terms and mistakenly ignore the structure of the market by sexual divisions. They treat sexual differentiation as determined largely outside the labour market by the sexual divisions of labour in the household. It is then incorrectly treated as a given which is unmodified by the workings of the labour market. There are two ways in which Barron and Norris do approach the problem of patriarchal structures, but fail to complete their analysis. The most important is the discussion of women's supposed lack of solidarism. This is always seen in terms of women not managing to organise, never in terms of men being organised against women in the labour market. The nearest they get to men being an opposing force is to suggest that male trade unionists do not assist women trade unionists to the point of being obstructive. They never mention men actively organising against women, despite its importance (Cockburn 1983; Hartmann 1979; Walby 1986). Barron and Norris do refer to general attitudes of hostility to women working, both in general and in relation to particular jobs, but this is seen as relatively diffuse rather than as organised. In fact, much of their article is about attitudes; it refers to ideological intervention in the labour market more than political and organisational interventions. I would argue that they are mistaken to see patriarchal intervention in the labour market as so confined to the level of beliefs. Another problem with Barron and Norris's work is to be found in the incorrect assumption that the primary and secondary division in the labour market extends across all jobs in Britain. For instance, clerical work in which such a high proportion of employed women are engaged does not fit into this dichotomy very well. Rather this division seems more appropriate when limited to the manual jobs in manufacturing for which it was originally developed by Doeringer and Piore (1971). 'Dualism' is not the best way to characterise the institutional rigidities of the labour market especially in relation to gender.

Marxist segmented labour market theory

Most Marxist writers on work have ignored the issue of gender relations in employment, and even fewer have addressed the issue of segregation. The orthodox Marxist approach has theoretically prioritised the relations between capital and labour, and infrequently considered the analysis of the inequality between men and women to be of importance. Further, the traditional Marxist focus on production rather than the market has assigned processes within the labour market a secondary place in any explanatory framework. Attempts to remedy the neglect of gender inequality in analyses of employment have typically involved an explanatory focus upon capital and the family, not the labour market. For example, Braverman (1974) explains the post-war increase in women's employment to be a result of, firstly, the deskilling of labour processes by capital and, secondly, the transfer of tasks from the household to capitalist production. Indeed, Beechey argued (in 1978) that the market was not a significant determinant of gender relations in employment. It is thus not surprising that with these theoretical principles most Marxist analyses have not addressed the issue of gender segregation in employment.

However, there is a significant exception in the work of Edwards, Gordon and Reich, in their Marxist analysis of gender and ethnic segmentation of the labour market. Edwards, Gordon and Reich combine the Marxist emphasis on capital labour struggle with a focus on labour market processes. Edwards (1979) provides a theoretical and historical account of the changing forms of labour market segmentation. He argues that different stages in the development of capitalism give rise to different forms of workplace relations and opportunities for both control by employers and resistance by workers. During early forms of capitalist development, workshops were small and forms of control varied and unsystematic. In so far as these conditions of employment still exist, as they do in some small firms, then these forms of employment relations also exist. Edwards argues that as firms grew bigger, and forms of resistance more effective, employers experimented with a variety of new forms of control, settling for more systematic and structured forms. The first of these was that of technical control, best exemplified by the control exercised over workers by the conveyor belt which regulated the speed and intensity of labour. However, this had the disadvantage from the employers' viewpoint, that it was open to collective resistance from organised workers. The other form of control, the bureaucratic, is based on countless small rules and expectations of regulated career advancement if these are successfully obeyed over a period of time.

Edwards suggests that each of these forms of control gives rise to a distinctive labour market segment, and to a specific class fraction based on each one. However, labour market segmentation is not the only basis of class fractionalisation for Edwards. At the end of his book he introduces the idea that women and blacks also constitute class fractions, and that these class fractions cut across the three labour market segments he has earlier identified. Edwards suggests that race and sex have their own dialectics, but declines to go into the bases of these, other than to suggest that, while they are intimately linked to the history of capitalism, they are not subsets of capitalist relations.

Edwards attempts to relate changes in the division of labour to both macro-developments in capitalism and forms of systematic social inequality in a historically sensitive and theoretically elegant way. However, there are various problems in his work. First, Edwards is profoundly ambivalent as to whether women and blacks suffer lower labour market positions as a result of employers' divide-and-rule tactics, or as a result of wider social processes. On the one hand, he unequivocally states the former; on the other, he announces the independent dialectics of race and sex. Secondly, it is unclear whether workers are divided by an employer within a firm, as part of a divide-and-rule strategy, or between firms which operate different forms of control over their labour forces. On the one hand, it appears that

Edwards is suggesting that employers have found a new mode of control which entails dividing the workforce (in the bureaucratic form) and which is distinctive from previous forms of the nineteenth century. On the other, it appears that Edwards is saying that there are different labour markets and labour segments which are divided according to which one of the three forms of control he has identified that the firm is using.

In later work, Gordon, Edwards and Reich (1982) more explicitly state that the strategy of segmentation of the labour market is a distinguishing feature of a specific time period: that from the 1920s to the present day. In this period the labour market is seen to become segmented into three sections: independent primary, subordinate primary and secondary, in a similar manner to Edwards (1979). This is seen to follow on from time periods during which initial proletarianisation took place, the 1820s to 1890s; and one in which labour was 'homogenised' between the 1870s and the Second World War. This work is a detailed account of the transformations in the capitalist economy as they affect the labour process and labour market organisation.

However, there is a problem in their work as a consequence of their failure to theorise explicitly the development of sexist and racist structures. Although Gordon, Edwards and Reich (1982: 32) note that 'Structural conflicts arising from relations among races, genders and nations, for example, are also likely to have their own independent logic and dynamics', they deliberately do not consider these, stating that their focus is elsewhere. However, this omission gives rise to difficulties within the terms of their own question. It is surely inappropriate to write of the 'homogenisation' of the labour force during the period from 1870 to the Second World War when divisions by ethnicity and gender are rife throughout this period as in the other two. Analyses of US census data by Hakim (1979) and Gross (1968) show ethnic groups and genders were segregated by occupation prior to, during and after this period. Gordon, Edwards and Reich (1982) note this phenomenon, but refuse to consider its significance for their periodisation of labour history. Indeed, they are somewhat cavalier in their use of evidence to support their claim that segregation by gender has increased in the post-Second World War period. For instance, they cite Davies's (1975) work on the entry of women to clerical employment in support, yet Davies is writing about the period up till the 1920s and 1930s, one which Edwards, Gordon and Reich elsewhere characterise as one of labour homogenisation.

If segregation by gender and ethnicity counts as segmentation, as the analysis (1982: 204–10) implies, then Gordon, Edwards and Reich's periodisation of segmentation and capitalist development is quite simply wrong; the differences between the periods are insufficient for their theory.

In their effort to reduce the explanation of segmentation to the struggle between capital and labour, Edwards, Gordon and Reich theoretically ignore the very divisions in the labour force which prompted the development of radical labour market analysis in the first place (cf. Doeringer and Piore 1971). Their analysis is not the grand theory of segmentation and capitalist development that they claim, but rather is limited to an explanation of forms of control in certain US companies. If, however, segregation and segmentation are treated as separate phenomena, as Edwards (1979) suggests, then segregation remains in need of an explanation.

Dual systems theory

Hartmann (1979b) pushes on the theoretical understanding of gender segregation with her analysis of patriarchal as well as capitalist relations. She is concerned that this synthesis of Marxist and feminist analysis should not be another 'unhappy marriage' in which one, Marxism, dominates the other, but rather be one in which they have equal standing in a more 'progressive union' (Hartmann 1981). Hartmann explains job segregation by sex in terms of the intersection of the two systems of capitalism and patriarchy, from which the dominant groups of each system, capitalists and men, benefit. Occupational segregation is constructed by men to keep the better-paid jobs for themselves. They are able to do this because they are better organised than women, and also have access to sources of power to support their claims, such as the state. Hartmann argues that segregation cannot be explained by a Marxist analysis of capitalism, because it predates it. For instance, men organised in guilds in medieval Europe were able to restrict women's access to the best jobs. Men benefit from job segregation in two ways. Firstly, they take the best paid jobs. Secondly, the lack of access to well-paid jobs drives women to marry on bad terms, so they have to service their husbands. Capital, as well as patriarchy, benefits from job segregation, because it enables employers to pay women low wages since there is an over-supply of women for the few remaining jobs. Finally, the system locks into a vicious circle in which women have even less access to the acquisition of the skills and experience necessary for the better jobs because of their work as housewives. The two systems of capitalism and patriarchy are seen to be in harmonious alliance, with a neat congruence of interests, with only occasional tensions. Hartmann supports her analysis with examples of the active struggles of men against women in the labour market over access to employment.

Hartmann's dual systems approach significantly advances our theorisation of gender relations, and is an especially powerful framework for an analysis of gender segregation at work. Hartmann's account has, however, been faced with some criticisms (see, especially,

Sargent 1981). The critical issue is whether she is able to sustain an analytic separation between capitalism and patriarchy. Young (1981) argues that this is not logically possible. Either dual systems theorists give capitalism and patriarchy the same base (for instance, the material sphere), in which case the systems are analytically inseparable, or they have separate bases (for instance, the economy as the basis of capitalism and culture for patriarchy), in which case they cannot explain the full range of features of both capitalism and patriarchy which fall outside these spheres. However, while Young identifies serious problems with existing dual systems texts, the problems she raises are not insuperable, if the theoretical analysis is more tightly specified.

While largely agreeing with Hartmann, I think there are some minor problems. Firstly, her analysis is too general to be able to account for the variations in the extent and forms of occupational segregation which exist. For instance, we need to know why women were able to gain entry to some occupations, such as clerical work and cotton weaving, but not to others such as engineering. Secondly, her analysis of the relations between patriarchy and capitalism overstates the degree of harmony between the two systems. The conflicts between the interests of capital in utilising cheap labour and those of patriarchy in restricting women to domestic labour or very limited forms of paid work is underestimated in her account. Thirdly, her analysis is limited by not considering changes in the middle and latter part of the twentieth century, which affect the balance of forces with both the capitalist and patriarchal systems and their interrelationship. However, these are relatively minor criticisms, suggesting a need for the development of Hartmann's approach, rather than its dismissal.

Race and segregation

A further problem with the work of Hartmann and many of the writers so far considered is their relative neglect of the significance of race and ethnicity. This is both a general problem in social theory, including feminist theory (see Amos and Parmar 1984; Carby 1982; Joseph 1981), and a specific one in relation to segregation. It is inappropriate to treat women as a unified category, segregated from men, where there are significant internal divisions on the basis of ethnicity. Indeed, ethnicity can be considered a basis of segregation in its own right (Phizacklea 1983b).

Some segmentation theorists have looked at the issue of race; indeed, the explanation of racial inequalities in employment was one of the initial stimuli for the development of this school of thought (e.g. Doeringer and Piore 1971). The Marxist segmentation theorists Edwards, Gordon and Reich treat ethnicity in a similar manner to gender; significant, but primarily exogenous to the system of employment relations they are examining. This meets the same problems as did their analysis of gender.

It is important that analysis of gender segregation at work take full account of the overlapping system of ethnic segregation.

Building a theory of segregation

Having critically discussed a range of social and economic theories of segregation, I now want to try to build a more adequate approach based on the synthesis of the best parts of each theory.

From neo-classical economists such as Mincer I would take the analysis of the sexual division of labour within and outside the family as a proper subject of study, and the necessity of the analysis of the relations between women's paid and unpaid work. However, this analysis is limited by its neglect of processes within the labour market, the power relations between the sexes and its ahistoricism. From Matthaei I would take the necessity for a historical analysis of the development of the sexual division of labour, although her analysis lacks sufficient appreciation of the power relations between the sexes and the processes within the labour market. From segmented labour market theorists like Gordon, Edwards and Reich (1982) I would take their focus on the development of segmented labour markets over time through social struggle, although they deal inadequately with structures of gender equality. From Hartmann I would take her approach to gender relations in terms of the intersection of patriarchy and capitalism, although I would emphasise the tension between the two systems to a greater extent than she does, and pay greater attention to the reasons for variations in segregation. In addition, the significance of ethnic division should be taken into account.

I shall now try to show how such a revised approach might work by comparing the development of segregation in three areas of employment in Britain.

Comparative segregation in clerical work, engineering and cotton textile weaving

I shall support and illustrate my claims by examining the process of sexual segregation in three areas of employment in Britain: cotton textiles, engineering, and clerical work. The issue here is why the different strategies of exclusion and of segregation were deployed in these various areas of employment with radically dissimilar outcomes. The textile occupations employ roughly equal proportions of men and women, engineering almost entirely men and clerical work disproportionately women. These are major areas of employment in contemporary Britain, occupying over a quarter of the workforce, and in the past employed still higher proportions of paid workers. Why should the workforce be segregated by sex in such different ways?

On the surface there are few obvious answers. Both textiles and engineering contain manual work at all levels of skill. If women can be skilled workers in textiles, entering the heavy working conditions of the nineteenth-century factory, there is no reason based on propensity to aquire skill, or physique, why they should not have been present in similar circumstances in engineering too. Indeed, in one area of the country, in one type of engineering, metalworking in the Black Country, women did perform engineering work. Yet textiles and engineering have strikingly different sex ratios. No explanations based on the level of ideological appropriateness, lightness of labour or relation to machinery can explain women's participation in one and not the other.

Why should women be disproportionately represented among clerks? Given that nineteenth-century clerical work was largely performed by men, why did this change so dramatically during the course of the twentieth century? Why did clerical work admit women and not engineering? Both were once the province of proud, skilled male workers; within both areas the skilled component of the occupation has shrunk disproportionately with the development of lesser-skilled forms of work. Why should one admit women to so much a greater extent than the other?

Explanations at the level of ideological appropriateness or propensity to acquire skill are not adequate answers to why these three areas of employment have such different sex ratios, since there are contrary cases within these three examples of areas of employment in Britain. Neither is it sufficient to assert that capitalists divided the workforce the better to control it, since this does not account for the variations in patterns of segregation or why some areas of employment get sex-typed female and others male. Nor is it sufficient to assert that the tendency of capital to deskill areas of work leads to their feminisation, since deskilling does not have the same consequence in each of these areas of employment. Nor is it enough to say that the proportion of women workers is explained by the level of patriarchal forces present in a given conjuncture, since this again cannot explain the differences in the sex-typing of these areas of employment.

Rather the variations in segregation are a result of the relative strength of patriarchal and capitalist social forces at particularly crucial moments in the development of these areas of employment. Further, there is no simple index of the level of patriarchal forces, since the institutional basis of these forces has changed over time.

The transformation of the sex composition of clerical work during the twentieth century is a particularly dramatic example of such a change. In the nineteenth century, clerical work was a skilled occupation monopolised by men, while today it is generally much less skilled and is largely performed by women. Some commentators (e.g. Davies 1975) have suggested that this transformation occurred as clerical work expanded and was transformed by the simple market pressure of the availability of suitably skilled (i.e. fully literate) women and the scarcity of such men who would take the wages the employers wanted to offer. This change is often described as taking place smoothly under such market pressures. That is, these analyses see capital as the dynamic part of the explanation, and the existence of such a gender-differentiated labour supply is treated as a given not in need of much explanatory attention.

The analyses are problematic in that they ignore the extent of male opposition to the entry of women to clerical work in the early twentieth century. The male clerks spoke, wrote, organised and even struck in order to prevent the entry of women into 'their' areas of work (Walby 1986). Their opposition had two bases; firstly that women's entry took work away from others like themselves (men) and would tend to lower the wage rate for all clerks, since it was possible to pay women less to do the same work as men; and, secondly, because it was seen to undermine the wider patriarchal order.

However, the men were relatively weakly organised, unlike the male opposition to women in engineering which was organised through the strong engineering unions. Further, the expansion of new forms of clerical work was very rapid, and it proved possible to employ women on the new forms of work and leave men on the old. Thus employers bought off the men's opposition, rarely directly substituting women for men (although this did happen on occasion), and segregating them and their conditions of work and pay from those of women. Segregation was thus the outcome of a threefold division of interests between the employers, the male clerks and the would-be women clerks. It can best be understood as the outcome of the articulation of patriarchal and capitalist interests and the compromise arrived at after struggle (see Walby 1986 for fuller account).

The situation in engineering was different in that the men who opposed the entry of women were effectively organised in unions which had substantial control over entry to the trade. Further, these unions were able to gain the support of the state when this control over entry was threatened by the dramatically increased demand for labour in engineering during the wars. The unions were able to gain government backing for an agreement to turn out women who entered the trade during wartime at its end. Although this was the subject of some controversy at the end of each war, and, in the case of the second, the men were somewhat outmanoeuvred by the employers over this, none the less it is an interesting example both of the effectiveness of certain forms of patriarchal unionism, and of the significance of the ability of one group of patriarchs to mobilise state power on their own behalf. The entry of women to engineering has continued to be of a very limited extent even today.

My final example of cotton textiles illustrates further the historical contingency of these balances of forces. In this, the first area of factory employment in the world, women were a large component of the paid workforce, and performed skilled work (weaving) as well. In this case there were no organised patriarchal forces within the factory to oppose the entry of women to this work until after the women had become an established part of the weaving workforce (although the situation in spinning was quite different). Such attempts as there were outside the factory (such as the drive to restrict the hours women could work to a greater extent than the hours of men) had a relatively limited effect, despite the eventually successful mobilisation of the state behind this restrictive patriarchal practice. However, more recently such restrictive legislation has had an effect on the gender composition of the textile workforce in conjunction with both the changing location of the textile industry in Britain in the world capitalist economy and the entry of migrant labour from the Third World. The decaying competitive position of the British textile industry and its reduced ability to pay high wages combined with the introduction of 24-hour shift working led to the recruitment of migrant male labour which was both legally able to work the night shift (barred to women without special arrangements) and which could (like white women) be paid less than white men. We see a simultaneous shift in the ethnic and gender composition of the workforce as employers turned from white women to black (often Asian) men. Thus, not only must both patriarchal and capitalist structures be taken into account when trying to explain sex segregation of the workforce, but racist ones also (see Walby 1986 for a fuller account of this comparison).

Conclusion

Many cherished assumptions of existing theories are significantly challenged by the existence of gender segregation at work. Neo-classical economic theory is challenged by the wages gap between men and women which cannot be explained by inequalities of human capital. Only a portion of the wage difference is attributable to this factor; most is due to the segregation of women into low-paid occupations. Traditional Marxist theory is challenged both by the significance of labour market processes, and by the irreducibility of gender inequalities – even, ultimately, to capitalism. The implications of segregation for class theory are immense. The division of labour is critically shaped by both capitalist and patriarchal forces. Since occupational structure is generally considered to be the backbone of the class structure, the structuring of this by sexual segregation potentially has important implications for class analysis. Traditionally feminist theory has explained women's position in the labour market as the result of their position in the family; the examination of segregation has seriously problematised that analysis. New and significant bases of gender inequality have been found within the workings of the labour market itself. Indeed, it is now argued that the labour market is as significant a determinant of women's position in the family as vice versa. However, there are aspects of the previous work which are useful.

The writers on culture have clearly demonstrated that the sexual division of labour is a social construct rather than a biological one, although their specific explanations of segregation do not engage with many significant structural issues. The human capital theorists were important in conceptualising women's housework as significant for an economic analysis, but the limitation of their focus to pure market forces incorrectly excludes the political and organisational structuring of the labour market itself. The dual labour market theorists were important in introducing the conceptualisation of a structured and segmented labour market, but dealt insufficiently with the social forces which produced this. The Marxist writers on segmented labour markets may be seen to contribute the importance of power and struggle in the structuring of the labour market, but their account is limited by their failure to theorise adequately the gender as well as class aspects of this inequality. Dualist theorists have been important in adding to this a theorisation of structural gender inequality, although existing accounts tend to overstate the degree of harmony between the two systems.

The theoretical arguments on gender segregation underpin some of the recent political activity around comparable worth. The wages gap between men and women is seen as critically due to the separation of men's and women's work and the prevention of comparison of wage rates between these forms of work. If this can be tackled by forcing the comparison of these segregated areas of work, then the expectation is that other aspects of gender inequality will be reduced.

3: The gendering of jobs: workplace relations and the reproduction of sex segregation

Cynthia Cockburn

'Sort of stuck in channels'

I recently talked with a sixteen-year-old, just as she began her year in a commercial office as a trainee on the Youth Training Scheme.[1] She said thoughtfully, 'It's funny, when you come to think of it. It's men doing this type of job and women doing that type of job. Sort of stuck in channels and they never get out.' Occupational segregation by sex had been one of the most striking impressions of her first week at work. What she barely guessed at, as yet, was how much the pattern she observed was likely to govern, even in the superficially unisex world of office work, her own future job, earnings, prospects and fulfilment.

Occupational segregation by sex is one of the most marked and persistent of the patterns that characterize our world, and its nature has by now been thoroughly rehearsed. Women and men tend to cluster in separate industries, separate occupations, different departments and different rooms. We use different toilets, wear different overalls and different hats. At the industrial level men are about 86 per cent of the labour force in the industrial group called 'mechanical engineering'. Conversely, women are about 67 per cent of the labour force in retail distribution and repair of consumer goods – even though this category includes vehicle repair. Clearly they cluster in shop work. Women employees are strikingly grouped in a handful of occupations. Of women part-timers for instance, all but 8 per cent are in selling; clerical; education, health and welfare; or cleaning, catering and hairdressing, etc. Men by contrast are engaged in a far wider range of activities, and there are few from which they are entirely absent (Equal Opportunities Commisssion (EOC) 1987b: 30–1).[2]

The finer the net is drawn the more segregation is found. Statistics of occupations show more separation between the sexes than those in which employment is specified by industry.[3] The Department of Employment/Office of Population Censuses and Surveys (DE/OPCS) survey reported by Jean Martin and Ceridwen Roberts was able to pose questions about sex segregation in such a way that they could focus down on the experience of individual women. Working women reported in 63 per cent of cases that they worked in 'women only' jobs. The occupational segregation was higher still if the professions and office work were weeded out. For instance, of semi-skilled factory workers no less than 73 per cent were working only with women in their particular jobs (Martin and Roberts 1984: 27–8).

I mention these well-known facts only as a reminder of two features of occupational segregation that will have a bearing on the argument of this chapter. First, while we have often noted hitherto that women's work appears to call for certain characteristics such as 'caring' or 'nimble fingers', the categories of work filled mainly by men are yet more identifiable, namely, those apparently requiring physical strength, technical competence or intellectual abilities, and that these are even more readily capable of ideological identification and representation than 'women's work'. This is a point to which I will return. In 1986 in Britain men were 89 per cent of the occupational groups 'general managerial' and 91 per cent of 'professional and related in science, engineering and technology'. They were 95 per cent of the labour force that processes, makes and repairs metal and electrical goods (EOC 1987b: 29).

Second, men are more segregated than women. If we think of occupations as being separate cells, each with its own cell wall, men reach out and penetrate into more of them. We could say that women do not 'defend' their cell walls so effectively against men as men defend theirs against incursions of women. In the DE/OPCS survey, for instance, the (rather small) sample of husbands revealed that 81 per cent of those working with other people worked only with men, and 98 per cent had male supervisors (Martin and Roberts 1984: 27–8). Catherine Hakim's figures show that in 1971 over half of all men were still in occupations where they outnumbered women by at least nine to one, while only a quarter of women were in occupations where women, as a sex, outnumbered men by this ratio (Hakim 1979: 23). Over the seventy-year period analysed by Hakim, the likelihood of working in an occupation where men predominated became proportionately greater for men.

As Hakim pointed out, there has been little reduction of occupational segregation by sex during this century. The phenomenon of sex segregation, besides, is remarkably universal. Reports from the USA (Gross 1968) and from European countries (Organisation for Economic

Co-operation and Development 1980) show a similar situation. In Third World countries, though the actual occupations of women and men vary widely, the existence of a clear sexual division of labour of some kind characterizes all (Boserup 1971).

There is by now a considerable body of writing of at least ten years' duration, attempting in various ways to explain occupational segregation by sex. We have work that, first, describes its forms and effects in manufacturing (Cavendish 1982; Pollert 1981; Westwood 1984), in office work (Crompton and Jones 1984), in medicine (Game and Pringle 1984) and in other fields. The particular skills and abilities developed by women during their childhood and in domestic life have been shown to be attractive to employers who are able to exploit them without paying for them (Elson and Pearson 1981).

The constraints placed on women by their domestic resonsibilities have been seen as making of them a distinct form of labour power, differentiated from men in the labour market by a preference for part-time work, a tendency to drop out and return to work as family needs dictate and an inability to work overtime and move location (Amsden 1980; Kahn-Hut *et al.* 1982; Myrdal and Klein 1970). Employers are shown to be ready to exploit these differences by paying women less and offering them inferior conditions and prospects. The role of employers in structuring sex segregation is illustrated by Glucksman (1986) and Liff (1986), each of whom shows, for the pre-war and post-war periods respectively, new industries being set up with clear intention from the outset of employing women in routine production jobs.

It has been suggested that job markets, as well as labour markets, tend to segmentation, some jobs being central to production, requiring high-grade and well-rewarded labour, others peripheral and hence an area of spasmodic recruitment and low pay (Friedman 1977, for example). 'Dual' labour market theories have been applied to women's work to show that women in particular can be seen as a secondary sector workforce confined to relatively low-paid, less secure, less 'skilled' and less rewarding jobs (Barron and Norris 1976).

It has been pointed out, however, that this work has tended to focus on manufacturing industry, ignoring the service sector in which women predominate (Beechey 1986). It has also been objected that such predominantly economic theories overlook the active part of craft unions in securing certain occupations for men (Rubery 1980). I demonstrated something of this process in work on the printing industry (Cockburn 1983). This account was within a train of reasoning that has developed in recent years that understands skill itself as a social rather than a technical phenomenon and sees the distinctions commonly made between men's 'skilled' work and women's 'unskilled' work as being a social construct in which men have played an active part (Phillips and Taylor 1980).

Looking for micro-mechanisms

In this chapter I want to suggest that, while none of the above theories are invalid and indeed each contributes some information to the analysis of occupational segregation, they are insufficient to explain the extra-ordinary resilience of sexual divisions in work.

We can show that occupational segregation pre-dates capitalism. In poll tax returns for Oxford in AD 1380, for instance, mention is made of 6 trades followed by women, 6 in which both women and men were engaged and no less than 81 pursued exclusively by men (Clark 1982: 155). Occupational segregation by sex also post-dates capitalism. In the USSR at the 1970 census, 98 per cent of nurses and nursery school personnel, 99 per cent stenographers and 91 per cent of catering employees were female (Lapidus 1976; Sacks 1976).

Occupational segregation also survives wars. In the Second World War, though women in the automobile industry entered hard and heavy male jobs, segregation by sex was quickly recreated 'for the duration'. So, as Ruth Milkman puts it, 'Rosie the Riveter did a man's job but more often than not she worked in a predominantly female department or job classification' (Milkman 1987: 9).[4]

Segregation also survives economic crisis, restructuring and technological revolutions. The application of computers was at first assumed to be a sex-neutral field of employment, but very soon sexual divisions developed, with men filling the more technical and knowl-edgeable jobs and women the more routine operating or simple programming jobs (Greenbaum 1976; Kraft and Dubnoff 1984). My own recent work shows that the introduction of new technology to certain workplaces as a survival strategy in recession, while it may have produced new kinds of job and new allocations of work to women and men, does little to reduce the *separation* of the spheres of the sexes.

We need to explain this survival power, How is occupational segregation by sex sustained and reproduced over time? I would suggest that something more can be learned by looking at small-scale, local mechanisms within the workplace itself and in particular at the relationship between women and men in the workforce. Certainly, employers do have an interest in some cases in sustaining the sex-typing of jobs. In other cases, however, they can be shown to be indifferent to the issue of which sex does what. Indeed, they sometimes clearly see advantage in actively changing the sex-typing of certain occupations (Cockburn 1983).[5] In such cases, what appears to sustain sex segregation is *the active engagement of male employees*.

This is not a new perception. Heidi Hartmann said as long ago as 1979 that 'male workers have played and continue to play a crucial role in maintaining sexual divisions in the labour process' (Hartmann 1979a:

208). She emphasised, however, the trade unions as the principle agents of protectionism. But trade unions cannot claim membership in many of the workplaces and occupations where segregation persists. There has been less effort made to understand how individual men as men, men in the workplace, unionised or no, act in such a way as to keep their separation from and superiority over women.

I believe that two mechanisms are important in this respect. First, the exploitation by men of horizontal and vertical differentiation in the occupational structure; and, second, the active gendering of both people and jobs.

Doing the quickstep

Catherine Hakim used the terms 'horizontal' and 'vertical' segregation to distinguish the situation where men and women are most commonly working in different *types* of occupation from those where they are working in different *grades* of occupation (Hakim 1979). For these forms of segregation to exist at all, workplaces must logically be subject to a division of labour of the kind that we, indeed, take for granted as natural. That is to say, jobs must be articulated as distinguishable tasks and responsibilities, and a grade structure must designate a ranking of posts and rewards. In fact, the hierarchisation of posts into quite detailed strata and the fragmentation of work into detail tasks are both highly characteristic of industrial capitalism. What is more, they are dynamic processes. Work is continually subdivided as technology 'advances'; levels are continually refined and chains of responsibility lengthened as firms expand and grow. Besides, jobs bear down on and shape each other. Thus the incumbent of the occupation of systems manager or production manager may create, shape and destroy other labour processes.

I suggest that we assume, for the purpose of this account, that workplaces are terrains in which are acted out the internal relations of two systems of power – that of class and that of sex; that they are the site of interactions between these systems. In this case we can see an informative meshing of the two sets of relations. Capitalist workplace relations involve fragmentation and hierarchisation; male power profits by this process, which enables men to move sideways or upwards to evade the incursions of women. These incursions, it should be added, may be the result of the will of employers (seeing advantage in replacing men with women), or of the state (sex discrimination legislation), and, in combination with either of these, the will of the female workforce, seeking new openings.

The principle that is at work here is male separatism. We may assume that men as a sex have an interest vested in maintaining superiority over women, a situation they must secure in a system where they themselves, as workers, are subject to domination by capital. Individual men therefore are under some social pressure to locate themselves in situations not only where they have greater bargaining power relative to capital but in which they are not directly comparable to women. If a man shares an occupation with a woman he feels his status tremble. He may be seen to do the job less well. He may, in the logic of things, sooner or later find himself answerable to a woman supervisor or forewoman. These things are uncomfortable for the individual male and bad for the relative stature of the sex. The tendency therefore is for any movement by women (usually sideways rather than upwards) to be countered by a movement of men out of the sphere contaminated by women.

An example of a horizontal escape route that is being used effectively by men is in medical physics. This is an occupation that women are slowly entering in greater numbers than before. Medical physics departments in hospitals are simultaneously obtaining responsibility for the supervision of the hospital's growing battery of high-tech equipment, including computers, scanners and linear accelerators. As women enter the profession they tend to be located in slots in 'nuclear medicine' which are those where members of the department have contact with patients. Men fill the newer slots that have more to do with the technology. There is more status attached to the latter than to the former, which is seen as being associated with nursing.

In the clothing industry, a curious situation is beginning to occur in which it appears that men are retaining their relative status as a sex, but partly at the cost of losing jobs. The clothing manufacturers have increasingly preferred to employ women as sewing-machinists. Men have disappeared from all but ethnic-minority sewing workshops today. Men for a long while, however, consolidated in the cutting room, where cloth cutting and the various processes associated with pattern making were linked parts of a craft occupation. Today, computerized systems are transforming pattern and cutting work in the more advanced firms, and, as this happens, women are being introduced to parts of the newly fragmented tasks: operating the spreading machine, doing the 'bundling' of the cut cloth. Some are operating the video-scopes of the pattern room and the big computer-driven knives. For a moment in some firms there is a unisex situation in the cutting and pattern area and even in some subdivisions thereof. But, in the view of more than one manager with whom I spoke, this is a temporary situation. The tendency is for occupations to re-establish a gender identity. Most of these particular jobs will become female.

In the interval, men have established themselves in certain slots: as plotter operator in the pattern room, say, or the one who mounts the fabric rolls on the spreaders. The point here is that individual men contribute to this process by their own choices. Many become disenchanted with the work as it becomes feminised. I interviewed a number of disaffected and disgruntled men who felt the industry had lost its masculinity. If they see an alternative job or an opportunity of early retirement they will take it – and leave the field to women.

While individually men have gradually lost their position in manual production work in these modern clothing firms, however, a process that their once-craft union has been powerless to resist due to the perilous economic condition of the industry, men as a sex have retained their superior position in the firm. They have almost exclusive hold over the new kinds of position that afford a degree of control over the labour process: those of maintenance engineer and systems technologist. These jobs are rapidly increasing in importance – a fact which is reiterated in the trade press.

An interesting situation occurred not long ago in which the re-establishment of sex segregation to the advantage of men has been scotched by the autonomous organisation of women workers. A large mail-order firm has recently introduced a new phase of materials-handling technology into its warehouse. It had, in the words of the woman shop steward, 'a devastating impact'. Among other things a new conveyor belt had been introduced in the receiving bay. This belt triggered a three-way struggle between management, women and men. Men and women had both been working, though on different tasks, in the receiving bay. The computerisation now made four women per belt surplus to need. Management stated the intention of moving them away, inevitably into another female ghetto. This time the women demanded and won the right to apply instead for the men's jobs in the receiving bay, unloading wagons and palletising at the end of the belt. Encouraged by this success they also obtained the right to apply for vacancies among fork-lift truck-driver jobs.

The really revolutionary step was yet to come, however. The management had a policy of offering voluntary severance pay to redundant workers only if no suitable alternative could be found for them in the warehouse. The women learned that some men were obtaining severance pay on the grounds that the only available positions were low-status women's jobs in picking and packing. Men were not expected to do these. The men had been saying it would make them feel degraded. They couldn't bring themselves to work alongside women. One said the idea made him feel giddy. He explained that he had a phobia about heights and in the same way he experienced a phobia now about women's work. But the women said to the company, 'If you allow the men to get away with this, if you allow them to move sideways into other men's jobs or out of the firm altogether with severance pay just because they refuse women's work, we will take you to tribunal.'

The women won this struggle. Some men were obliged to join them on the despised picket line. They had achieved this by having a strong woman shop steward who was not afraid to call women-only meetings and to confront male workers as well as management. As a result the criteria on which jobs have been allocated in the firm since that date have completely changed. It will be interesting to see what moves men generate to re-establish separation in coming years. They will no doubt try.

Vertical moves

Where horizontal segregation fails, a second option remains for those men who have the abilities to climb. Vertically, work affords a series of ladders with distinct rungs up which men can step out of reach of direct comparison and equivalence with women. Even in the most feminine field of work the higher the rank the more masculine becomes the occupation.

Radiography was another of the occupations I studied in my recent research on gender and technology. Radiography has long been considered 'women's work'. But in the last decade, prompted in part by an improvement in pay and conditions in the professions supplementary to medicine, an increasing number of men have begun to apply for training and jobs. They bring certain practical advantages over women – freedom to do overtime, no career breaks due to child bearing – and so they tend to climb rapidly over them. Men as a result are represented disproportionately in the higher posts and in the upper ranks of the professional organisation. Likewise, in hairdressing, where women are 86 per cent of the workforce, men cluster at the top of the trade, and anxiety is expressed about the lack of boys in the lower ranks only because 'they are tomorrow's managers and owners' (Attwood and Hatton 1983: 119).

Apart from simply climbing existing ladders, men may respond to pressure from women by actively creating new vertical subdivisions. This may happen in technology as women succeed in entering it in greater numbers. Sally Hacker has shown how, in the USA, more and more advanced mathematics has been introduced into the engineering curriculum as a way of stratifying the qualifications. The élite groups are those who have the maths; the rest fall to a lower status. Given their backgound, women are more often disadvantaged by this than men. As a result, women who get some purchase on technology do not gain as much from it as they might. 'As the ratio of engineers to technicians declines, women and minorities are being actively recruited to become the technicians – that is the engineering aides – who form a growing proportion of the new technical workforce.' Hacker points out that the pay differential between the engineer and the engineering aide is almost exactly the differential between the national average pay of men and women (Hacker 1983: 39).

This instance is a reminder that the many occupational niches created by hierarchisation and fragmentation of work cannot be seen simply as a pattern of cells, each to some extent self-contained and autonomous. In fact, they represent a struggle for ascendancy, and the relationship between them is, besides, continually manipulated from above – by the employer. In particular, many men, by being in positions superior to many women, are able to create and destroy, form and deform, the occupations done by women. The upper ranks of the engineering profession were precisely those which fostered the creation of the lower-ranking 'aides' through changes in education and professional structure.

The gendering process

The second mechanism to which I pointed as assisting the reproduction of sex segregation was the social process of gendering. The horizontal and vertical manoeuvrings of men would not alone suffice to keep women out of their sphere – such an effect presupposes simultaneous cultural activity.

While people are working, they are not just producing goods and services, pay packet and career, they are also producing culture. The relations that surround technology and technological work are made up both of things people do and of things they believe and say. What they do gives rise to what they feel, and of course their feelings and ideas also partly determine what they and other people do. The ideas produced by men, because men are the more powerful sex, tend to be hegemonic. Women's ideas sometimes reflect this dominant gender ideology, but those of many women (and indeed of a minority of men) run counter to it.

I will not rehearse here the arguments concerning the nature of gender, but simply affirm what is by now widely accepted: that gender is not the same thing as biological sex; that it involves a dualism, complementary and mutually exclusive masculine and feminine forms; and it is first and foremost a social fact (Connell *et al.* 1982; Kessler and McKenna 1978). It is appropriate to use 'gender' as a transitive verb. People are actively gendered during their childhood and youth. Three facts that are less often acknowledged are that the gendering process, first, extends into adult life; second, it applies to many phenomena by extension from human beings; and third, it is a medium of male power.

The result of the gendering process is that all behaviour beomes gendered and all interpretations of behaviour likewise. Woman and man become a 'couple' and are seen as complementary to each other, regardless of the fact that in many transactions between women and men (working, training, shopping, enjoying recreation) there is no real need to see them as couples, or indeed to distinguish the sexes as different at all. It is very difficult to stop ourselves seeing things in this way, because gender is part of our cultural tools for thinking, for ordering and understanding the world.

Things are gendered materially (sized or coloured differently, for instance) and also ideologically. We can use objects as gender metaphors: a pink ribbon, for instance. In a world where so many things are gendered, from shampoo and deodorants to entire environments as local as the 'ladies toilet' and as large as the North Sea oil rig, it is not surprising that occupations are often gendered too. It is of course a two-way process. People have a gender, and their gender rubs off on the jobs they do. The jobs in turn have a gender character which rubs off on the people who do them. Tools and machinery used in work are gendered too, in such a way that the sexes are expected to relate to different kinds of equipment in different ways. An eighteenth-century man probably felt effeminate using a spinning-wheel, though he would have felt comfortable enough repairing one. In a training workshop where I have been doing fieldwork, it is impossible to get a teenage lad to wipe the floor with a mop, though he may be persuaded to sweep it with a broom. Any woman lifting a crowbar is likely to have some gender-conscious thoughts as she does so.

When a new invention arrives in the workplace it is already gendered by the activities and expectations of its manufacturers and its owners. It may even be ergonomically sex-specific, scaled for the average height or anticipated strength of the sex that is to use it. Even if it arrives apparently gender-neutral it quickly acquires a gender by association with its user or its purpose. The computer was the brainchild of male engineers and was born into a male line of production technology. The fact that it has a keyboard rather like a (feminine) typewriter confuses no one for long. When a computer arrives in a school, for instance, boys and girls are quick to detect its latent masculinity. Their own relationship to each other and to the new machine quickly confirms this. The boys soon elbow the girls out of the way. But when they use the keyboard they often take care to do so with two fingers only, so that they cannot be thought to be typists.

The many technologists and technicians I have interviewed (almost all males) have expressed time and again their identification as men with technology and of technology itself with masculinity. The effect can be summed up in the advert for the Ford Sierra car: 'Man and Machine in Perfect Harmony'. A natural affinity is often proposed between men and machines. A classic of ideological work is Smiles's *Lives of the Engineers* in which he celebrates those famous Victorians like Isambard Kingdom Brunel, 'strong-mined, resolute and ingenious, impelled to their special pursuits by the force of their constructive instincts' (Smiles 1986 [1862]: v).

Men likewise actively construct femininity as non-technical and 'woman' as essentially a non-worker. 'On the whole, women are happy with nine-to-five jobs and maybe a family and a home. They are not that interested in being on top, or running things,' said one senior engineer in his forties. Add to this the words of a sixteen-year-old lad just entering his first training placement: 'I really think it's better if men are all together, you see. If it's all men, all of them can speak frankly and express their feelings. If there's a woman there, you know, it can be different.' The workplaces in which these two males spent their days reflected both their preferences and their preception of reality, and undoubtedly also the ideas grew out of the practice of separate spheres.

This cultural work assists the sideways and upwards movements by which the male sex maintains a separation from women. In engineering, for instance, masculine ideology makes use of a hard/soft dichotomy to appropriate tough, physical engineering work for masculinity. It runs into a contradiction however when it comes to evaluating its 'opposite': cerebral, professional forms of engineering, desk-bound and sedentary. The masculist ideology copes with this by calling in to play an alternative dichtomy, associating the masculine with rationality, with the intellect, femininity with the irrational and with the body — incidentally turning an almost complete conceptual somersault in the process.

This kind of ideological work has certainly assisted the step whereby electronic engineering – light, clean, safe work, apparently the very opposite of manly mechanical engineering – has been successfully appropriated for masculinity. An over-arching dichotomy of course that men everywhere and always are able to deploy to their advantage is quite simply: masculine equals superior, active and powerful; feminine equals subordinate, submissive and directed. Lowly jobs may be pink or blue, and men manage to establish a compensatory advantage for masculinity even at this lower level in the heroisms of heavy manual labour (Willis 1977). Top jobs in any field, however, are deepest blue.

Implications for strategy

What then of breaking down occupational segregation and helping women out of the cramping confines of their characteristic stuck-in-a-rut, low-paid jobs? In particular, what of getting women technical competence?

The arguments of those of us who promote 'women into engineering' and 'women into manual trades' are sometimes felt to be fatally flawed by the uncomfortable fact that, on the whole, women do not want to be technologists. While some pioneering types can be shown to be keen to break into non-traditional work, the great majority of women do not appear to want to. Nor do they seem ambitious for top jobs. The research on which my analysis is based indicates that it is important not to bury away this embarrassing fact, but rather to acknowledge it. There is a good reason for women's reluctance. It is not that women are set against the idea of non-traditional fields of work. Many, all other things being equal, for instance, would have taken up technical training and done well at technical work. They are simply aware, however, of the high social costs that we all pay if we disobey gender rules. The gendering of jobs (most energetically by men) advertises loudly where women are not to enter. If we ignore the message we are made to feel silly, pushy, unnatural – all by turns. There is a relentless low-level background noise of harassment. We become unlovable.

Unless these costs are taken into account (and they are costs that have to be paid on top of the ordinary weariness of a hard day's work) we do little more than lead women into difficulties they can ill afford to encounter.

The logic of the analysis suggests that what must change is the relations of work. In particular, ending job segregation by sex would be helped by moves that leave men fewer escape routes: reintegrating tasks; restructuring the content of jobs and the relationship between them; and levelling out the hierarchies, reducing differentials in responsibility and pay. Such a system is easiest to establish in co-operatives, but it is not beyond all reason to wish it to be placed on the trade union agenda when bargaining with employers.

An interesting action-research project set up by the Engineering Industry Training Board with funding from the Manpower Services Commission moves in this direction. It involved pilot firms in redesigning the jobs of machine operators to include more technical tasks such as setting and first-line maintenance of the machine. It then proceeded to train some women operators for these enhanced roles (Sinclair n.d.). It is notable that male-dominated trade unions have in the past pushed in a very contrary direction – to increased demarcation and steeper differentials.

Secondly, we need to work towards a relaxation of gender differentiation both in jobs and in people. Where women enter work that men continue to define as their own, a struggle will occur over either the gender of the job or that of the person. In some cases women will be masculinised, made into 'honorary men', and in a similar way the handful of men who cross into traditionally female areas of work at the female level will be written off as effeminate, tolerated as eccentrics or failures. Sometimes the gender of the job will swivel round in some way to deal with the problem of assimilating new entrants, or simply to explain them.

An instance of this is reported by Joseph Corn, who found that after a few determined women had clocked up enough thousands of flying-hours to be considered at last for training as commercial airline pilots, airlines began to see advantage in using the existence of women pilots to counter the bad publicity from plane crashes. It was supposed that a nervous public would be reassured to see that flying is perfectly safe; any fool can do it (Corn, cited in McGaw 1982: 805).

The way radiography, for instance, is perceived in future is likely to depend in part on the proportions of women and men in the profession. The more men, the more it will be seen as a technical job. The more women, the more it will be seen as a routine push-button job or a 'caring profession'. No solution works so long as we have pronouncedly gendered jobs and gendered people, where the masculine is overvalued and the feminine undervalued, and where men have power over women.

To this of course has to be added that a further prerequisite of ending sex segregation at work is ending the broader social division of labour by which masculinity is associated with economic production and femininity with reproduction and domestic life. This is a point that is often made when considering the more economic aspects of women's difference in the labour market. But it is also a factor in gendering. The gendering process that pursues us into adult life catches us as much at home as at work. 'His' are the lawnmower and the electric drill; 'hers' are the washing-machine and the ironing board. The tool shed has an aura of blue, and the kitchen of pink. The dichotomies, separations and power inequalities that occur at home and those that occur at work are related and mutually reinforcing.

Occupational desegregation is unlikely, by this analysis, to occur simply as a result of economic and technical change, shifts in the interests of capital, though these things may help. It cannot go very far without the further development of the women's movement. Behind occupational segregation is gender differentiation, and behind that again is male power, which has to be confronted directly. The slow and steady route to change is undoubtedly through women's autonomous organisation outside and inside trade unions and political parties, changing the nature of demands concerning training and work. Teachers and parents too can do much to change gender relations and occupational choice. But the short cut, favoured by many women, is women's autonomous training initiatives in non-traditional fields of work. There are perhaps a score of these in existence today, where women train in various aspects of technology. Most have been set up within the last three or four years, often with European Social Fund support and matching funding from left-Labour local authorities. Some of the women who receive training in such workshops go on to set up women's working co-ops. It is only in these circumstances, they feel, that the conditions are prefigured for changing occupational structures, relations and cultures and detaching job from gender.

Notes

1   This paper draws on two research projects, each funded by the Economic and Social Research Council and the Equal Opportunities Commission between 1983 and 1986. Many of the points made here are discussed at

greater length in the reports of those projects, namely: Cynthia Cockburn, *Machinery of Dominance: Women, Men, and Technical Know-How* (1985) and Cynthia Cockburn, *Two-Track Training: Sex Inequalities and the Youth Training Scheme* (1987).

2   All these figures derive from the Department of Employment's *New Earnings Survey*, which are summarised in EOC 1987b.

3   For instance, percentages go as high as 74 per cent female in 'clerical and related', 99 per cent male in construction and mining (EOC 1987b: 29)

4   In shipbuilding in the war years women gained access to high wages, equal pay and jobs from which they had formerly been excluded. But the employers achieved war production, working with an inexperienced labour force, by introducing new techniques and fragmenting tasks. As a result occupational segregation was reintroduced even during the war years in a new form (Skold 1980).

5   The substitution of computer-aided 'cold' typesetting for 'hot metal' processes in printing has stimulated and been stimulated by the possibility of substituting 'semi-skilled women' for craftsmen (Cockburn 1983).

4: Gender, racism and occupational segregation

Annie Phizacklea

Women workers are by no means an homogeneous category, with the impact of racism and ethnicity clearly etched on the employment profiles of black women in British labour markets. What we have witnessed over the last twenty years is (a) the development and reproduction of 'ethnic' niches within the larger body of 'women's' work; (b) an accelerating rate of unemployment for black as compared to white women, due to black women's confinement to certain industries and sectors; (c) that racial discrimination further increases the likelihood of black women losing their jobs when compared with white women; and (d) that this situation is pushing many black, particularly Asian, women into unorganised sectors of manufacturing industry.

It is suggested here that one cannot apply pure capital logic in explaining these processes. Instead we must turn to the way in which racism and sexism combine to confine black women to a uniquely subordinate position prior to their entry into the labour market. In addition, we need to look at the way in which the state has institutionalised this within its own practices.

The analytical focus of what follows is the employment position of black women in the UK, black referring to both Afro-Caribbean and Asian women. While both groups of women experience widespread racial and sexual discrimination within British labour markets, the actual work that they do is largely ethnically specific, which in itself requires explanation.

Black women, ideology and the state

Black women in Britain today either originate from or have their ancestral origins in ex-British colonies. An important feature of the colonisation process was the development of an ideology alleging the 'innate' inferiority of the dominated. Thus the plundering of whole sections of the globe could be justified in terms of 'imperial trusteeship' for the betterment of 'backward peoples' (Fryer 1984: 165). This pseudo-scientific racist ideology propagated the view that the world was divided up into distinct and permanent 'races', some superior to others; but only those with white skin were capable of intelligent thought. Such views were shown to be totally spurious and therefore the result of totally non-scientific influences only in the twentieth century, by which time they were culturally entrenched and widely believed by all classes in Britain. Thus when black men and women began to migrate to Britain in the 1950s in response to shortages of labour in certain sectors of the economy they were received within a particular ideological context: a context which not only cast them as a 'race' apart, measured by their being labelled 'coloured', but members of those 'inferior races' in the Empire who in the past had supplied slave or 'coolie' (inferior) labour for the enrichment of the metropolitan society (Miles and Phizacklea 1984: 13). This racist categorisation served to justify their exclusion from equal access to jobs, housing, education and other facilities and resources. Rather than indigenous labour extending the warm embrace of international brother- and sisterhood, black men and women were met by exclusionary practice within the trade union movement, a concern with 'numbers' and repeated references to the refusal of the 'immigrants' to conform to the 'British way of life' (Phizacklea and Miles 1987). The 'problem' was rarely identified as one of white racism.

The Commonwealth Immigrants Act of 1962 withdrew from Commonwealth citizens the right of entry to Britain unless they possessed a Ministry of Labour employment voucher or were a dependant of such a person. The Act appeared to 'rationally' control labour migration without reference to 'race'. In practice this was not the case. The legislation was introduced only after a political campaign to reduce 'coloured colonial immigration' and did not apply to Irish labour migration. In the words of Hugh Gaitskell, then leader of the Labour opposition in Parliament: 'It is a plain anti-Commonwealth measure in theory and it is a plain anti-colour measure in practice' (ibid: 42). And as William Deedes, a government minister at the time, recalled in 1968: 'The Bill's real purpose was to restrict the influx of coloured immigrants. We were reluctant to say as much openly' (ibid: 44). The legislation was racist in intent and effect. Racism had been institutionalised from the top.

The sop to these controls was the introduction from 1965 onwards of 'measures to aid integration' of black people in the UK. But the contradictions inherent in this dual policy are clear cut. By banning the entry of certain categories of persons they are officially stamped 'unwanted surplus'. Whatever measures exist to aid the 'integration' of the same category of persons already resident, their very presence is deemed 'problematic', with the state expending considerable energy in reminding them of this. Tactics include regarding all family and relatives exercising their right to family reunion as possible illegal entrants (Commmission for Racial Equality, CRE, 1985), deportation (Gordon 1984; WING 1985), denying access to the welfare state (Gordon 1985), and regarding black youth as a 'law and order' problem (Gilroy 1982).

While all black people in, or exercising their right of entry to, Britain are singled out for this special treatment, black women are subject to even more fundamental forms of discrimination within immigration and nationality law than men. All British immigration law is framed on the assumption that women are chattels of men. The fact that historically hundreds of thousands of women have entered Britain in search of work is not recognised in immigration law, nor the fact that those same women might want to be joined by their husbands and/or children. For instance, when employment vouchers were introduced for Commonwealth citizens in 1962 women voucher holders had no automatic right to bring their spouses or children into the country, while men did. The same sexual discrimination applies to work permit holders (WING 1985).

In the run-up to the 1979 general election Margaret Thatcher spoke of the legitimacy of 'people's fears' of 'being swamped' and pledged that if elected her government would ban the entry of all foreign husbands and fiancés. A blanket ban would of course have led to the exclusion of white as well as black husbands. Opposition to her proposals reflected this concern, and the rules were voted down in Parliament later in 1979. The government hurriedly amended the proposals so as to exclude only the husbands and fiancés of women without British ancestry or, put differently, mainly black women. The rules were changed again in 1983 to allow all women with British citizenship regardless of ancestry to bring in foreign husbands or fiancés, but the burden of proof to produce satisfactory evidence whether or not the primary purpose of the marriage was immigration was shifted from the immigration officer to the applicant. In the case of the genuineness of an intended marriage it is unlikely that positive proof can in any case be found. The overriding philosophy is that all applicants are bogus (CRE 1985).

Thus black women, according to British immigration law, should stay in their or their ancestor's country of origin and look after a husband and children. Their role as individuals with rights, as workers, as persons who might want their husbands, fiancés and/or children to join them, is denied ideologically and often in practice. It is within this context of institutionalised racism and sexism which defines black women's rights as of lesser value than white women's that we can begin to understand the extent of structural racism in British labour markets.

Black women, racism and British labour markets

Since the late 1960s the Policy Studies Institute (PSI) has carried out three national surveys comparing the socio-economic position of black and white Britons. The last survey in 1982 concluded that Asian and Afro-Caribbean women in Britain remain largely confined to the jobs available to them or their mothers on entry to Britain. Their unemployment rate in 1982 was nearly twice that of white women, and the difference was even greater for the under-25 age group. Brown concludes: 'The processes of direct and indirect racial discrimination in employment operate as if to recognise the legitimacy of recruitment of black workers to some jobs but their exclusion from others (1984: 316).

Having said this at an aggregate level, the gap in job levels between black and white women is far less marked than that between black men and white men. In fact, between the 1974 and 1982 surveys there appears to have been some bridging of the gap between black and white women's job levels. But, as Brown points out, this is largely illusory: much of this change is caused by the fact that many black people in the poorest jobs have become unemployed and those in the better jobs have therefore become a larger proportion of all blacks in employment (1984: 179).

The 1982 PSI study found that, while more white women are in non-manual jobs than black women, the percentage of Asian women in professional and managerial jobs is almost as high as that of whites. In addition, while there is a higher proportion of black women workers in semi-skilled jobs, there are slightly more white unskilled women workers compared to black, which is explained by the higher proportion of white women in part-time employment (Brown 1984: 158). The same survey shows that 44 per cent of white women worked part-time against 29 per cent of Afro-Caribbean and only 16 per cent of Asian women.

In the Greater London Council *London Labour Plan* (1986) it is argued that the apparent similarity in the low status of black and white women

> comes from the fact that white women often find themselves trapped in low status part-time jobs. Black women are trapped in low status jobs by another mechanism – that of racial discrimination. They are much more likely to have to bring in a second wage, and to work full-time, partly because black men are also trapped in low status, low paid jobs. While full-time work lifts white women out of some of the worst low paid areas, this is much less true for black women.
>
> (GLC 1986: 114).

Sectorally there are marked ethnic differences, with Afro-Caribbean and white women divided between the manufacturing and service sector in a similar way, while Asian women are highly concentrated in manufacturing, particularly textiles and clothing. The category 'professional and scientific' services, accounts for 40 per cent of Afro-

Table 4.1 Job levels of women: all employees by ethnic group (column percentages)

Job level	White	West Indian	Asian	Indian	African Asian	Muslim	Hindu	Sikh
Professional, employer, manager	7	1	6	5	7	(7)	8	3
Other non-manual	55	52	42	35	52	(36)	49	19
Skilled manual and foremen	5	4	6	8	3	(1)	4	10
Semi-skilled manual	21	36	44	50	36	(52)	37	66
Unskilled manual	11	7	2	1	3	(5)	2	2
Base: female employees (weighted)	1,050	1,020	760	431	237	102	322	229
(unweighted)	495	502	340	195	102	45	146	105

Source: Brown 1984: 198.

Caribbean women, 25 per cent of white women, 19 per cent Indian and 7 per cent of African Asian women (Brown 1984: 160). While these figures reflect the distribution of these ethnic groups within the National Health Service, they hide ethnic groups' differential occupational distribution within it. Thus, while a high proportion of white women in this group are administrative workers, only 5 per cent of Afro-Caribbean women occupy such a post, the majority being found in nursing jobs. Outside of nursing most Afro-Caribbean women are confined to manual work in the service sector, particularly cleaning and catering (Brown 1984: 164; GLC 1986: 114).

In 1982, 14 per cent of Asian women compared to 7 per cent of white and 1 per cent of Afro-Caribbean women were self-employed. This figure represents a substantial shift for Asian women into self-employed status, a point to which we will return later.

The most marked differences between black and white women's employment profiles lie in unemployment levels. Not only are black women twice as likely as white women to be unemployed, but as unemployment has increased nationally it has affected black women far more severely. Why?

Explaining black women's unemployment

Racism and racial discrimination can be shown to explain virtually all the variance in black and white women's unemployment rates. While racism confined black women on entry to British labour markets to certain sectors and industries which have been most affected by recession, the persistence of racism has denied them the possibility of breaking out of gender-specific and ethnically segregated low-pay labour markets and into expanding areas of 'women's work'.

Thus first we must examine how and why black women were incorporated as workers into the post-war economy. In the inter-war years neo-Taylorite working practices were introduced into many British factories. As the economy expanded after the Second World War, production and managerial control in medium- and large-scale factories was organised in accordance with the principles of subdivided tasks and the deskilling of labour which afforded the possibility of enhanced control by management.

Because of its 'deskilled' character much of the work available was regarded as 'women's work' with correspondingly low rates of pay. The role of women, either as semi- or unskilled operatives or as routine office workers, expanded. While work that 'women did' became automatically defined as low skilled, there were further socially and legally constructed definitions of who did what within that occupational ghetto. White women sought work in the more 'desirable' world of the office, while black women were largely confined by legal subordination (in the form of either employment vouchers or work permits issued only for jobs for which no native, or now other European Community national, labour can be found – in other words, work shunned by white women) and/or racial subordination to semi- and unskilled jobs in manufacturing and the service sector (Phizacklea 1983a).

Whatever the difference between the two, in both instances women were being drawn into the labour process at one moment in a continuing trend towards further mechanisation. By the mid-1970s semi- and unskilled manual jobs in manufacturing had become the principal focus for the application of the new automation technologies which are both productivity-enhancing and labour-displacing. But, as Ralph Fevre has indicated in his study of the textile industry, the new jobs that go with the new technology go to white (predominantly male) not black workers, the latter being deemed unsuitable for new work requiring 'mental' attributes, (Fevre 1982). Thus the introduction of new technology reproduces and extends an existing racial division of labour and the traditional sexual division as well. Women's jobs predominantly require little or no technological competence (Cockburn 1985). Black women lose out on both counts, as is evidenced by the PSI findings which showed that, if white workers were as widely represented within those sectors, industries and job levels as black workers, their unemployment levels would still not be as high as those of black workers (Brown 1984). In short, while racial discrimination has confined black workers to low job levels, further discrimination results in black workers being more likely to lose their jobs than whites (Newnham 1986).

Young black women with few educational qualifications experience staggeringly high levels of unemployment. A Department of Employment survey carried out in 1984 indicated that 87 per cent had not found a job within a year of leaving school (*Employment Gazette* 1984). Well-qualified young black women fare little better. Shirley Dex's longitudinal analysis of the labour market experiences of a sample of educationally matched young black and white women indicated that the black women were last in the hiring queue and, in economic downturns, first in the firing queue (Dex 1983).

Even in those manual sectors of service work less susceptible to automation, for instance cleaning and catering, the increase in 'contracting out' to agencies has led to deterioration in pay and conditions and job losses (Coyle 1985; Lander 1986).

Thus, as work in the formal economy contracts, many black, particularly Asian, women have found work in the 'ethnic economy' as the only alternative. Whether or not this can provide the escape route for black women in the same way that it has for some black men is an open question.

Black women and the 'ethnic economy'

Entrepreneurship constitutes an escape route for many black men confined to dead-end manual jobs by racism and racial discrimination. Nevertheless during the 1980s entrepreneurship has become a necessity for many shaken out of labour-intensive manufacturing industries in which they were located. Black residential concentration in the inner cities has further reduced the alternatives for those made redundant. In many ways, entrepreneurship is then a form of disguised unemployment, with earnings often much lower than those that prevailed during wage-labouring days (Aldrich, Jones and McEvoy 1984).

But black women have not escaped the experience of dead-end, low-paid manual work and redundancy either, and work in the 'ethnic economy' is very often the only work to be had. With meagre start-up capital, minority entrepreneurial projects include small-scale manufacturing enterprises (clothing being the most important), service and retail outlets. Such projects have low entry barriers and are highly labour-intensive, with continuing access to a cheap and flexible labour force crucial to their economic viability.

But, as I have argued elsewhere (Phizacklea 1988: 22), ethnic business is predominantly male-controlled and labour-intensive; men are bosses, and women either are workers or can expect to control or give orders only to other women. This is not unique to 'ethnic' business, in so far as fewer women than men are entrepreneurs in the population as a whole. But it is argued that those ethnic groups deemed to be more 'successful' in the world of business than others are characterised by social structures which give easier access to female labour subordinated to patriarchal control mechanisms.

The publication in 1984 of the third PSI survey (Brown 1984) testified to the rise in self-employment among Asians in Britain compared to the 1974 survey. Ten years on, Asian men and women were more likely to be self-employed than white men and women, while Caribbean men and women remained under-represented within the ranks of the self-employed. Labour Force and other surveys also indicate over-representation of Turkish and Greek Cypriot men (22 per cent) and Chinese among the ranks of the self-employed.

Obviously, self-employment is not synonymous with enterpreneurship, though it is often casually adopted as a measure of such. For instance, many clothing workers report their employment status as self-employed, but this is a subjective definition for a situation where their boss is not interested in shouldering the costs or responsibilities of being an employer; they are left to their own devices. In reality they receive work from only one company; many are actually working on its premises and if they are they are supervised. Thus they are expected to behave as employees without any of the benefits of employee status (Phizacklea 1988).

In addition, in the clothing industry many wives and daughters of Asian, Turkish and Greek Cypriot entrepreneurs supply unpaid labour as machinists, finishers and also supervisors. The evidence suggests that such women do not receive any 'independent' reward but view any surplus that might accrue from their labour as an essential contribution to the family income. Thus female members and young male members of the family work under patriarchal relations of production, remaining dependent for their maintenance on the boss, who is usually also the head of household, in return for their efforts.

But men and women working in these circumstances usually have differing expectations of their jobs. The woman machinist might at best expect a supervisory role, while the male machinist's confinement to low-pay 'women's work' is a necessary part of an entrepreneurial apprenticeship. The 'fringe benefit' of entrepreneurial training is reserved for men.

But not all male entrepreneurs serve such apprenticeships, their entry into the clothing industry being based entirely on access to the sewing skills of female family and co-ethnics and meagre redundancy payments. In the West Midlands a whole new clothing industry has 'taken off' on this basis since 1978. Asian male-workers were recruited throughout the 1960s to work in the West Midlands metal manufacturing and engineering industries. Yet between 1975 and 1982, 74 per cent of all industrial job losses in the area were in industries and areas of Asian concentration, and unemployment rates here rose to between 40 and 47 per cent (Gaffikin and Nickson n.d.).

A small redundancy payment is enough to set oneself up as a clothing producer if there is also access to skilled, cheap and flexible labour. Asian women have become the predominant suppliers of that labour in what has become the only manufacturing growth area in the whole of the West Midlands economy. It is estimated that at least 20,000 new jobs have been created in small clothing firms in the area since the late 1970s (West Midlands Low Pay Unit 1984). The 1984 West Midlands Low Pay Unit survey indicated that pay for long hours and intensive work was below the minimum in such firms. Nevertheless this type of exploitation must be seen within the context of staggeringly high levels of unemployment within the region for Asian men and women, racism and exclusionary practices in other sectors of the labour market. The threat of unemployment and the knowledge that there are other minority women who can be substituted for the same job act as a powerful deterrent to resistance among an already vulnerable workforce. However, such pressures have not deterred Asian women from struggling for union recognition in their workplaces in a number of notable disputes in the area. In the majority of cases, employers have won by sacking all the workers or by using the tactics of closing down the firm and re-opening under a new name and with a new workforce (Bishton 1982). In other cases, employers have used husbands to bring women workers 'into line'. As Swasti Mitter (1986: 57) has argued, 'the servility, subservience and passivity that the communities expect of wives towards their husbands, daughters-in-law towards father-in-law in the home, were reproduced to an important extent in the factories.

I would suggest that access to family or community members as low-wage workers under what resemble patriarchal relations of production provides a key competitive advantage as far as the labour-intensive 'start-up' business is concerned. Ethnic groups with different social structures, for example Afro-Caribbeans, will be at a disadvantage, research indicating that Caribbean businesses are not characteristically labour-intensive (Ward and Reeves 1984).

Finally, we will turn to the position of black women and homeworking, homeworkers constituting one of the most vulnerable sections of the labour-force.

Black women and homeworking

According to the 1984 Labour Force Survey (Newnham 1987: 1) 66 per cent of white women are economically active, 71 per cent of Afro-Caribbean, 58 per cent of Indian, but only 17 per cent of Pakistani and Bangladeshi women. While all recent official surveys confirm these figures, we know that in the case of Asian, particularly Pakistani and Bangladeshi women, these figures constitute a gross underestimate. For instance, in his study of Rochdale, Anwar (1979) states that most Pakistani women in that town are homeworkers. Community workers in Tower Hamlets assured me that this was also the case with Bangladeshi women residents, who take in homework out of financial necessity (Phizacklea 1988).

Obviously it is not only Asian women who are homeworkers (see Allen and Wolkowitz's study of white women homeworkers in Yorkshire, 1987). The findings of a recent Department of Employment report suggests that the homeworking labour force differs to a small degree from the labour force as a whole 'in being slightly less likely to be members of ethnic minority groups' (Hakim 1987a: 94). In addition, it is claimed that manufacturing homework is a 'relative rarity' (Hakim 1984). Evidence from local homeworking support groups directly challenges this official view (see, for instance, Armstrong (Leicester Outwork Campaign) 1982; Greenwich Homeworkers Project 1987; Wolverhampton Homeworkers Research Project 1984). And we must therefore ask, why the apparent gap between this official view and reality? There are, for a start, some obvious sampling problems with the survey. The report is based on interviews with 576 people drawn from the 90,000-strong 1981 Labour Force Survey. The latter was based on a random national sample, whereas manufacturing homeworkers are concentrated in inner cities and certain discrete areas of the country associated with clothing and hosiery production. In areas such as inner London, the response rate was only 43 per cent; for many black women, fear of racial attack deters them from answering the door to a stranger. In addition, unless mother-tongue interviewers are used in particular localities, there is no possiblity of interviewing homeworkers. Finally, because so much homeworking is 'off the books', fear of reprisals makes many homeworkers reluctant to declare themselves.

The experience of all the local homeworking projects is that only after many years of building trust between the project workers and homeworkers will the latter feel able to talk openly about their work. The Wolverhampton Homeworkers Research Project was built on this kind of trust and drew on information gathered by Asian women from fifty Asian women homeworkers. The project set out to ascertain why women became homeworkers and to examine their employment conditions and rights. Forty-seven of the fifty women had children, the majority having three or more children; 72 per cent gave child care as the main reason for working at home, while only three women mentioned cultural or religious reasons for homeworking. The majority had worked outside the home before the birth of their first child. None were currently members of a trade union; nearly all had to purchase their own sewing-machine at an average cost of £300, and yet their pay varied between 25p and £1 an hour. 60 per cent of the women described themselves as self-employed or did not understand the relationship between themselves and their employer. All of the women were involved in an unwritten contractual relationship with their employer (Wolverhampton Homeworkers Research Project 1984).

Conclusion

Women generally are confined to low-skill and low-paid work. Structural changes in the economy, particularly the growth of the service sector, simply reproduce the traditional sexual division of work and rewards. For black women, the most marked changes in their employment profile over the last ten years has been that even more have been excluded from employment in the formal economy altogether. While we have shown that work in the 'ethnic economy' may pick up some of this unemployment, the shift could hardly be said to constitute an improvement for black women given the characteristic pay and conditions in this highly competitive sector of the economy. In addition, many black, particularly Asian, women's work is hidden in the home, homeworkers constituting the most vulnerable section of the labour force. Racism and racial discrimination result in black women finding it harder to get any job and being more likely to lose their jobs than white women. For this reason any programmes aimed at combating sex discrimination and gender segregation must by definition aim simultaneously to combat racial discrimination and segregation too. If not, then the future for black women in British labour markets is very bleak.

5: Gender divisions and wage labour in English history

Chris Middleton

Wage labour is not an invention of the capitalist economy.[1] As far back as the thirteenth century large feudal estates would meet part of their labour need by employing staffs of wage workers known as *famuli*.[2] But the *famuli* were in no sense proletarians. They were bonded labourers, prohibited from selling their services on any labour market.

Among the lists of *famuli* still surviving are a set for eighteen manors on estates belonging to the Earls of Cornwall, the Abbots of Crowland and the Bishop of Winchester (Postan 1954: appendix II). They shed some interesting light on the sexual division of labour under feudalism. Wage labour had little status in this society, and most *famuli* would probably have been recruited from poorer families in the community (Britton 1977: 92), yet the records list a considerable number of labourers who were recruited for their special skills. Nearly all the 'specialists' so listed were engaged in activities conventionally defined as men's work (ploughmen, shepherds, herdsmen, millers, etc.). Openings for skilled women (chiefly in the dairy and garden) were few in comparison, and the majority of women workers were simply recorded as 'servants'.[3] Thus (even though a servant was not necessarily a domestic drudge, and some may have been employed in predominantly agricultural tasks) there is evidence here of a pattern of job segregation by sex which has a remarkably familiar ring:

- Recruitment to most positions was governed by sex.
- There were fewer opportunities for women in this relatively secure (though hardly prestigious) form of paid employment.
- The *range* of specialist work open to women was far narrower than that for men.
- Most women were recruited to service positions of an unspecified nature (e.g. 'one woman-servant'), whereas adult males were widely employed in specialist capacities.
- There was a marked tendency for women to be employed in domestic services.

The purpose of this chapter is to assess the relevance of such evidence to the debate about gender divisions in the labour markets of contemporary capitalism. Most contributions to that debate claim either that labour market segmentation is itself a function of capitalist development or that the source of gender divisions within the labour market can be traced to a family-household system specifically associated with capitalist formations. The validity of such accounts must be brought into question if it can be shown that patterns of gender segregation and inequality are not confined to a single mode of production.

The argument that follows falls into three parts. First, I examine various 'class-derivationist' accounts of gender segregation in the labour market and suggest that they share more common ground with feminist approaches than is generally supposed. In particular, both traditions have regarded the conditions goyerning women's entry into the labour market as the key to understanding gender divisions within it. A range of historical evidence is then advanced to suggest that the terms of entry may not, in fact, be critical. The evidence indicates that the patriarchal organisation of wage work in pre-industrial England was remarkably similar to that informing the labour market under industrial capitalism, yet was compatible with significant variations both in the character of the labour supply and in the conditions under which labour 'offered' its services. Finally, we consider the implications of this finding for feminist theories of patriarchy. While, superficially, the evidence seems to confirm the existence of an autonomous system of patriarchal oppression (one, in particular, that operates independently of class), the logical grounds for drawing such an inference are flawed. In fact, that conclusion can be sustained only if the evidence is wrenched from its proper historical context.

Theories of gender segregation in the labour market

Capitalist labour markets are stratified, and the divisions within them coincide (though never perfectly) with the segregation of the workforce on the basis of ascriptive characteristics such as gender, race, age and disability. These two observations form the bedrock of contemporary labour market theory. How and why labour markets became structured as they did, and the mode of their articulation with gender and other differences, form the key areas for debate.

Theories of labour market stratification have generally been developed in isolation from feminist accounts of the sexual division of labour. They may be described as 'class-derivation' theories in so far as they locate the source of segmentation within the imperatives of capital accumulation and/or conflicts between capital and labour. Some of them focus on capitalist initiatives, while others prefer to emphasise strategies evolved by workers endeavouring to improve the terms on which they sell their labour power. Both varieties have been criticised by feminists for incorporating gender divisions into a predetermined structure of labour market relations, i.e. as a 'by-product of the dynamics of capital accumulation and capital restructuring' (Beechey 1983: 41) or else as 'a by-product of struggles between capital and labour' (Walby 1983: 158). I am not convinced, however, that this properly represents the 'class-derivationist' position. These theories do not, in fact, view the imperatives of capital accumulation or class struggle as major determinants of *gendered* segregation in the occupational sector. It is the segmentation of the labour market, not gender divisions as such, which they see as deriving from the capitalist process. Thus we need to distinguish three possible positions:

(1) Gender divisions in the labour market are a by-product of processes of capital accumulation and/or class struggle.
(2) Segmented labour markets are created by processes of capital accumulation and/or class struggle. Gender divisions become superimposed on the market for reasons which lie *beyond the scope of the model*.
(3) Patriarchal forms of segmentation are neither derivative of class relations nor superimposed upon the labour market. They reflect an independent process of structuration.

As indicated, 'class-derivation' theories are often accused of adopting position (1), but position (2) is actually more typical of their approach. All major studies within this tradition argue that gender becomes relevant within the labour market because of conditions *external* to it: namely, the differential characteristics of men and women workers or the circumstances governing their availability for wage work – neither of which is seen as determined wholly by capital accumulation or class struggle.

Theories focusing on employer initiatives include dual labour market theory (Barron and Norris 1976; Doeringer and Piore 1971), radical theory (Gordon, Edwards and Reich 1982; Reich, Gordon and Edwards 1973), the deskilling thesis (Braverman 1974) and many accounts of the industrial reserve army. Whatever the nature of their disagreements, all treat gender divisions in a fundamentally similar way. They explain developments in the structure of the labour market in terms of 'demand-side' economics, while identifying its gendered dimension as a function ultimately of labour supply – and hence constructed by social processes beyond the province of labour market theory. Edwards provides the clearest acknowledgement of this. He believes that 'to understand the historical forces that established and maintain the divisions [within the labour market], we must look to the job structure'. On the other hand, 'for both blacks and women, the separate dialectics of race and sex condition their participation in the capitalist economy . . . *and require separate analysis.*' (Edwards 1979: 166, 197, 195, my emphasis). In this interpretation, then, distinctions of gender are superimposed on a predetermined framework of labour market divisions.

Theories which concentrate on capitalist initiatives may under-estimate the degree to which gender divisions in the labour market are attributable to working-class action. Rubery, for instance, suggests that workers are threatened by the deskilling process and may be induced to take 'defensive actions . . . to stratify the labour force, control entry to occupations and maintain skill status long after these skill divisions have become irrelevant' (Rubery 1980: 257). In this case, segmentation arises because the existing labour force protects itself against competition from new influxes of workers (comprising, in the recent history of capitalism, female and immigrant labour). Likewise, nineteenth-century workers resisted the cheapening of labour power by attempting to limit the number of married women entering the labour market (Humphries 1977). Though this would not cause segregation *within* the labour market, it might help to explain women's poorer market capacity and thus their consignment to secondary sector occupations. Once again, gender discrimination in the labour market is explained in terms of the determinants of labour supply.

In all these accounts, labour market stratification becomes *gendered* because of processes occurring in the wider society. Indeed, for Rubery and, to some extent, Edwards, women's recruitment into the secondary sector can be viewed as historically contingent – a product of their previous exclusion from the labour market and the particular timing of their re-entry into the waged labour force. However, radical theory's main explanatory thrust focuses on monopoly capitalism's 'divide-and-rule' strategies. Edwards suggests that pre-existing divisions of race and sex are manipulated in order to foment working-class disunity, though it was 'the lack of any effective bargaining strength among blacks and women [that] made discrimination possible' (Edwards 1979: 195). From this perspective there was nothing fortuitous about segregation; gender discrimination was the result of deliberate policy on the part of employers. But the latter's success is still seen as conditional on *extraneous* processes that have resulted in differential market capacities for men and women. It is, of course, important to distinguish between the actual characteristics of workers and the stereotypes which are held of them. Both Piore and Edwards tend to accept that workers in the secondary labour market lack stable work habits, while Braverman and Rubery assume that women provide a cheap and unskilled workforce. But even where care is taken to avoid this particular pitfall, as in Barron and Norris's account, the characteristics of women workers (real or ascribed) still enter the analysis as an exogenous 'given'.

Perhaps it is to be expected that theories emphasising the employers' responsibility for segmentation will treat conditions governing the supply of labour as peripheral. But even studies which privilege supply-side economics by concentrating on workers' strategies tend to refer somewhat casually to 'traditional' family forms and 'traditional' patterns of job segregation (Humphries 1977; Rubery and Tarling 1982). It is implicitly accepted that the source of women's poor bargaining position and/or low level of motivation can be traced to the family-household system and women's continuing responsibility for the domestic welfare of its members. Few analyses of labour market segmentation have actually investigated this wider sexual division of labour, though Brenner and Ramas's recent article (1984) is a major exception. In their view the labour market operates in a 'sex-blind' way. Segregation arises because, at the point of entry, women are in a poor bargaining position owing to historically specific domestic responsibilities. Brenner and Ramas's argument is thus similar to others reviewed here. The novelty of their approach lay in their willingness to pursue the analysis beyond the labour market.

To summarise the argument thus far: 'class-derivation' theorists do not normally claim to explain gender as a principle of stratification in the labour process. Rather, *they have taken as given* various attributes of women as a supply of labour (meagre or unrecognised skills, a readiness to accept low pay, low bargaining strength, domestic commitments, etc.) which result in their allocation to the secondary sector. These characteristics presuppose a patriarchal division of labour or ideology operating beyond the boundaries of the labour market. Yet these are exactly the areas that many feminist critics have been keen to explore and which many have privileged within their own analytical approaches. One thinks perhaps of Delphy's domestic mode of production; of Barrett's discussion of familial ideology; and of Beechey's earlier emphasis, since qualified, on the special characteristics of married women workers. On this reading, then, a theoretical *rapprochement* between 'class-derivation' theories of labour market segmentation and feminist analyses of the sexual division of labour seems quite feasible.

But are the circumstances governing women's entry into the labour market really the critical factor? Here a broader historical canvas may prove illuminating. A reassessment of labour market theory would certainly be required if it were shown that comparable patterns of gender segregation and inequality had prevailed in the wage-labouring sectors of non-capitalist economies which often lacked a market in labour and where family-household structures were so markedly different.

Wage labour in feudal England

Let us return first to the case of the medieval *famuli*. It should perhaps be emphasised that most of the farmworkers recruited for their skills would not be 'specialists' in any modern sense of the word. Many farming skills had a seasonal application only, and versatility was essential. Moreover, since desmesne farming in most regions relied on the unwaged labour of bonded tenants, the *famulus* was not the most typical figure in the rural landscape. Yet it would be unwise to belittle the significance of these estate records for they testify to the fact that the rudimentary elements of occupational specialisation (and perhaps of occupational identity too) were present in one of the few sectors of the rural economy where such a development could be sustained, i.e. where the unit of labour was sufficiently large and the technical division of labour sufficiently advanced to allow for the frequent and regular use of specialist skills. The records show clearly that these embryonic occupational identities were largely confined to men.

Apart from the *famuli* two other kinds of wage labour supplemented the basic system of rental exploitation: namely, skilled artisans and day-labourers. The occupational experiences of the former varied enormously. Smiths, for example, might be full-time craftsmen plying their trade from a single village, whereas thatchers and common carpenters normally provided their specialist services on a seasonal or part-time basis, engaging in farmwork for the rest of their time. Other craftsmen, especially masons, more specialist carpenters and those engaged in the building trade, tended to form a migratory but highly paid labour force. Women are sometimes recorded as assistants in these trades (thatching, in particular), but otherwise all these craftworkers were male.

At the other end of the wage labouring scale was feudalism's version of the reserve army. This was drawn from a class of landless labourers and cottars whose subsistence depended on a combination of grazing and gathering rights supplemented by income from day wage-labour. These, the poorest labourers of all, included a high number of women, and it is unlikely that the sexual segregation of labour was as strict among them as it was among other groups of wage-workers. Yet even here there were distinct patterns of recruitment for men and women. Regular paid day-labour seems to have been a male prerogative, and the only work available to women and children was of a seasonal kind. (Rogers 1866: Vol I, 289 ff.; 1894: 169–70). The circumstances of female cottars and labourers living alone, of whom there may have been considerable numbers, must have been particularly dire (Hilton 1975: 27–36; Russell 1948: 61–9).

Information on wages in medieval England is too sketchy for any detailed comparison of male and female rates to be possible, but certain broad patterns do emerge clearly. The best series of data is an extensive, but frustratingly patchy, listing of payments for the years 1259–1400 compiled by Thorold Rogers. The difficulties in interpreting these listings are formidable, and so the following comments are confined to data which can be expressed unequivocally as the day-rate for an individual labourer. One fact stands out sharply: wages for work normally performed by women were significantly lower than those paid for men's work. In the eighty years prior to the Black Death (1268–1347) the median day-rate for men's work was 2.5d (N = 25; range: 1d–4d), while that for women's work was only 1d (N = 17; range: 0.75d–1.5d). Rates rose sharply thereafter (1349–94) to medians of 3d for men's work (N = 13; range: 2d–8d) and to 2d for women's work (N = 5; range: 1d–2d) (adapted from Rogers 1866: Vol. II, 576–83). Other figures in the listings resist even the simplest computation but certainly bear out the general impression of inequality between male and female earnings.

It is hard to tell whether differences in wage rates were solely a function of the sexual division of labour, or whether women were paid less even when they performed identical work. Rogers believed that male and female harvesters were paid equal rates during the thirteenth century, and Hilton came across a similar example for the 1380s involving some Gloucestershire reapers, though this may conceivably have been due to labour shortages (Hilton 1975: 102–3; Rogers 1866: Vol. I, 281; 1894: 170). But, against this, we have the anonymous author of a late thirteenth-century farming guide, entitled *Hosebondrie*, advising estate managers to employ women for certain tasks because they would accept 'much less money than a man would take' (Oschinsky 1971: 427, citing Bennett n.d.).

In sum, women are rarely documented in medieval records as performing agricultural work of a skilled or prestigious nature, and they appear to have received considerably less pay than men.

The expansion of wage labour: farm servants and day-labourers

Feudal relations in England never recovered from the havoc wrought by famine and plague over the course of the fourteenth century. The fifteenth century became, above all, the age of the yeoman farmer, i.e. of the middling peasant relying heavily on family labour, though signs of the incipient commercialisation of agriculture were already visible by the century's end (Tawney 1912). This development was associated with, and arguably responsible for, a vast increase in the proportion of the rural population who were dependent on wage labour.

Despite the disappearance of bonded labour the crucial separation of the wage-labouring population into 'living-in' servants and day-labourers persisted. Indeed, this division became a key organising principle of agricultural labour in a way that had never been true of the medieval economy. By the sixteenth century farm service involved a far higher proportion of the labouring population than before, and had also acquired new functions and meanings. The farm servants who lived in, 'servants in husbandry', were hired annually, but cannot be regarded as proletarians with long-term contracts.[4] Mostly, they were young single persons entering households as dependants, their time placed at their master's disposal for the duration of the contract. They became, in effect, hired members of a working family, and many, especially women and girls, would have been kept busy round the house as well as in the fields.

Farm service had become the main institutional source of continually available labour in a social structure where co-resident families were generally small.[5] It flourished because of the importance of the small farmer, offering a flexible solution to cyclical imbalances between labour needs and resources arising from the family's developmental cycle. One historian succinctly expressed it thus: 'Service in husbandry solved the cyclical problem by eliminating it. The family was simply redefined' (Kussmaul 1981: 24). From the servants' point of view their term of employment offered a training in farmwork and domestic production. But the arrangement was hardly one of their own choosing, and there can be little doubt about the stigma attached to service, for women quite as much as men (Hajnal 1965: 132).[6]

The position of day-labourers was quite different. Typically, they were married adults, living independently of their employer and hired only when he needed them – thus their experience of work was likely to be seasonal, intermittent and dependent on the vagaries of the weather and their own state of health. The division between service and day-labour had become, for the majority of agricultural workers, a matter of successive stages in their personal biography; a position characterised by relatively secure employment but semi-servile status was exchanged, on marriage, for an uncertain and often poverty-stricken independence.

Women were particularly associated with household service (Kussmaul 1981). Although unmarried persons of both sexes were supposed to be placed under a master's authority, young women were more vigorously coerced than men and fewer remained unplaced (Emmison 1976: 147–64; Scott 1973: 41).[7] Gregory King estimated that there were 300,000 female servants in 1695 compared to 260,000 male (King 1810: 39). Thus the protection which service afforded against the uncertainties and irregularity of the labour market was extended to rather more women than men, but only by reaffirming their subservient status. Girls in service were expected to acquire not only the skills they would need as a farm labourer's wife, but also the virtues of a submissive demeanour.

The experience of independent labourers was generally one of chronic underemployment, but women appear to have fared even worse than men. On average they worked fewer days in the year, and it was rare indeed for them to find regular employment outside their own homes. Where they did manage to do so it was usually by combining agricultural work with menial household tasks such as washing and scrubbing, or with cooking for the field-labourers (Scott 1973: 128–30).

Between the sixteenth and eighteenth centuries the preponderance of the large capitalist farm in the agrarian economy advanced inexorably through discontinuous but cumulative processes of dispossession and amalgamation, expanding especially in the south-eastern counties of arable farming. Farming methods and technology became subject to the competitive 'disciplines' of the market, though, as we shall see, adherence to those disciplines was sometimes overridden by patriarchal ideology and conventions. The large estates employed proportionately fewer servants-in-husbandry than smaller farms and relied heavily on day-labour. The trend towards occupational specialisation was also at its most marked here, though regular full-time work in a single job was still the exception.

Few of the opportunities arising on these estates were open to women, who continued to be confined to the dairy and market garden. In fact, the pattern of occupational specialisation on the large capitalist farms seems to have resembled, but in a more entrenched form, the model of gendered segregation that we observed among the medieval *famuli* (Everitt 1967: 430 ff.). However, the work experience of women could not remain unaffected while prospects for men were improving. Changing technology and divisions of labour often meant a deteriorating situation for women within the labour process. As agriculture grew more specialised and the distribution of tasks less fluid, the work of ordinary labourers tended to become even less varied and rewarding than it had been before.

Harvest labour: a case study of day-labour

A clear illustration of the effects advancing technology and specialisation could have is provided by the history of the harvest, always the season of greatest demand for day- or weekly labour. The harvest called for the involvement of all members of the community, and at no other time of the year could so many women be found working outside their household. It was also the season when wages tended to be most buoyant.

The focal work of the harvest, and the best paid, was the actual cutting of the crop. This could be done either by *reaping* with a sickle or by *mowing*, two-handed, with the heavier and more productive corn-scythe. Male harvesters predominated in this part of the work, but at the beginning of our period they certainly held no monopoly. The records contain numerous references to female reapers and even a few to female mowers.[8] But the gradual replacement of sickle by scythe had a deleterious effect on women's involvement (Roberts 1979). Wherever the new corn-cutting technology was introduced, which happened with gathering momentum from the later Middle Ages, women ceased to be employed as shearers. In the opinion of Michael Roberts, and also in that of many contemporary writers, the critical factor in this was the additional size and weight of the scythe which 'emphasised the strength and stature required of the mower, effectively confining its use to the strongest men' (Roberts 1979: 8). However, the adoption of the corn-scythe did not eliminate women from the harvest entirely. Although a mower could cut larger quantities of corn more quickly than a reaper, he 'left the corn he had cut in more disarray and, as a result, more subsidiary workers were needed to gather the produce of a mower than were necessary for each individual reaper' (Roberts 1979: 13). Thus the introduction of the new technology had complex implications for the pattern of women's work in the harvest fields. Women were displaced from the highly paid work of shearing but, for a long period, were even more in demand as poorly paid rakers and followers. A classic case of deskilling following the introduction of new technology?

Research by Snell (1985) has demonstrated that the trend towards male domination of the harvest accelerated during the latter half of the eighteenth century in the grain-growing counties of the south and east. The harvest had traditionally been a time of low unemployment for both men and women, but from 1760 the seasonal curve of women's unemployment continued to rise during the summer and early autumn in contrast to the male curve which reflected an ever greater job security during the harvest months. These curves show that in many parishes women wage-workers had not just become marginal to the harvest effort but had been eliminated from it altogether – apart from the very short-term work of gleaning. Frequency indicators from the 1834 Report of the Poor Law Commission further suggest that their activity had come to be concentrated on hay-making and stone picking, on the spring work of weeding corn, and gleaning (Snell 1985: 55–6). The lowest rates of female unemployment were now in the spring, which, as Snell emphasised, was 'a period of the year characterised . . . by relatively slight labour costs and by a low demand for labour' (1985: 22). Or, to put it from the women's perspective, they had less work and less money.

Thus we have shown how, over the course of several centuries, the sexual division of harvest labour was transformed through two distinct processes. Initially, segregation was intensified by a technological change; the gradual introduction of the corn-scythe led to a channelling of female harvesters into subsidiary activities; and, whatever we may think of Roberts's explanation that women are less likely to have the physical capacity to mow, the *hierarchical* ramifications of this process still need to be analysed sociologically. The second and subsequent movement entailed the exclusion of women from the harvest fields. This process was relatively abrupt and confined for the most part to the corn-growing counties. Snell's analysis gives more weight to socio-economic forces. The shift to specialised crop farming had exacerbated seasonal fluctuations in the demand for labour at the same time as agricultural labourers were being turned into a proletariat wholly dependent on wage income. Seasonal unemployment simply pushed them on to the parish. In effect, an economy of underemployed labour had been transformed into one of structural unemployment. If the level of women's agricultural involvement had been maintained under these circumstances, male vulnerability to seasonal unemployment would have been even greater, and Snell thinks it likely that pressure arose from within the male labour force itself to exclude female competition (Snell 1985: 57–66).

Wage discrimination: servants and labourers

Evidence on wages in pre-industrial England after the mid-fourteenth century comes in two forms: direct evidence of wages paid from account books (which is fairly reliable, but scarce) and the indirect evidence of legally assessed maximum wage rates. While early attempts at wage regulation enjoyed limited success and so give little indication of actual wage levels, payments in excess of the prescribed rates became relatively uncommon after the Statute of Artificers (1562–3) had devolved responsibility for setting maximum wages to county level (Clark 1919: chap. 3; Kussmaul 1981: 35–9). From then on maximum rates seem to have reflected local conditions and practice.

Estimates of gender inequality among agricultural wage-workers must distinguish clearly between the incomes of servants (among whom women and girls were disproportionately represented) and those of day-labourers. Farm servants were in the singular position of being half family members, half hired helps. Provision of their food and board was part of an obligatory relationship as well as a material necessity. For the most part it appears that servants were well fed, reasonably well housed according to the standards of the day and abysmally low paid. Gender inequality among servants hinged on the last of these, and the evidence is unambiguous. Women received only a fraction of men's wages.

On a random sample of thirty assessments in various English counties between 1564 and 1724, Kussmaul found that the median female servant's wage was only 57 per cent of the median male wage (mean = 61 per cent; range: 30–83 per cent), while two later sets of figures for Lincolnshire at the end of the eighteenth century show even higher average discrepancies (Kussmaul 1981: 37, 182, appendix 2). Figures presented by Roberts over a roughly similar period, but on a narrower sample, produce a median of 57 per cent and a mean of 52 per cent

(Roberts 1979: 19). These last assessments, selected because they allow valid comparisons to be made over time, show that the extent of inequality in each county remained remarkably stable for several decades (see Figure 5.1). Yet, at any one time, men's wages were much more variable than women's, partly because young boys could anticipate substantial wage rises as they grew older, while female wages rose little with age.

Day-rates for independent labourers were higher than those for farm servants, but show a similar pattern of gender inequality. Some of the fullest surviving estate records are those kept by the Yorkshire farmer Henry Best. Here the median wage for female harvesters was 75 per cent that paid to men; the mean was 72 per cent.[9] This suggests a somewhat narrower differential between male and female day-rates than existed for servants, and this pattern is reflected in other parts of the country.

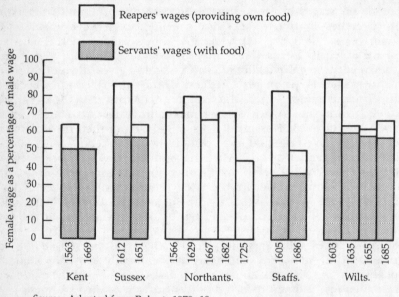

Source: Adapted from Roberts 1979: 19

Figure 5.1   Ratio of female to male assessed wages, 1563–1725

The direct, same-year comparisons of gender differentials for harvest reapers and servants for four of the counties recorded in Figure 5.1 indicate that sex discrimination in wage levels was significantly greater among servants than it was among day-labourers.

However, Figure 5.1 also tells a story of widening differentials between male and female harvest labourers in the midlands, south, and east. The growing segregation of work in the harvest fields, and the marginalizing of women's activities there, had the predictable result of heightening wage inequalities between the sexes. This pattern is confirmed by fuller series of data for agricultural wages in general which indicate that gender differentials remained more or less constant until about 1760, when male rates began to surge ahead while female wages declined steadily in real terms until the first decade of the nineteenth century, clearly reflecting women's exclusion from harvest labour and their removal to the low-paid, low-demand spring season (Snell 1985: 29–34).

Principles of gender stratification in the history of wage labour

The most striking empirical point to emerge must surely be the sheer longevity of some highly familiar features of gender stratification. Segregation and inequality in the organisation of wage labour have persisted with remarkable tenacity through profound changes in the wider social order of class and gender relations. Let us now recapitulate the main findings and assess their implications for theories of occupational segregation.

(a) Wage labour has consistently been stratified on the basis of gender. This has been so even in the absence of a labour market. We saw this most clearly in the organisation of *famuli* labour on the feudal desmesnes and, later, within the farm-servant class (for it seems most unlikely that the servant-hiring fairs functioned as impersonal labour markets) (Kussmaul 1981). In these contexts it seems inappropriate to talk either of factors governing the terms of women's 'entry' into the labour process or of the relative 'bargaining strength' of different groups of workers.

(b) Until the late eighteenth century the economy was characterised by chronic underemployment. Thus, even where labour markets were emerging, it is unlikely that the 'availability', 'commitment' or 'dispensability' of different groups of workers were a major factor in determining their variable conditions of employment.

(c) Male workers have also been stratified by skill, status and income despite the lack of a labour market. Indeed, the extent of differentiation among male workers appears to have been consistently greater than that among female workers. The experiences of men as a group have been more diverse than those of women, with regard both to the variety of jobs available to them, and to the range of incomes they have been able to secure.

(d) Stability and security of employment in early modern England were not associated with skill, high overall wages or status. Many skills could be utilised only on a seasonal basis, and most farmers relied on day-labour for work requiring these skills. Many skilled labourers, therefore, belonged to a seasonal reserve army of labour. Farming households employed servants on annual contracts to meet their needs for routine agricultural labour.

(e) Women have long been associated with the household and domestic tasks, but there is no evidence that women's disadvantaged position in the occupational structure was a consequence of their responsibility for or commitment to their families. In pre-industrial England their connection with the household was intensified by marriage (Middleton 1979), but certainly not dependent on it; single women regularly performed domestic services in the households of strangers. Women in service were almost invariably unmarried and childless, but gender still provided a template for occupational segregation in this sphere. Indeed, differentials between men and women servants were wider than those for other contemporary groups of wage workers.

(f) There is little evidence that segregation in the countryside was ever caused by male workers closing ranks against unskilled and low-paid female competition. (The towns and professions were another matter entirely.) The one exception we encountered was the highly proletarianised harvest labourers discussed by Snell. But this example is interesting for its reversal of the more recent process of male working-class defensive action described in the combined writings of Humphries and Rubery, where the channelling of women into secondary sector jobs is interpreted as a consequence of their earlier expulsion from the labour market. For female harvest labourers this sequence was reversed; they suffered exclusion only *after* a long and secular process of increasing segregation. The sense of historical contingency which we remarked in Rubery's position is rather undermined by this observation – it appears that sex discrimination could be directed quite as much against established women workers as against outsiders and newcomers.

Studies of economic life in pre-industrial England show that gender has been a basic principle of occupational division and inequality from as far back as the thirteenth century. In most cases, the organisation of labour was inseparable from questions of political authority and marital status. Gender, most emphatically, was *not* a distinction to be grafted on to a pre-existing framework of segregation because of the particular attributes of women workers or the circumstances under which they sold their labour. The utter durability of this principle despite profound changes in the mode of production must cast doubt on the validity of models that attribute its occurrence under industrial capitalism to class dynamics or family-household systems that are specific to that mode.

Interpreting historical data on the control of women's labour

These findings on long-term trends in the organisation of wage labour show that patriarchal forms may have a remarkable capacity for survival, and appear to confirm the existence of an autonomous system of patriarchy that is largely independent of the mode of production and class structure. The data presented are so vulnerable to this kind of misreading that they cannot be left to speak for themselves. I will therefore end by indicating some of the problems with this interpretation.

The concept of patriarchy was born from a perception of male dominance as virtually ubiquitous. Some radical feminists readily embraced the ahistorical implications of this by identifying women as an invariably oppressed sex, but the more historically minded Marxist-feminist tradition has understandably proved more wary (Alexander and Taylor 1982; Beechey 1979; Rowbotham 1982). Should the concept be repudiated as inherently ahistorical, or can it be developed as a vehicle for exploring the relationship between gender oppression and modes of production? Writers like Hartmann (1979) and Cockburn (1983) have argued that patriarchy is an essential concept for historically conceived feminist research and have vigorously defended the formulation of distinct feminist categories on the grounds that previous attempts to *integrate* feminism and Marxism have led either to the marginalisation of feminist concerns or else to their incorporation within the latter's conceptual framework.[10] This accurately diagnoses the limitations of much past work in the field, but their solution, nevertheless, is logically flawed.

Marxist-feminists who favour the concept of patriarchy are engaged in two distinct though closely related projects. The first is to historicise the concept so as to invest it with *explanatory* power in historical and comparative research. 'Patriarchy' would then possess a theoretical status within feminist theory similar to that enjoyed by the concept of 'class' within Marxism. The second objective is to establish the existence of patriarchy as an *independent* order of inequality and control so as to avoid the kind of reductionist theorising that analyses 'the sexual subordination of women . . . as a by-product of class processes' (Cockburn 1983: 6). The following discussion examines this theoretical programme in relation to patriarchal labour processes.

There have actually been rather few attempts to trace the pattern of job segregation and control by sex through the course of a transition from one mode of production to another. Hartmann's has been one of the most influential. She argues that

> before capitalism, a patriarchal system was established in which
> men controlled the labour of women and children in the family,
> and that in so doing men learned the techniques of hierarchical

organisation and control . . . the problem for men became one of maintaining their control over the labour power of women.

(Hartmann 1976: 138)

This seems fairly representative of Marxist-feminist approaches to patriarchy on three counts: in its sense of the patriarchal order as a system functioning on its own account; in its awareness of the historical specificity of patriarchal forms; and finally in its stress on men acting collectively *as men* (rather than as capitalists, peasants, trade unionists, etc.) in order to maintain their privileges and control.

Let us deal first with the explanatory potential of this perspective. This is problematic since the concept is required to meet two contradictory objectives. As we saw, the term first found favour because a language was sought that would reflect the sheer prevalence of male-dominated institutions across a wide range of social structures and modes of production. 'Patriarchy' is an idea rooted in a sense of continuity and sameness, and sustained by the kinds of evidence presented in this article. But Marxist-feminists are alert to cross-cultural variations and historical diversity, and acknowledge that the different manifestations of patriarchy cannot be dismissed as unimportant. Thus, in an attempt to devise a theory which would grasp both continuity and change, they have frequently defined their research project as one of tracing and explaining the changing *forms* of patriarchy (Beechey 1979; MacKintosh 1977; McDonough and Harrison 1978: 26). But this solution actually places strict limits on the significance of history and, ironically, of 'patriarchy' too. If it is only the form of patriarchy that undergoes change, the patriarchal *essence* must presumably remain constant – immune as it were from historical influence. The concept fails to acquire the explanatory power it is intended to have since things have to happen *to* patriarchy to precipitate the observed changes. It is not a motor of history itself.

The theory also lacks any means of showing *why* men should control women's labour or seek to organise purely on the basis of their sex in order to maintain it. Some have argued that the power men enjoy over women makes their commitment to patriarchy self-evident. After all, the argument runs, we do not feel it necessary to ask why capitalists seek to maintain control over their workers.[11] On closer examination, however, this defence of the concept proves to be tautologous, and the comparison with class cannot be sustained. Logically speaking, we cannot explain men's control over women's labour by pointing to the power that it gives them, for this conflates an explanation with the explicandum. 'Patriarchy' is a mental construct that categorises a set of related phenomena in a particular informative way. This is not to gainsay the existence of patriarchal relations since the phenomena referred to are real enough; but if patriarchy's existence has been inferred from evidence showing women's oppression by men, then the concept cannot properly be used to *explain* that evidence.[12]

The comparison with Marxist theories of class structure is also inappropriate. Hartmann herself has acknowledged the essential difference while failing, apparently, to recognise its full implications. Marxist categories of class are 'empty places' in the sense that they do not specify the characteristics of the particular individuals who fill them. A class is *defined* by its social relationship to another class, and it is that relationship which provides the category with its internal conceptual unity. Class categories, moreover, are theoretically contingent. Their explanatory power is contained within a particular model of social development, and they have no utility outside that framework. But this is hardly true for the distinction between men and women. The categories of gender are defined, in the first instance, according to biological criteria, while the nature of the social relationship between them has to be empirically demonstrated, and only then explained. A concept such as 'patriarchy' that is designed to portray that relationship should be seen as a descriptive rather than an explanatory term. Certainly, it cannot be both.

Even if it is accepted that the concept of patriarchy has no explanatory value it would still be possible to interpret our findings as evidence for an institutional order of patriarchy that was independent of the mode of production. There can be no brooking the central empirical point that Hartmann makes: women's labour was under male control. Her deductions, however, are not substantiated and actually fly in the face of the evidence. First, there is the dubious suggestion, explicitly argued elsewhere (Hartmann 1979b: 11–12), that *all* men shared in the control of women's labour. The history of pre-capitalist England does not support this contention. Here was a society, especially in the era of high feudalism, where a substantial minority never married at all, and there is no evidence whatsoever to suggest that single men held any authority over women's productive or sexual labour. Moreover, a man's marital status or prospects were intimately bound up with the system of landholding; those without land or other means of livelihood could not normally expect to marry. A man's access to the control of female labour was thus conditional on his position in the class structure. Since the patriarchal organisation of labour cannot be understood except in relation to the matrix of feudal property relations, it seems incongruous to elaborate a separate theory of patriarchy. Hartmann's insistence on conceptualising men as a cohesive and homogeneous group leads her to gloss over these differences, and she ends up by describing men as sharing objectives and problems that have no basis in real life.

The impression of continuity in the patriarchal organisation of wage labour is very strong. It is all the more important, therefore, to retain a proper empathy for cultures that are remote to us. The past is really a

foreign country, and we cannot assume that familiar signs are indicative
of a familiar reality. Continuities need to be explained, but historical
regularities are no more amenable to universalising concepts than are
the vagaries of historical change. It may prove necessary to provide
different explanations for apparently similar findings according to their
social context. Gender segregation and inequality may be grounded in
different structural relationships at different times, may have different
rationales and mean different things to their participants.

In effect, what I am proposing reverses the conventional formulation
of Marxist-feminism's project as the examination of changing forms of
patriarchy. It suggests that even when patriarchal forms persist more or
less unchanged, we cannot assume that the underlying structure
determining women's oppression has remained constant. This is not to
deny the feminist claim that men act together as men, but it is to suggest
that they rarely, if ever, act together *just* as men, purely on the basis of
their sex. The position I am advocating is not a reductionist one. It does
not analyse patriarchal relations as a by-product of class processes any
more than it would allow class relations to be analysed without
reference to gendered structuring. Peasant men in feudal England did
not seek control of women's labour simply because they were peasants,
but neither did they do so because they were men. They did so because
they were male peasants striving to carve out their futures according to
male peasant values under constraints imposed by a particular mode of
production. Similar perspectives are necessary, of course, on male
landlords, farmers and agrarian capitalists. Patriarchy and class are
neither 'relatively autonomous' nor reducible one to another. They
comprise an integrated set of relationships.

Notes

1 An expanded version of this article can be found in Pahl (1988). It includes
  both a more detailed presentation of the historical evidence and a fuller
  elaboration of the theoretical issues.
2 *Famulus* (m)/*famula* (f). I have used the generic masculine case either when
  referring to original documentation or where it would be misleading to
  imply both sexes, because few women were involved.
3 References to skilled work in this chapter rest on what appear to be the
  contemporary definitions of skill or specialist work.
4 The labels 'servant' and 'labourer' were not applied with quite such
  discrimination as the discussion here might imply, but the institutional
  distinction was drawn sharply enough.
5 The new consensus describes the family in early modern England as
  'nuclear'. This is quite misleading, as the only significant continuity with the
  modern nuclear family is the size of the co-resident unit. The label ignores
  all other aspects of familial institutions including even the co-resident unit's
  internal structure.

6 Thus Moll Flanders's aversion to service was a fiction based solidly in social fact (see Roberts 1985). Many of the rural poor preferred a precarious independence to the protection of service; there were very few older servants.

7 Stone (1977) has suggested that service was an important institution for controlling unruly male youth. Be that as it may, it was still more important for its control over young women.

8 Roberts (1979: 6 and n. 24) has queried the reliability of some of these references.

9 The source here is Robinson (1857). The figures are calculated from account lists in Roberts (1979: appendix B).

10 Cockburn prefers the notion of sex/gender systems developed by Gayle Rubin to that of patriarchy, as it escapes the inbuilt assumption that men are always dominant. She is happy to use the term 'patriarchy', however, when referring to male-dominated sex/gender systems and she observes that they are very long-lived. Most of the points made here in respect to patriarchal theory apply equally well to theories of the sex/gender system, since this system is regarded as being separate from the class structure (Cockburn 1983: 8).

11 At the Economic and Social Research Council symposium where this chapter was first presented, certain women greeted the suggestion that there was a need to ask why men should seek to control women's labour with some amazement. In their eyes the question seemed utterly superfluous.

12 The implicit structure of circular reasoning runs as follows:
Men enjoy power over women and benefit from it.
Why do men have power?
Because men have organised to obtain and retain power.
Why have men so organised, and how have they succeeded?
Because men have power over women and benefit from it.

6: Patriarchal relations and patterns of sex segregation in the medical division of labour

Anne Witz

This chapter investigates the extent to which patterns of sex segregation in the medical division of labour have been historically constituted as a patriarchal structure. The centrality of occupational sex segregation to analyses of gender relations in paid employment is now widely recognised (cf. Bergmann 1980; Connelly 1978; Hakim 1979, 1981; Hartmann 1979b; Oppenheimer 1969; Walby 1983, 1986). Hartmann (1979b) has argued that job segregation by sex secures male dominance in the labour market, and Walby (1983) that the segregation of men and women into different and far from equal occupations constitutes a patriarchal labour market structure. It is important, however, not to confuse processes with outcomes as their structured effects. Job segregation by sex is the *structure* of gender-differentiated positions which should properly be regarded as the outcome or the sedimented form of ongoing *processes* of gendered occupational closure in the labour market. It is to recent developments in neo-Weberian closure theory that we may look to provide a useful set of concepts which to analyse the different ways in which male power has been utilised in distributive struggles in the labour market.

Gender and occupational closure

Neo-Weberian closure theory usefully illuminates forms of *gendered* distributive struggles in the arena of the labour market. Utilising concepts of closure, a minimal definition of occupational control strategies is one which defines these as processes of closure within the labour market. Modes of closure are defined by Parkin as 'different means of mobilizing power for purposes of staking claims to resources and opportunities' (1974: 5). In his earlier formulation of closure processes Parkin distinguishes between strategies of exclusion as the attempts by a social group 'to maintain or enhance its privileges by the process of subordination – i.e. the creation of another group or stratum of ineligibles beneath it' (1974: 4), and strategies of solidarism as 'collective responses of excluded groups which are themselves unable to maximize resources by exclusion practices' (1974: 5). Parkin, in his later work (1979), subsequently abandons the term 'solidarism' in favour of the term 'usurpation' to describe forms of countervailing social action engaged in by negatively privileged, excluded groups. Murphy (1984), another closure theorist, has criticised Parkin for failing to specify the structural relations between different closure practices and attend to what Murphy refers to as the 'deep structure of closure'. Murphy (1984, 1986) offers further refinements to the closure concept, distinguishing between principal, derivative and contingent forms of exclusion,[1] as well as between revolutionary and inclusionary forms of usurpation.[2] Kreckel (1980), who discusses closure concepts specifically in relation to processes of labour market structuration, is critical of the failure of closure theorists to identify the social sources of power underlying closure processes. So, whilst Kreckel welcomes the recent neo-Weberian conception of the market as 'intrinsically a structure of power' (cf. Giddens 1973), he also insists that the social sources of what are in fact unequal bargaining strengths in the labour market will have to be identified. In particular, Kreckel observes the failure of closure theorists to consider 'why certain groups within the labour sector of the labour market are in a better position to make successful use of strategies of closure than others' (1980: 531). The major innovation of Kreckel is the distinction he draws between three different strategies of closure which may be pursued within the labour sector of the labour market. These are exclusion, involving the downwards use of power and a process of subordination, demarcation, directed at potential competitors in the labour market but involving processes of mutual differentiation rather than subordination, and, finally, solidarism, an essentially defensive collective response of upwards pressure mounted by a disadvantaged group within the labour market.

So how might concepts of closure be employed to conceptualise the gendered dimensions of occupational closure in the labour market? Parkin's (1979) distinction between *exclusionary* and *usurpationary* processes of closure may usefully be retained. However, Murphy's further distinction between principal, derivative and contingent forms of exclusion does not prove immediately useful in analysing gender struggles in the labour market. Indeed, Murphy is unable to specify whether gendered forms of exclusion are derivative or contingent in relation to the principal mode. Kreckel's (1980) contribution discusses exclusionary closure processes within the orbit of the labour market and is important for this reason. His notion of *demarcationary* strategies of closure is a particularly innovative one, but should not be regarded as necessarily involving the absence of subordination. However, Kreckel's continued use of the rather clumsy term 'solidarism' is best abandoned in favour of Parkin's later term, 'usurpation'.

We are now able to make with a broad distinction between *exclusionary, demarcationary* and *usurpationary* closure processes. But I want to offer tighter definitions of these closure processes as they occur in the terrain of the labour market, and to establish their specifically gendered dimensions. The grounds for distinguishing exclusionary from demarcationary closure are as follows. Exclusionary closure strategies are mechanisms of intra-occupational control, which means that they are primarily concerned with control over the sphere of an occupational group's own labour. Demarcationary closure strategies describe processes of inter-occupational control which extend beyond the sphere of control over an occupational group's own labour and touch upon related labour or occupations.[3]

Modes of patriarchal closure in the labour market are generated and sustained by means of *gendered* strategies of exclusionary and demarcationary closure. Gendered *strategies of exclusionary closure* serve to create women as a class of ineligibles and secure for men privileged access to rewards and opportunities accruing from activities in the sphere of paid work. These employ gendered collectivist criteria of exclusion *vis-à-vis* women and gendered individualist criteria of inclusion *vis-à-vis* men. Male exclusionary shelters in the labour market are created by excluding women from routes of access to resources such as skills, knowledge, entry credentials or technical competence, thereby precluding women from entering an occupation. They provide the key mechanism whereby men of all classes have been able to secure and sustain competitive advantages over women in the labour market.

Patriarchal modes of occupational closure are also sustained by the pursuit of *gendered strategies of demarcationary closure*. These are mechanisms of inter-occupational control concerned with the creation and control of gendered occupational boundaries in a division of labour. This notion directs attention to the possibility that power asymmetries between men and women may underscore the creation and control of occupational boundaries and relations. As the distinction between these two processes of closure suggests, male strategies of exclusionary closure seek to exclude women from certain spheres of competence in the labour market, whereas those of demarcationary closure turn upon the inclusion of women within spheres of competence and the possible subordination of these to male-dominated spheres of competence.

I wish to stress that we may speak of *patriarchal* modes of occupational closure when male power is mobilised as a resource in staking privileged claims to resources and opportunities in the labour market and when closure strategies incorporate gender-specific modes of control. When male power is mobilised in the pursuit of strategies of closure in the labour market, then the social source of this power is patriarchy. In this way, the concepts of closure theory are pressed into the service of identifying the socio-political instance of male power (cf. Cockburn 1983), in particular the ways in which male power is organised and institutionalised within the labour market.

Usurpationary closure processes describe the actions of an excluded group in response to its outsider status and entail the mobilisation of power by one group against another that stands in a relation of dominance to it (Parkin 1979: 74–8). Modes of patriarchal closure may be challenged by gendered strategies of unsurpationary closure. In the face of exclusionary closure, women, who do not simply acquiesce to patriarchal practices in the labour market, may engage in usurpationary strategies. One form of usurpationary struggle, is where women challenge the operation of gendered collectivist criteria of exclusion and seek to replace these with non-gendered individualist criteria of inclusion in a structure of occupational positions from which they are excluded solely on account of their gender. In this case we may speak of a gendered strategy of *inclusionary* usurpation (Murphy 1984).

I now want to relate the distinction between gendered strategies of exclusionary and demarcationary closure back to the phenomenon of occupational sex segregation. Hakim (1979) has made an analytical distinction between two different dimensions of occupational sex segregation. There is a *horizontal* and a *vertical* dimension. The former describes the fact that men and women simply do different jobs, whilst the latter describes the hierarchical ordering of predominantly male and predominantly female jobs, with men's occupations typically commanding higher rewards, both symbolic and material, than women's. The analytical distinction I have offered between processes of exclusionary and demarcationary closure enables a distinction to be drawn between gendered strategies which have different structured effects along these two dimensions. Gendered strategies of exclusionary closure have the structured effect of horizontal sex segregation as women are simply excluded from jobs monopolised by men and do different jobs. They provide some of the clues as to why women have been or are 'not there' in certain occupations. But the structure of job segregation by sex is also a hierarchical structure in which relations of male domination and female subordination are embedded (apart from the fact that it maintains these relations at a societal level). Women are typically hedged into low-paying and low-status jobs with little autonomy which invariably stand in a subordinate relation to related male occupations. It is precisely this vertical, hierarchical dimension of sexually segregated occupations that is generated by gendered strategies of demarcationary closure.

The following analysis of the gendered dimensions of the sociopolitics of occupational closure in the formative period of the modern medical division of labour demonstrates the utility of some of the refinements to closure concepts which I have just outlined with reference to processes of occupational closure. Three episodes of gender conflict in the late nineteenth and early twentieth centuries are examined. The first occurred within the profession of medicine between 1858 and 1876, when aspiring women doctors challenged the exclusive male prerogotive over medical education and practice and so engaged in a usurpationary struggle. The second occurred between medical men and female midwifery, as medical men engaged in strategies of demarcationary closure in relation to the unregulated but adjacent occupation of midwifery. The third was a gender struggle between male and female radiographers in the 1930s and is, ironically but interestingly, a case study in the absence of gendered exclusionary closure in a new occupation in the medical division of labour.

Gendered strategies of exclusionary and usurpationary closure in the nineteenth-century medical profession

Professional closure in medicine was also constructed as patriarchal closure, sustained by means of gendered strategies of exclusion of women. The 1858 Medical (Registration) Act in effect established an exclusive male prerogative over legal medical practice (Manton 1965). Although rules of sexual exclusion were not explicitly codified into the 1858 Medical Act, these operated within the context of the universities and medical corporations that made up the nineteen portals of entry to the medical profession. These admitted only men to courses of medical instruction and examination. The right to legitimate medical practice as a 'legally or duly qualified medical practitioner' was conditional upon the possession of a university medical degree of licentiateship, membership or fellowship of one of the medical corporations (Stansfeld 1877). The exclusive male prerogative over legitimate medical practice was immediately challenged by aspiring women doctors, who engaged in a protracted struggle to gain admission to the medical profession (cf. Bell 1953; Jex-Blake 1886; Thorne 1915). This took the form of a female usurpationary struggle in the face of male strategies of exclusionary closure in the medical profession. The professional project in medicine was secured partly by means of the legalistic tactic of state sponsorship, and partly by credentialist tactics located within the institutional sphere of civil society – in the universities and medical corporations, such as the Royal Colleges of Physicians and of Surgeons, as these provided the medical education and examination necessary to qualify as a doctor under the terms of the 1858 Medical Act. Women also employed both legalistic and credentialist tactics in their usurpationary struggle.

Credentialist tactics inclusionary of usurpation were conducted on the terrain of civil society and challenged the exclusion of women from the system of medical education and examination. Between 1869 and 1873 a group of aspiring women doctors led by Sophia Jex-Blake struggled to receive medical lectures and present themselves for medical degrees at the University of Edinburgh (cf. Jex-Blake 1886). It was an equal rights tactic of credentialism because it sought to secure access to medical credentials for women in a male-dominated institution from which women were excluded. Following their defeat at Edinburgh, aspiring medical women set up the London School of Medicine for women in 1874 (Jex-Blake 1866; Thorne 1915) in order to provide women with a gender-specific route of access to medical education. This amounted to a separatist tactic of credentialism, to which women resorted in the face of the resilience of gendered exclusionary strategies in the modern university system.

Women also had recourse to legalistic tactics, conducted on the institutional terrain of the state legislature, and attempted to secure access to registered medical practice by Act of Parliament. As women were not explicitly excluded from registered medical practice, one of the legalistic tactics resorted to in their usurpationary struggle was the attempt to secure by Act of Parliament a separate route of access to the medical register. This separatist tactic sought to capitalize on the fact that, by 1870, women could gain medical degrees from a number of European universities and that, under Schedule A of the 1858 Act, anyone already possessing a degree of MD from a foreign university and practising in Britain before 1 October 1858 was eligible for registration. In 1874 and again in 1876 William Cowper-Temple introduced a Bill into Parliament which sought to secure women's access to the medical register by proposing that foreign degrees were to be recognised once again, but this time only when they were held by women.[4] This Bill sought to bypass those patriarchal structures that excluded women from routes of access to educational credentials and institute another gender-specific or twentieth portal of entry to the medical profession. Cowper-Temple's Bill was easily deflected by the General Medical Council (GMC), which could safely hide behind the cloak of liberalism and decry the injustice of such a proposal which called upon the Council to grant to women a privilege that was refused to men (Minutes of the GMC 1875).

Between 1874 and 1876 other Bills which this time aimed to secure women's access to the existing system of medical education and examination were introduced annually into Parliament.[5] The government eventually admitted that the subject of medical education for women demanded their consideration (Stansfeld 1877) and requested the General Medical Council to consider the general question of 'whether women ought to be able to look to medical practice, or certain branches of it, as open to them equally with men as a profession and means of livelihood' (Minutes of the GMC 1875: 89). The General Medical Council then felt bound to consider the whole question of the admission of women to the medical profession (Minutes of the GMC 1875) whereas up until that point it had been able to rely on the resilience of gendered exclusionary strategies operating within the patriarchally structured institutions of the modern university and medical corporations. The committee empowered to consider this issue subsequently recommended that 'The Medical Council are of opinion that the study and practice of medicine and surgery, instead of affording a field of exertion well fitted for women, do, on the contrary, present special difficulties which cannot be safely disregarded' (Minutes of the GMC 1875: 94). However, the question arose at this point as to whether the phrase 'cannot be safely disregarded' should be taken to imply the necessity for the legal elaboration of sexual exclusionary rules. It was at this point, argued Stansfeld perceptively, that 'the position of the opponents of medical women became untenable and the legalised admission of women to the ranks of the profession only a matter of time' (Stansfeld 1877). An amendment was put to and carried by the General Medical Council that the phrase which 'cannot be safely disregarded' be deleted and the phrase 'but the council are not prepared to say that women ought to be excluded from the profession' be inserted (Minutes of the GMC 1875). Russell-Gurney's Bill was passed in 1876, as an 'Enabling Bill', which established that the universities and medical corporations could not use their existing powers to *exclude* women, *but neither could they be forced to include women.*[6]

Patriarchal demarcationary closure: medical men and female midwives in the nineteenth century

By the early 1870s sexually segregated spheres of competence within the emerging medical division of labour were clearly in evidence, with women engaged in the four spheres of midwifery, nursing, dispensing and the management of medical institutions, all of which were considered by the General Medical Council as 'services for which women are specially adapted' (Minutes of the GMC 1873: 171). However, what was not clear at this point in time was the precise nature of the relationship between these female occupations and the male medical profession. Additionally, as I have shown, the sexual division of labour itself was being contested as women, in the pursuit of their strategy of inclusionary usurpation, were challenging the exclusive male prerogative over medicine. In the latter part of the nineteenth century, then, medical men were simultaneously defending patriarchal exclusionary closure within the medical profession and, as the following account of the debate around midwives' registration demonstrates, pursuing gendered strategies of demarcation.

The division of labour between female midwives and medical men, some of whom came to be known as 'men-midwives', had been a focus of struggle since the seventeenth century (Donnison 1977) as female midwifery practice became subject to the encroachments of medical men. By the mid-nineteenth century the division of labour between medical men and midwives had been constructed as a division between *assistance* and *intervention* in the process of labour, corresponding to a division in the process of parturition itself into 'normal' and 'abnormal' conditions. 'Normal' labour was constructed as a 'natural' process requiring attendance or assistance and remained within the sphere of competence of the midwife, whilst 'abnormal' labour was constructed as those conditions requiring intervention, frequently by means of instruments such as forceps, and incorporated within the exclusive sphere of competence of medical men.

The debate around midwives' registration in the latter half of the nineteenth century reveals that the medical profession was divided over the issue of the desirability or otherwise of a state-sponsored system of registration for midwives. Medical men pursued two different gendered strategies of demarcation in relation to midwives. The first was a *demarcationary strategy of incorporation* which entailed the absorption of virtually the whole gamut of tasks associated with independent female midwifery within the exclusive sphere of competence of the medical profession. If successful, this demarcationary strategy would have signalled the demise of midwifery as a distinct occupational role. The second was a *demarcationary strategy of de-skilling*, which sought to restrict female midwifery practice to the sphere of 'normal' labour whilst 'creaming off' practices surrounding abnormal labour and locating these within the sphere of competence of the medical profession. The de-skilling strategy did preserve the role of midwife, although with a diminished sphere of competence and subject to medical control over the education and regulation of midwives. Both strategies were articulated with reference to the gender composition of the occupation of midwifery.

Medical men's pursuit of a gendered strategy of incorporation aimed to establish an exclusive male prerogative over the provision of midwifery services by incorporating the 'medicalised' portion of midwifery tasks within the sphere of competence of the medical practitioner and delegating the 'nursing' portion to the 'monthly' or 'obstetric' nurse who, 'under the charge and supervision of a medical man, carries out that portion of attendance *which is more suitable to a mere woman*, the changing of sheets and the attending of the patient, and attentions of that kind' (Select Committee on Midwife Registration 1892: 133). The independent midwife was to be replaced by the 'obstetric' nurse, whose duties were restricted to nursing the mother and baby under the direct supervision of a doctor (*Nursing Notes* 1890: 86). As midwifery and nursing were both female occupations, it was feasible to propose that certain functions currently associated with midwifery should be relocated within the occupational sphere of competence of nurses.

This strategy, which would have brought about the demise of the midwife as an independent practitioner with her own clients, failed largely because the medical profession could not in fact see a way to meet the total demand for midwifery services. One of the effects of medical professionalisation has been to contract the supply of doctors relative to the population (Waddington 1984). It was estimated that seven out of every nine births were attended by midwives, whether trained or untrained, and that there were 10,000 midwives in England (*Nursing Notes* 1888: supplement). Many medical men were reluctant to place themselves in a position where they would be called upon to meet the total demand for midwifery services. The work itself was regarded as excessively time-consuming (Select Committee on Midwife Registration 1892: 22), a problem that had much to do with the essentially unpredictable duration of labour. The devolution of tasks associated with attendance and assistance during labour on to midwives served to relieve reluctant medical men 'from the necessity of attending parturient women for hours, and waiting for nature to complete a process which they could neither assist nor prevent' (*British Medical Journal* 1873: 406). Potentially at any rate, all women regardless of their social class might demand midwifery services; and if doctors had made it incumbent upon themselves to meet this demand, they would have been providing midwifery services for rich and poor alike. The way out of this dilemma reveals the real nub of the de-skilling strategy which, whilst seeking to preserve midwives as a distinct occupational group, also sought to *stratify* both the demand for and the supply of midwifery services; the rich would employ the services of doctors, whilst the poor would employ those of midwives. It was argued that 'a class of educated midwives would be of great advantage to poor women, and would relieve medical men of a large amount of hard and unremunerative midwifery practice' (*Nursing Notes* 1890: 38).

Interestingly medical men advocating a more drastic demarcationary strategy of incorporation opposed midwives' registration on the grounds that it would create an inferior class of midwifery practitioner for the poor and that midwives would continue to pose a competitive threat to general practitioners, depriving them of a considerable amount of midwifery practice (*British Medical Journal* 1873: 354; Select Committee on Midwife Registration 1892: 56). But the de-skilling strategy aimed to preserve midwives precisely in order to meet the bulk of the demand for midwifery services from the poor. However, by segmenting both the demand for and supply of midwifery services, it simultaneously precluded the possibility that midwives would pose a competitive threat to doctors.

Medical men's demarcationary strategy of de-skilling aimed to preserve midwives as a distinct occupational group by devolving certain midwifery tasks on to women and permitting the midwife a limited degree of autonomy in the daily practice of midwifery, in the form of discretion at the level of execution. The problem then arose of ensuring that midwives did not transgress occupational boundaries and encroach upon medical men's exclusive sphere of 'intervention'. It was argued that 'Everything must be done to limit the midwife severely to the simple duties of a natural case' (*The Lancet* 1890). This was not a problem for medical men advocating a strategy of incorporation and the transformation of midwives into obstetric nurses, for this entailed the incorporation of normal as well as abnormal labour within medical men's sphere of competence. This was because medical men would superintend the whole process of labour and delegate certain tasks to obstetric nurses acting only under their supervision. However, for those medical men who conceded the impracticality and undesirability of such indiscriminate medical control over the total process of parturition, there was the thorny problem that the very process of labour was, by definition, normal up until the point when it could be construed as abnormal and required medical intervention. This meant that, if the midwife was employed in the first instance to attend labour, it was the midwife herself who had to decide when a labour qualified as abnormal and required a doctor to be present. For the de-skilling strategy to be realized, the *boundaries* between midwifery and medical practice had to be clearly prescribed and rigidly maintained by the medical profession.

It was the resolution of this problem of inter-occupational *control* over the sexual division of labour between midwives and medical men that explains why some medical men championed the cause of a system of midwives' registration. They sought to control both the registration and education of midwives in order to preclude any encroachments into the doctor's sphere of competence. In 1872 medical men of the Obstetrical Society started their own course of instruction and diploma for midwives. The Obstetrical Society of London was founded in 1857 and by 1873 was composed of around 600 fellows, including many eminent obstetricians (*British Medical Journal* 1873: 676). The Obstetrical Society's scheme for the education and regulation of midwives accorded midwives a minimal occupational role which amounted to the management of the process of natural labour and the care, as distinct from the treatment, of mother and child (Minutes of the GMC 1877, appendix: 51–5). The knowledge base of midwifery was to be kept as minimal as possible, for 'What you want to educate midwives for is for them to know their own ignorance. That is really the one great object in educating midwives' (Select Committee on Midwives Registration 1892: 101). The Obstetrical Society advocated and provided a medical education where 'the range is kept necessarily and designedly limited' (Select Committee on Midwives Registration 1892:

121). It sought to ensure that midwives were instructed by medical men, examined and licensed by a body appointed by the General Medical Council and subject to both compulsory registration and the possibility of erasure from the register on the grounds of misconduct (*British Medical Journal* 1874: 186; Minutes of the GMC 1877, appendix: 51–5). The most serious misconduct of midwives would be that of 'exceeding their duties' (*British Medical Journal* 1874: 186) by transgressing occupational boundaries through failing to call on medical assistance when necessary or administering medical treatment to their clients.

The case of medicine and midwifery demonstrates the utility of the concept of demarcationary strategies of occupational closure. It also suggests how the gender of occupations involved in demarcationary struggles is not a fortuitous or contingent, but a necessary factor in relation to both the form and the outcome of demarcationary strategies. The radical restructuring of occupational boundaries entailed by the demarcationary strategy of incorporation was possible because of the feasibility of shifting functions of female midwifery on to the female nurse, thus rendering the independent female midwifery practitioner obsolete. Medical men of the Obstetrical Society, who advocated the demarcationary strategy of de-skilling, could realistically aim to control the education and regulation of midwives because midwives had proved unsuccessful in providing for their own education, and had no option but to avail themselves of the Obstetrical Society diploma if they wished to be educated and examined.

Gender stratification in radiography in the early twentieth century

The occupation of radiography between the years 1900 and 1940 provides a case study in the absence of patriarchal closure. Radiography has never been an exclusively male occupation but had a mixed gender composition from the very early days of the application of X-ray techniques in medical diagnosis and treatment. By the 1920s it had become a predominantly female occupation. The case of radiography shows how, in the absence of patriarchal exclusionary closure, patterns of internal sex segregation may arise within an occupation. Gender struggle occurred in the occupation of radiography during the 1930s, when male radiographers engaged in a strategy of internal demarcation, which may be treated as a sub-type of exclusionary closure. It did not hinge upon the wholesale exclusion of women from an occupation (indeed, this had failed) but upon the exclusion of women from certain jobs and their inclusion in others within an occupation. As a sub-type of exclusionary closure male radiographers' strategy of internal demarcation was concerned with internal occupational control and sought to differentiate between different types of radiography skills, to gender these skills and to differentially evaluate these gendered bundles of radiography skills.

The following account of sexual divisions within radiography picks up on two questions: first, how did women gain access to radiographic work during the early days of unregulated practice and maintain access to regulated practice; and secondly, did non-gender-specific criteria of entry into the occupation of radiography indicate non-gender-specific forms of practice within it?

Before focusing on processes of intra-occupational demarcation within radiography, it should be noted that processes of inter-occupational demarcation between the paramedical occupation of radiography and the medical occupation of radiology have been examined by Larkin (1978, 1983). Larkin's analysis of the social organisation of X-ray work concentrates on the dual process of the emergence of radiology as a specialism within the medical profession, and the emergence of radiographers as process workers acting at the behest of radiologists in a capacity of technical aides (Larkin 1983). Larkin's discussion of sexual divisions in radiography is perfunctory. At one point he suggests that radiography attracted middle-class daughters in search of a husband, but admits there is no evidence for this! Larkin also notes that the manual skills of radiography that had been shed by the medical profession 'were redefined as "scientific" yet in some sense "suitably female" ' (Larkin · 1983: 83) and observes that the pre-dominance of women in radiography 'buttressed the authority of the pre-dominantly male medical profession and a much smaller group of male radiographers' (Larkin 1983: 85). But Larkin fails to unpick the significance of gender relations in his analysis of the emergence of inter-occupational control relations between medical radiologists and X-ray technicians. The *mediating* role of patriarchal relations in modes of demarcation in the medical division of labour is glossed over by Larkin. The intensification of radiographers' subordination to medical radiologists was accompanied by an intensification in the gendered imagery of radiographic work. So by 1952 the description of radiographic work finds an explicit parallel in housework: 'Like the housewife's tasks, a technician's work is never done' (*Radiography* 1952: 135). The advice meted out to the radiographer is to 'Keep him [the radiologist] in clean white coats, see that his hair, possibly askew by removal of lead apron, head mirror or red goggles, is combed before he confronts a patient', and reads like the advice to a young radiographer-bride embarking on the hazardous career of pleasing her radiologist-husband who'll 'pout and fidget at these things and say he is henpecked, but he will like it' (*Radiography* 1952: 137)!

Women were involved in operating X-ray apparatus from its inception. The earliest record of women working in radiography is cited as 1896 'when a woman assisted in the taking of radiographs' (*Radiography* 1935: 155), shortly after the discovery of X-rays by Roentgen in 1895. As X-rays became more widely used as an aid to medical diagnosis, two forms of radiography practice emerged. There was private practice where the lay radiographer, chemist or engineer purchased, operated and maintained X-ray apparatus and provided information directly to the client or to the doctor. There was also hospital practice as X-ray apparatus was purchased by hospitals. The increasing use of X-ray apparatus in hospitals, together with the absence of specially trained technicians, meant that it 'was often operated by a nurse, a porter, a dispenser or any handy-man' (*British Journal of Radiology* 1942: 351) or by hospital engineers and electricians (*Radiography* 1937: 127). The widespread use of nurses to operate newly installed X-ray apparatus in hospitals is particularly significant because this meant that women originally gained access to radiographic skills and practice by way of the nursing profession and within the context of hospital rather than private practice. By 1921 X-ray work was described as 'a vast field open to nurses' (*British Journal of Nursing* 1921: 59).

However, although women clearly had been involved in radiography from the very outset, men struggled to establish a male *prerogative* over X-ray work. Male radiographers formed themselves into a Society in 1921 primarily in order to regulate the practice of radiography. Despite a declared willingness to use legalistic tactics where necessary (Minutes of the Society of Radiographers 1921), the Society relied mainly upon credentialist tactics and the patronage of hospital radiologists — medical men who specialised in X-ray diagnosis and treatment. The Society promptly instituted its own diploma in radiography, and, in 1921, 50 men and 9 women received the first Diploma of the Society of Radiographers (Minutes of the Society of Radiographers 1921). However, from 1922 onwards there were at least three times as many women as men qualifying as radiographers annually (Larkin 1983). But the presence of women in unregulated X-ray practice, particularly in hospitals, had not gone unnoticed (Minutes of the Society of Radiographers 1921), and male radiographers hoped that the formalisation of routes of access to radiography would exclude women (cf. *British Journal of Radiography* 1932). But credentialist tactics in the pursuit of gendered strategies of exclusionary closure failed to effectively exclude women from radiography training.

Then, in the 1930s, male radiographers' retrospective accounts of the early days of radiography emphasised the precarious and unpredictable nature of the new X-ray apparatus and presented a male image of the pioneer X-ray worker, who 'wrestled' with and 'tamed' the unpredictable and frequently unreliable X-ray apparatus, setting radiography on a surer scientific and technical footing (cf. *Radiography* 1937: 110). This male image of radiography centred around an association between technical knowledge or competence and maleness. The perpetuation of this particular association between gender and technical competence during the 1930s amounted to a mystification of radiographic skills which served to bolster male radiographers' strategies of internal demarcation between gendered spheres of competence. Their claims were not completely illegitimate in that the Institute of Electrical Engineers was a prominent interest group in the early days of radiography (cf. Larkin 1983), and electrical engineering had indeed provided men with a different route of access to radiographic skills and practice than women. However, male radiographers' retrospective reconstructions of the early days of X-ray work ignored the fact that

> when X-ray departments were very young, the work which today has reached a degree of efficiency in the hands of qualified technicians was then carried out for the most part by nurses. These nurses had no theoretical knowledge of the work they were doing. They were taught practically and they got on with the job. Often they became very interested in their work, their departments grew, and they became 'Sisters-in-charge'.
>
> (*Radiography* 1937: 74)

Male radiographers' exercise in retrospective sex-typing acquires particular significance when considered alongside the simultaneous attempts to challenge the legitimacy of nursing as a route of access to radiography. Together these provide the basis of their strategy of internal demarcation between male and female spheres of competence within radiography.

Women's route of access to radiographic skills and practice had initially been by way of nursing in hospitals, and there continued to be considerable overlap between nursing and radiographic skills as far as women were concerned. Increasingly, women accessed radiographic skills through the formal route of the Society of Radiographers' diploma because it was hospital workers who felt it necessary to obtain this new qualification (*Radiography* 1935: 156). Women were able to take advantage of the Society of Radiographers' hospital-based training. This explains why credentialist tactics of gendered exclusionary closure failed to exclude women from training and qualifying as radiographers.

Some women practised as 'nurse-radiographers' and held dual qualifications as State Registered Nurse (SRN) and Member of the Society of Radiographers (MSR). The tradition of nurse-radiographers and X-ray sisters is crucial to an understanding of processes of sex-typing within radiography and male radiographers' pursuit of a strategy of internal demarcation. This tradition arose largely out of the practice of integrating X-ray duties into a ward-sister's duties rather than appointing a radiographer when new X-ray apparatus was installed in hospitals, particularly in smaller hospitals. Indeed, it was even argued that the X-ray sister preceded the radiographer in hospitals, and that the emerging distinction between the two was a dubious one (*Radiography* 1937: 74). Many X-ray sisters took advantage of the training and formal qualifications offered by the Society of Radiographers from 1921 onwards, and some hospitals would advertise specifically for X-ray sisters in preference to a radiographer. If they could not appoint an X-ray sister with dual qualifications, they frequently preferred to appoint an SEN who had experience working with X-rays rather than a radiographer who was not a trained nurse (*Radiography* 1937: 75). Such practices put women at a distinct advantage in the market for X-ray workers because the demand for nurse-radiographers, X-ray sisters and trained nurses with practical experience of X-ray work was a *sex-specific demand for female X-ray workers*, whilst the demand for radiographers was potentially non-sex-specific. Male radiographers, then, not only had to compete with women for posts as radiographers, but had to compete for some of these posts at a considerable disadvantage where custom and practice favoured the employment of trained nurses either with or without formal qualifications in radiography. Women with dual qualifications in nursing and radiography enjoyed a distinct competitive advantage over male radiographers. Accordingly, male radiographers' pursuit of a strategy of internal differentiation within radiography aimed at removing the distinct competitive advantage enjoyed by nurse-radiographers. The problem for male radiographers was essentially that, 'of two radiographers of otherwise equal ability, the one trained as a nurse, and the other not, the former would be unquestionably more valuable in every instance' (*Radiography* 1937: 190). This was reinforced by the practice of appointing women with dual qualifications in nursing and radiography at the lower salary of nursing.

Male radiographers' appeal to the engineering origins of radiographic skills, together with their insistence that nursing skills had no value and legitimacy in radiography (*Radiography* 1937: 111–12, 189), amounted to a gendered strategy of internal demarcation which aimed at removing the competitive advantage for posts (as distinct from any real advantage in the form of salary) enjoyed by female nurse-radiographers, and particularly for senior hospital posts held by X-ray sisters. On the other hand, nurse-radiographers defended their competence as radiographers by arguing that nursing skills were essential in X-ray work which required medical knowledge and, most crucially, patient care. 'Radiography is not only a matter of locating breakdowns, turning knobs, and saving films – an engineer can do the first two, and anybody the third – there is also the patient for whose sake this expensive apparatus is congregated together' (*Radiography* 1937: 160). This argument proved a powerful one and, together with the increasing articulation of the radiographer's subordination to the medical radiologist within the parameters of patriarchal authority relations, enabled women to legitimate their role within radiography and consolidate their distinct competitive advantage over male radiographers.

Conclusion

It has been a central contention of this chapter that concepts borrowed from closure theory provide valuable insight into some of the complex historical processes which have generated job segregation by sex in the medical division of labour. But I have also stressed that the social sources of unequal bargaining powers in the labour market must be identified. Consequently, it is necessary to ground an analysis of gendered strategies of closure within the historical and structural matrix of patriarchal capitalism. Patriarchal relations mediate both the form and the outcome of gendered strategies of closure.

The case of medicine demonstrated the utility of concepts of gendered strategies of exclusionary and usurpationary closure, and also served to specify how medical men and aspiring women doctors had recourse to credentialist and legalistic tactics of closure. The case of midwifery illustrated how the concept of gendered strategies of demarcationary closure alerts attention to the fact that occupational boundaries between midwifery and medicine were negotiated with reference to the gender of the providers of midwifery services. The principle of an exclusive male prerogative over midwifery services advocated by the medical men engaged in the demarcationary strategy of incorporation proved to be inexpedient, and so it was the de-skilling strategy of demarcation which prevailed. This stratified the market for midwifery services according to the social class of the client and the gender of the provider of midwifery services. The principle of sexual segregation underscored and demarcation of occupational boundaries between female midwifery and male medicine. The case study of radiography provides insights into processes of gender segregation within an occupation, which Hakim (1979) refers to as internal vertical job segregation by sex. This was an occupation in which male radiographers had failed to secure patriarchal exclusionary closure, but within which they engaged in a strategy of internal demarcation, attempting to demarcate between gendered spheres of competence within the occupational labour market for radiographers. This response to the presence of women within an occupation may usefully be regarded as a sub-type of exclusionary closure, because it is still concerned with intra-occupational control over an occupation's own labour, rather than with demarcation between occupations.

In conclusion, there are further observations to be made, highlighting the necessity of grounding closure practices within broader sets of patriarchal relations. The case of medicine provides the best illustration of this. First, patriarchal closure in medicine was sustained within the institutional sphere of civil society, specifically in the modern university and the professional corporations and associations of the medical profession. Larson (1977) identifies both these institutions as key locations for the mobilisation of the autonomous means of professional closure.[7] But these were also key locations for the institutionalisation of male power, and proved resilient to the usurpationary claims of women. Second, it was the state, which Larson (1977) identifies as the institutional location of the heteronomous means of professional closure, which proved most susceptible to women's usurpationary claims in medicine and was the weakest link in the chain of patriarchal closure in medicine. Hence, in view of the success (limited though this was) of women's equal rights legalistic tactic of usurpation, Eisenstein's (1981) assertion that the modern state is more relative than autonomous along its patriarchal dimensions must be questioned.

Notes

1 The principal form of exclusion is the main determinant of access to or exclusion from power, resources and opportunities in society. It is backed by the legal apparatus of the state. Legal title to private property is the principal form of exclusion in capitalist market societies. Contingent and derivative forms of exclusion are defined in terms of their relation to the principal form (cf. Murphy 1984).
2 Inclusionary usurpation involves a struggle by the excluded group to become involved in a structure of positions from which they are excluded, whereas revolutionary usurpation involves the excluded group calling for the radical restructuring of those positions, not simply their inclusion in them.
3 This distinction between exclusionary and demarcationary closure picks up on Freidson's emphasis on the Janus-headed nature of professional control, that a profession is characterised not only by occupational monopoly but also by a position of dominance in a division of labour (cf. Freidson 1977: 24).
4 The Medical Act Amendment (Foreign Universities) Bill.
5 The Universities (Scotland) (Degrees to Women) Bill in 1875 and the Medical Act (Qualifications) Bill in 1976.
6 The General Medical Council's reluctance to adopt a legalistic exclusionary strategy in relation to the general question of women's admission to the medical profession was matched by its unwillingness to sanction any real challenge to the patriarchal modes of closure that did exist in the universities and medical corporations. Its response to Russell-Gurney's Bill 'to remove restrictions on the granting of qualifications for registration under the Medical Act on the ground of sex' was that, as long as such measures were *discretionary* rather than compulsory and did not interfere with the 'free action' of universities and corporations, then they could see no ground for opposition.
7 Larson (1977) usefully distinguishes between autonomous means of professionalisation, which are defined or created by professional groups themselves, and heteronomous means, which are chiefly defined or formed by other social groups.

7: Keeping women in and out of line: sexual harassment and occupational segregation

Elizabeth A. Stanko

Introduction

The purpose of this chapter is to explore the issue of sexual harassment at work and its implications for thinking about segregation in employment. As a significant factor in women's experiences of working, sexual harassment is a form of sexual discrimination in employment. Closely tied to issues of gender, power and control, sexual harassment surfaces as the metaphor for gender relations and sexuality in the wider society. Issues of maleness, femaleness, sexual power, economic power and social control coalesce within often mundane, seemingly ordinary, work situations.

Women's experiences of sexual harassment are not bound by traditional or non-traditional occupational spheres. They are bound by the wider experience of male dominance. This wider reality must be recognised in discussions of women's experiences of occupational segregation, and in the discussions about how to expand women's participation in the world of work. Do, for example, women's chances of being sexually harassed increase or decrease when they enter non-traditional employment? Can we reduce impediments to women's segregated employment by making previously all-male occupations safe for women? These and other questions will be addressed in this chapter.

Sexual harassment

What is sexual harassment? Broadly defined, sexual harassment is *unwanted* sexual attention. Its behavioural forms are many and include visual (leering); verbal (sexual teasing, jokes, comments or questions); unwanted pressure for sexual favours or dates; unwanted touching or pinching; unwanted pressure for sexual favours with implied threats of job-related consequences for non-co-operation; physical assault; sexual assault; rape. The behavioural manifestation may be a singular event or a continuous series of events. How such behaviour is 'backed up', notes Edwin Schur, by male power to 'hire and fire, promote and demote, reward and punish, also can vary greatly' (1984: 136).

Just as the form of sexual harassment varies widely, so does its effect. If one were to construct a continuum of sexual harassment, one might construct a scale with leering, non-physical forms of behaviour on one end of the scale and sexual assault/rape at the other end. This scale of severity of sexual harassment, some might also assume, is directly related to how an individual would respond to such behaviour. Not so. Research in the USA and the UK indicates otherwise (Collins and Blodgett 1981; Cooper and Davidson 1982; Farley 1978; Hadjifotiou 1983; MacKinnon 1978; Read 1982; Sedley and Benn 1982). The form of sexual intrusion is often immaterial. Women are sometimes greatly distressed by persistent low-level harassment – leering, for instance – and exhibit stress symptoms similar to women who have experiences of sexual and physical assault (Silverman 1976–7).

What is an intrusive leer or a pressure for a date? The labelling of a man's behaviour as intrusive, offensive and harassing arises from women's experience. In and out of work, women constantly negotiate what men consider acceptable male sexual attention and interest (Wise and Stanley 1987). Sometimes women successfully fend off what they feel is intrusive · sexualised behaviour without any job-related consequences. Other women, in refusing to respond to sexual interest of co-workers or superiors, learn too late that their co-operation in men's sexual interest is a job requirement.

Farley (1978) reports the experience of Carmita Wood, a woman who ultimately left her job because her complaints about her supervisor were considered unreasonable:

> He would make her feel exceedingly uncomfortable by making sexual gestures, he would often lean against her, immobilizing her between his own body and the chair and desk. He would never look her in the eye but would instead move his eyes up and down her body below the neck. He would also stand with his hands in his pockets as if rubbing his genitals.
>
> (Farley 1978: 93).

While harassing behaviour varies widely, the pattern of the behaviour and its effects on those harassed all represent a serious violation to personal integrity. In each instance, a woman is no longer made to feel like an employee or a colleague. She is immediately transformed into a sexual object. One police woman, for instance, quit her job after she came to work and found a photograph of her head pasted to a pornographic picture and posted throughout the police station. At this point, her gender, her sexual being, was the focus of attention, not her work performance. Her sexuality becomes part of her labour. Her work context includes a previously hidden part of the job description; the employee must be willing to field any and all sexual advances, wanted and unwanted.

How many are actually affected by sexual harassment? It is, for women, an all too common experience. Research in the USA indicates that somewhere between one in five and four in five women have experienced sexual harassment at some time in their working lives. In Britain, the Alfred Marks Bureau queried 799 managers and employees of its branches throughout the UK; 66 per cent of the employees and 86 per cent of the managers reported that they were aware of various forms of sexual harassment present in their office. Fifty-one per cent of the women admitted to having experienced some form of sexual harassment. Cooper and Davidson (1982) found 52 per cent of women managers they studied had experienced sexual harassment. Leeds TUCRIC (1983) found 59 per cent of their interviewed women experienced harassment.

Imposed sexuality at work has many consequences. Feelings of humiliation, anger, self-blame, perhaps a loss of self-confidence and a drop in job performance, are coupled with uncertainty about retaining one's job. Most concrete are the economic consequences; some women quit jobs, some find they are transferred or demoted, some lose their jobs when they do not co-operate with sexual advances. Few women have been successful in fighting cases of 'unfair dismissal' which have resulted from sexual harassment.

As it stands today, despite growing awareness, few women complain about sexual harassment. The Alliance Against Sexual Coercion, a Massachusetts-based group, comments:

> Women are conditioned to feel that if they confront the issue directly, it will most likely escalate, for sexual harassment in the workplace is an issue of power, and experience shows that pressing the issue will bring on an intensified response. It seems easier to do nothing than to complain, because complaining is stepping out of line, and stepping out of line brings on a display of power and control in our society.
>
> (Alliance Against Sexual Coercion 1981: 19)

Gendered work: job segregation and sexual harassment

While complex and complicated in our everyday lives, the configuration of gender, power and sexuality poses particular problems when they locate themselves at work. Awareness of sexual harassment has grown over the past ten years (Farley 1978; Hadjifotiou 1983; MacKinnon 1978; Read 1982; Seddon 1983; Sedley and Benn 1982). While introducing sexualised behaviour into the working environment does not always constitute sexual harassment, recognising its potential for misuse is one key to sorting out what behaviour is threatening and coercive to workers. The potentially coercive nature of sexuality within unequal power dynamics must be understood within the context of stratified gender divisions which have consequences within both engendered working spheres and definitions of sexuality and their appropriate and expected displays.

Since many occupational spheres remain largely male or female in composition, solidarity among workers on the job may be built by drawing upon what is assumed to be mutual heterosexual interest in sexuality. In this context, heterosexuality must be situated within a patriarchal structure which elevates the men above the women. Gender, to Catharine MacKinnon, 'is power division and sexuality is one sphere of its expression' (1978: 221). Men's sexuality and men's sexual interest take precedence over women's. In most contexts, this power is enhanced by control over women's economic well-being.

Confusion still remains about whether sexualised behaviour between workers automatically constitutes sexual harassment and how sexuality at work might contribute to segregation in employment. Some light can be shed on this confusion, I believe, by posing some questions about work and sexuality. First, to what extent do men's and women's working spheres – recognised as segregated by gender into 'men's' versus 'women's' work – contain, encourage and reproduce tacit assumptions about sexuality and displays of sexualised behaviour? Second, to what extent do we still view sexualised behaviour, largely assumed to be heterosexual behaviour, as coequally exchanged or negotiated among mutually consenting, non-threatened individuals without regard to the resulting beneficial or detrimental economic consequences?

One further note: while I will be focusing on sexual harassment of women by men within assumptions of heterosexuality, I do not mean to ignore nor belittle the experiences of women and men who may experience sexual harassment from other women and/or men, heterosexual or homosexual. I do, however, wish to use sexual harassment as another example of how male domination locates itself in *women's* everyday lives. As such and as a reflection of gender stratification, both within work spheres and within concepts of appropriate sexuality, sexual harassment is one form of sexual/physical abuse which is largely directed to women by men, a form of 'intimate intrusion' which serves to keep women in and out of line (Stanko 1985).

Women's occupations and sexual harassment

Engendered working spheres set the stage, but not the script, for men's use of coercive sexuality. Because men as a gender continue to have power and control over women as a gender, sexualising women who work in traditional occupations serves to eroticise women's subordination (MacKinnon 1978; Schur 1984). Women's employment spheres, largely composed of care-giving and service jobs, contribute to promoting the sexualisation of women in those positions. Waitresses, for instance, particularly those who are cocktail waitresses or barmaids, might find that their own sexuality and/or personal attractiveness is part of the expected service and therefore part of the job requirements. Similarly, secretaries to some extent become office wives (Kanter 1977). The periodic sex scandals which hit the newspapers, for example, where an influential man's affair with his secretary brings him particular embarrassment, are rarely viewed as unusual. Apparently the roles of secretary and wife are easily integrated. How many secretaries unwillingly have this expectation imposed upon them and have left jobs because of it? Being female, in women's work, may in fact be a 'set-up' for harassment. As one woman remarks, the men in the office 'seem to be under some impression that they're [the women in the office] as available as the morning coffee' (Read 1982: 57).

If women are employed, they are most likely to be employed in traditionally female arenas, lower paid and of lower status than men, typically supervised and controlled by men, doubly jeopardised by job and by gender. Job protection, access to grievance procedures and complaints officers, and marginality contribute to the silence around the prevalence of sexual harassment. But there may be advantages which women who occupy previously all-male occupations do not have. There is the possibility that a woman may find safety in numbers or at least some sanctuary among female co-workers. By no means is this situation a guarantee or a shield from sexual harassment. Many women's experiences tell us otherwise.

Sue Read's (1982) account of Polly illustrates how the atmosphere within a previously female-dominated working environment may change when it suddenly becomes predominantly male. Polly's experience exemplifies the distress of being surrounded by what others might characterise as 'seemingly harmless male bantering'.

> When I first joined the laboratory and was working with about fifteen other people, three of them male, everything was fine. Then two of the men and myself were moved to a department on our own with our head of department, a nice bloke of about 29, the same age as the other two men. After about four months another young man joined us, and almost immediately, he started passing sexual comments to the other two men, talking loudly across the lab. It made me feel very embarrassed, but I ignored them hoping they would get bored eventually and stop. But I started to change. I

became very wary and careful of whatever I said, because they'd pick it up and turn it round to have a double meaning.

Then the comments got worse and were directed at me, my body, questions about my private life and sexual likes and dislikes. I just ignored them all. And one day, I don't remember how, they got round to the fact that they decided that I was obviously a virgin, but they would make sure that didn't last. They began bringing *Playboy* magazine into work and leaving it lying around open, and little sexual drawings began appearing scribbled on my desk diary. I don't know which one of them was doing it, they egged each other on all the time.

(1982: 70–1)

It comes as no surprise to hear that women entering previously all-male work sites, which are likely to bring higher wage packets and prestige, may also face sexual harassment.

Men's occupations and sexual harassment

While many women in traditional employment spheres report experiencing forms of sexual harassment, women entering non-traditional employment report that they too are subjected to men's intrusive, sexualised behaviour. According to the Leeds TUCRIC study (1983), 96 per cent of women in non-traditional spheres versus 48 per cent in traditional spheres of employment experienced forms of harassment ranging from leering to actual sexual assault. The most comprehensive US survey to date, the US Merit System's Protection Board survey of 23,000 federal workers, also found higher reported levels of sexual harassment among higher-educated women in professional positions (Martin 1981).

What do these experiences and surveys tell us? Perhaps women in traditional employment have less power to complain about men's sexualised attention and are less likely to report the behaviour as harassment. Women in traditional employment may have already found a number of different strategies to negotiate men's behaviour. They may also assume that being annoyed or bothered by men in these jobs, as cocktail waitresses often do for example, is part of the job. Women newly employed in men's occupational spheres may assume that because they are employed on par with men, sexual harassment – at least that kind of behaviour they see directed to women subordinates – will not be part of their experiences. But women entering previously all-male occupations may confront hostility and resentment from men, and thus are subjected to greater levels of sexual harassment. Women who receive harassment in non-traditional jobs may expect, naïvely, to be given the same opportunities and treatment as men. This may be one reason why they characterise their co-workers' behaviour as unacceptable and label it as harassment.

In many respects, men's working environments become part of men's territories. Displays of heterosexual interest are part of that territory. Work is the place where men are together and away from home, swap stories, tell jokes, share experiences of or commentary about sport or women or both. Male working culture, particularly within employment spheres primarily occupied by men, support and to some extent may promote the sexualisation of women who may also be their fellow workers. Controversy concerning 'pin-ups' of female nudes in work sites, for instance, shows how, until challenged, displays of male heterosexual objectification of women become part of building and maintaining male solidarity on the job.

Thus, within male-dominated, primarily heterosexual work environments, male behaviour is typically unquestioned, particularly if it is directed at women sexually. Sexual jokes, comments, teasing or touching of women are part of building and sustaining male solidarity. Certainly not all men participate, but few men intervene. Women who are targets of this behaviour are characterised as 'asking for it' or thought of as being flattered by any display of men's sexual desire. This behaviour, too, is considered not intrusive but deserved and welcomed. Women, it is commonly assumed, by entering into men's territory, must expect and accept these displays of healthy male heterosexuality. It is, after all, harmless to men and important to the construction of their working environment. From a male point of view, the harmful effects of sexual harassment are not understood as intrusions, just male 'fun'.

Both Farley (1978) and MacKinnon (1978), two ground-breaking authorities on sexual harassment, have noted the use of sexual harassment to try to drive women away from invading previously all-male work spheres. Clearly, sexual harassment becomes one way for men to 'defend the territory'. These tactics are not unlike the tactics used to keep women in the home and off the streets (Stanko 1985) – men who harass use strategies which they know will humiliate, frighten, coerce and terrify women at work. MacKinnon more eloquently states this position:

Sexual harassment exemplifies and promotes employment practices which disadvantage women in work (especially occupational segregation) and sexual practices which intimately degrade and objectify women. In this broader perspective, sexual harassment at work undercuts women's potential for social equality in two interpenetrated ways: by using her employment position to coerce her sexually while using her sexual position to coerce her economically.

(1978: 7)

Safety at work: against sexual harassment

Women's experiences of male violence outside the work context also reflect patterns of reported victimisation related to whether women lead traditional or non-traditional life-styles. Women leading more traditional life-styles are most likely to experience various forms of criminal violence in the home, but are less likely to report them to official criminal justice agencies (Hanmer and Saunders 1984; Russell 1973, 1982). Women leading non-traditional life-styles report higher levels of violence outside the home (Hall 1985; Widom and Maxfield 1984). It is, however, impossible to guarantee that any woman, regardless of life-style and occupation, will escape the exposure to various forms of men's sexually intrusive behaviour (Russell 1984; Schur 1984; Stanko 1985).

In this way, sexual harassment becomes a potential safety hazard for women who work in both traditional and non-traditional occupations. Feelings of anxiety, fear, helplessness and loss of control essentially make the working environment one which becomes dangerous to women's physical and mental health. Indeed, some women should receive additional combat pay for some of their work experiences.

Curiously, objections to women entering non-traditional employment focus on women's safety from those they might contact in the course of their employment. The Leeds TUCRIC study, for example, found that postwomen were asked at interviews 'how they will cope with being the only woman working all night with three hundred men in the parcel office or with the threat of being attacked when walking through the worst areas of town at 5 a.m.' (1983: 65). While those interview questions might lead one to believe the interviews are concerned about women's safety from unknown abusers loose on the street, the postwomen stated they received frequent comments from men about sex and women's appearance during their working days. Women are left with the responsibility for their own safety – from fellow workers as well as those encountered on the job.

Safety from male violence on the street, at home or at work, is a major concern for women (Stanko 1985, 1987). Adopting precautions — in dress, manner and perhaps even choice of job or occupation – is one way to cope with threatening situations. Choice of job may be affected by women's perceived and real vulnerability to various forms of male violence including sexual harassment. It might be interesting to inquire when studying gender and employment whether feelings of safety or uncomfortableness are considered in the selection of an occupation or employment site. We know women quit jobs because they are leaving harassing situations; do they also choose jobs to minimise their confrontations with harassers?

In the interest of precaution and safety, predicting which men will harass is not always possible. Harassers, while often managers and supervisors, are just as likely to be co-workers; some are subordinates, customers, clients, patients or students. Most harassers are not behaving in 'aberrant' ways, but in a manner typical of men's treatment of women in a heterosexual encounter. At the most dangerous and frightening end of the spectrum, one study of undetected rapists indicates that these men are aware that what they are doing is indeed coercive sexuality (Smithyman 1978). Rapists get away with rape and harassers get away with various forms of harassment (which might also include rape) simply because they can. This is not to say that rape or harassment may even constitute a significant part of these men's lives. Smithyman's research indicates that thinking about rape is one small aspect of the undetected rapist's life (1978: 49).

Women, both in and out of employment, have become specialists in avoidance so that they can minimise their confrontation with sexual harassment. Thus, sexual harassment, like woman-battering, incest, rape and sexual assault, is primarily a display of male control and intrusion into women's lives. In a sense, work is no different than everyday dilemmas of safety concern to women. Sexual harassment remains a common experience of working women. Crime surveys indicate that women are more afraid to be on the streets alone at night. So too research on incest, rape and sexual and physical assaults on women shows that the most dangerous place for women is in their own homes. Work, like home and the street, is yet another location where women are subjected to abuse because they are women. Since sexual harassment is located well within women's commonplace experiences, it is even more difficult to find a way to specify how men's typical behaviour at work is any different from their behaviour outside work. As the issues of segregation and employment continue to be debated, women need to keep in mind how to combat sexual harassment along with economic segregation.

8: Sex discrimination in youth labour markets and employers' interests

Ken Roberts, Deborah Richardson and Sally Dench

There are contrasting views on how gender divisions in employment are most likely to be affected by broader economic and social trends in the 1980s.[1] On the one hand, there are those who predict that traditional gender divisions will be maintained and possibly consolidated, with new technologies and occupations being absorbed within existing patriarchal relationships (Equal Opportunities Commission (EOC) 1985). Widespread unemployment is confronting most sections of the workforce with fiercer competition. However, groups with privileges to defend can adopt closure strategies to protect their positions. Marginal workers, including newcomers to the labour market, and women, may be forced out completely, or may find their routes out of secondary employment becoming narrower than ever. Many females have minimal job security. They are sometimes first out in redundancy situations. Older women may be pressured back into domestic roles by their inability to obtain or retain jobs. For some young women, it has been argued, high unemployment can make the traditional escapes into marriage and parenthood appear more attractive than ever (Griffin 1985).

There is, however, a different, more optimistic view of women's prospects. The compression of childrearing into a brief part of the life span has now brought the majority of adult women into the workforce where their treatment has become 'an issue'. Women are no longer acquiescing before unequal opportunities. Feminist pressure has helped to produce equal pay and opportunity laws. This legislation may not have delivered instant changes, but it can be used by women seeking wider opportunities, and allows their aspirations to be presented as 'rights'. The 1980s are proving a decade of persistent high unemployment and also a period of rapid economic, technological and occupational change. Many firms have been obliged not only to prune, but to restructure, their workforces. Former divisions of labour are being unfrozen, which, it can be argued, creates favourable conditions for women to make a stand, politicise their grievances, claim their rights, break through traditional divisions and out of secondary segments (Game and Pringle 1984).

Women's share of employment has been increasing throughout the twentieth century, but up to the 1980s, as previous chapters have explained, there was no weakening of the division between men's and women's occupations (Hakim 1979). At the beginning of the 1980s over two-thirds of female employees were still in jobs where 90 per cent or more of the workers were women (Martin and Roberts 1984). Up to now most women have remained in second-class segments, on the secondary sides of dual labour markets. Over 40 per cent are still part-timers. The majority are still in non-skilled manual, clerical, retail and other service jobs, with poor rates of pay and promotion prospects. All this is generally agreed and, indeed, is probably too well known to require further corroboration. However, the processes that have created, and sustain, gender divisions in employment remain matters for debate. And different assessments of the likely significance of economic conditions in the 1980s are related to different analysts' views on the sources of gender divisions. Those who believe that patriarchal relationships have arisen from some kind of alliance between males' interests and the rationality of an exploitative capitalist system are unlikely to regard new technologies, or the replacement of old by new industries, firms and occupations, as sufficient to break the barriers between men's and women's occupational enclaves. In contrast, those who attribute some autonomy to stratification by gender, and who believe that changes in the market positions and political efficacy of different groups of workers, including women and men, can lead to significant changes in their life-chances, are far more likely to envisage women breaking out from their formerly subordinate labour market positions during the economic restructuring that is currently in process.

One might expect any unfreezing of gender divisions to be especially visible in youth labour markets where the occupational restructuring provoked by macroeconomic trends and new technologies is interacting with government measures intended to promote youth training and employment. These measures, it is officially claimed, or hoped, will be of special assistance to formerly disadvantaged groups, and should offer wider opportunities to school-leavers who used to be denied systematic training and further education. Female school-leavers are obvious candidates for such benefits. If, on the other hand, high unemployment and defensive strategies by existing job-holders are consolidating existing divisions, this should also be apparent in youth training and employment. Since the mid-1970s youth unemployment has been well above adult levels.

Our fresh evidence offers clear indications of whether or not there are any trends towards gender divisions dissolving in the youth labour markets of the 1980s. Equally important, it clarifies the interests and circumstances that are crucial in determining whether changes occur or fail to do so. The evidence is from interviews during 1984 in 308 firms – a quota sample covering all the applicable size-bands in thirteen business sectors, and from three local labour markets: Liverpool, Walsall and Chelmsford. This survey of firms was part of a larger research project into the changing structure of youth labour markets (Roberts, Dench and Richardson 1987). The principal objective in the survey of firms was to chart and explain changes in levels and types of demand for beginning workers. However, addressing these questions generated a wealth of more general information about trends in the size and composition of the firms' workforces and recruits, training practices and rates of pay in different sectors, together with the reasons for any changes. As a result, we have data on the proportions of males and females, full- and part-time, in different age groups, already employed, recently recruited and being trained for different occupations.

The information that we shall present is from and about employers only, the demand side of the labour market. It relates to employers' perspectives and practices which structure young people's and other would-be workers' opportunities, but this bias will not be the source of our main conclusion – that employers' interests and practices are crucial in reproducing gender divisions in employment in most cases; while, in a smaller number of firms, these interests are leading to changes. If most of the firms that we studied had been keen to promote equal opportunities, this would have been apparent in our evidence. In practice, the majority of the employers were well aware that gender divisions were being reproduced within their firms, and they did not regard this as *their* problem. Indeed, our evidence illustrates how desegmentation would clash with most employers' real and self-defined interests, which is not to say that employers are the sole obstacles to equal opportunities. Boys and girls are still not being brought to the threshold of their working lives with equal qualifications and aspirations. However, our evidence suggests that, even if this occurred, gender divisions would soon appear once the individuals were in the labour market, for the demand for labour remains anything but gender-neutral. Unless and until employers' interests and equal opportunities are aligned, we expect little progress towards sex equality in employment. Moreover, we shall argue that it is not just employers' perceived interests, but their real interests, that will need to be changed.

Our evidence confirms that employment opportunities for males and females are certainly changing in the 1980s. Most of the firms that we studied were changing in shape and size, sometimes dramatically. However, the changes in process were not towards more or less discrimination and segmentation. They simply followed the macro-economic and occupational trends which were altering the numbers, relative proportions and locations of men's and women's jobs. Our firms' adult workforces contained all the familiar gender divisions. This was probably too predictable even to deserve comment. The reproduction of these divisions was less predictable, but there were no signs of any general trends towards desegregation in youth recruitment and training or in remuneration. Nor were many firms endeavouring to initiate such trends.

Recruitment

The most recent government statistics show that male and female school-leavers are still entering different industries and occupations. Ask employers why and they will usually explain that it is still rare for men and women to apply for each other's jobs. We will return to this explanation later. It is not an outright lie, but it is rarely the whole truth.

We did not ask directly whether the firms that we surveyed were guilty of sex discrimination. Our questions focused on recruits' ages rather than their sex and were phrased as general queries about the types of personnel sought at different levels. The employers were asked the age groups from which they preferred to recruit, whether any qualifications or experience were required or preferred and, incidentally, whether they were looking for men, women or either. Many managers were quite prepared to state their preferences. Most jobs appeared to be open to male or female applicants, but the 1975 Sex Discrimination Act had certainly not eradicated blatant sexism. Whether males, females or either were sought varied with the type of occupation and the type of firm. Eighty-three per cent of firms were equally willing to recruit men or women to sales jobs, but only 63 per cent to skilled manual occupations. Large firms were relatively free of overt gender discrimination, whereas small companies often made no secret of their preferences. The proprietors explained how they 'used their loaves' and, in public, kept quiet. When one sex was preferred, this was usually operating to women's advantage in clerical jobs. Married women were considered best for typing and clerical work, and equally suitable for computer operating. For unskilled posts the employers were as likely to be biased towards women as men. The latter tended to be preferred when the work was heavy, whereas women were considered the more nimble and accurate at intricate assembly jobs. At all other levels – management, professional, technical, skilled and semi-skilled – there was a general preference for men.

Discrimination when hiring from external labour markets was only one way in which recruitment methods operated to women's disadvantage. Internal labour markets (Kerr 1954) also favoured men.

These markets are created when access to certain jobs is limited to personnel already within an organisation. The jobs are never advertised externally. Outsiders are not considered no matter what their capabilities, skills and experience. Trade unions are sometimes regulators of internal labour markets (Loveridge 1983). Members in specific industries and occupations may combine to defend 'their' jobs from outside competition and define the pools from which labour can be hired. However, trade unions' influence should not be exaggerated; they had some say in recruitment in only 12 per cent of our firms. We do not doubt that the processes sustaining gender divisions in employment include the collective efforts of males to defend 'their' occupations. Some males may feel that their sexual identities would be undermined if women were admitted. Many undoubtedly realise that their generally superior earnings, and their dominant masculine status at work and at home, would be threatened. There are few recorded cases of male workers *en masse* opposing methods of recruitment that are known, by all concerned, to favour their own sex. Efforts to change these recruitment methods are often resisted by the males with vested interests to protect. However, male workers do not always have the power to control occupational recruitment, or any other aspects of their work situations, so as to protect their interests. Our evidence suggests that male workers' interests are reflected in recruitment methods only when these interests coincide with employers' preferences. According to our evidence, employers are the main architects of internal labour markets. These are created to reward and retain skilled staff, and to ensure that key posts are filled by known and reliable personnel. In addition, the promise of internal careers can aid recruitment to lower-level jobs.

Among the firms that we investigated internal labour markets were more strongly associated with certain grades of employment than with any specific business sectors, or establishments of a particular size. Eighty-four per cent of the firms normally promoted from within to supervisory posts. Managers and professional staff were usually trained internally, then promoted, in 58 per cent. In contrast, less than 10 per cent normally recruited internally to clerical, semi-skilled and unskilled jobs. When it occurred, internal promotion to these posts was usually from temporary or casual grades, though some firms had recently begun using the Youth Opportunities Programme and the Youth Training Scheme (YTS) to assess recruits, then select the best for retention or promotion. Girls may be as well equipped as boys to negotiate these particular hurdles, whereas regulating access to *higher*-level jobs through internal labour markets will favour employees with unbroken careers, which in practice must usually mean men.

Training

At the time of our inquiries and in the firms investigated, female entrants were still being denied equal training. Three sets of reasons accounted for this. Firstly, girls were still more likely than boys to be recruited by sectors with relatively poor training records, usually because their workforces were mainly unskilled. Food, distribution, and hotels and catering are prime examples. British industries offering prolonged and systematic training to high proportions of their young recruits, which include coal, shipbuilding and construction, remain male dominated.

Secondly, within most industries girls were being channelled into occupations where training tended to be basic, if any was offered. Engineering apprentices are still overwhelmingly male, while the majority of the industry's female staff are unskilled (EOC 1983). In sales and clerical employment, which tend to be women's occupations, our firms' recruits were unlikely to be offered anything beyond basic inductions. Staff were then expected to pick things up informally as they went along. Clerical and sales apprenticeships were rare. Off-the-job training was sometimes offered in these occupations, but it was usually selective and voluntary rather than universal and compulsory.

Thirdly, we found that, within the same occupational grades, boys were given the longer training, and were the more likely to benefit from off-the-job opportunities. Even when boys and girls were initially recruited on apparently equal terms and then worked side by side, informal discrimination often asserted itself before long. Males were encouraged to apply for day release, to attend short courses and evening classes. Managements seemed to assume that boys were interested in getting on. In contrast girls had to push themselves forward or display exceptional talent before equal opportunities were offered.

Most of the employers were fully aware that their male recruits received the longer and better training. They often justified this discrimination in terms of the boys' and girls' aspirations. However, many also draw attention to the firms' own longer-term interests and personnel requirements. Males were expected to remain for extended careers within the companies. Training girls was considered more risky. Some firms, from among the minority that trained substantial numbers of female recruits, were concerned that they would run short of career staff to promote. Less venturesome companies regarded training girls as a waste of everyone's time.

Forty-seven per cent of the firms were involved in the YTS, but the scheme was making virtually no impact on gender divisions. Girls may appear to be deriving as much benefit as boys. Those who enter the labour market at age 16 are just as likely to participate. However, there is extensive gender differentiation within the YTS. Boys and girls tend to be channelled into different schemes, and trained for different occupations. Usually, girls' training either is for 'women's work' (Fawcett Society 1985) or leads back to external labour markets, which may mean unemployment. If our firms are representative there must be few managements that are prepared to review and change their entire training regimes and personnel practices merely because the government launches a new scheme. Most firms were either assimilating the YTS into their own ongoing routines, ignoring it or compartmentalising youth training.

Very few managements subscribed the ideology with which the Manpower Services Commission had surrounded the YTS. The firms were simply not interested in training young people in transferable skills. The employers argued that many of the skills they required were specific to the companies, and that the main advantages of in-house training included trainees becoming thoroughly conversant with the firms' own methods and, in the process, developing company loyalty. Many managements failed to see any point in broad-based training. Some regarded the compulsory off-the-job elements as pointless. Few could see any reason why they should provide training in skills for staff to transfer to competitors. Hence the general preference for males when the YTS year was the first stage in longer training programmes which led to genuine career opportunities.

Pay

All firms were asked about pay in the occupations to which their largest numbers of young males, then young females, were recruited. Most companies supplied information about sales, clerical, apprentice and skilled or unskilled rates. Few 16- to 18-year-olds were being recruited directly into the technical, management or professional grades. We noted rates of pay for 16-year-olds, 18-year-olds and adults. For present purposes, the principal issue is whether male and female recruits were being rewarded with equal pay for equal work, and in general males were being offered superior income opportunities.

In sales, clerical and unskilled jobs, male and female rates were similar until age 18, after which males climbed ahead. Our firms were offering men the longer income careers, a difference that was related to their superior training. This will be why there are wider age differentials in pay among male than among female employees, and why there are much wider income inequalities between adult males and females than among young workers.

In skilled manual occupations, females were being paid less than males at all ages, from 16 onwards. For girls, training in manual skills is still concentrated in a limited number of trades such as clothing, hairdressing and leather goods. Rates for apprentices and adults in these occupations were not only far lower than in equivalent male jobs, in engineering and construction for example, but also beneath women's average earnings in sales, clerical and even unskilled employment.

According to this evidence, nominally equal training will not deliver equal pay while women remain clustered in women's occupations. Hairdressing has a long record as a major source of apprentice training for girls. The industry has an apparently excellent training record. Virtually all its young recruits receive systematic training lasting several years. Yet the industry has some of the lowest wages in the country. The attractions, apart from the glamour, include opportunities for self-employment. This can be a route towards the top of the women's pay league. However, merely providing training, whether within or outside the YTS, is clearly no guarantee that either the status or pay of women's work will be enhanced.

Custom and practice

Why were gender divisions surviving the unfreezing of occupational structures, the clamour for women's rights and government measures intended to alleviate disadvantages? Three sets of factors must be combined in a fully comprehensive explanation, but not with equal weight. The separation of men's and women's work is often described as traditional. This means more than the practices having persisted for ages. Custom can then become its own justification. Why change practices that have stood the test of time? Campaigners for equal opportunities often feel that they are battling against tradition. We agree. But we doubt whether the relevant traditions will be undermined if only employers can be persuaded to reappraise customary practices and reconsider their necessity or whether they might have become counter-productive in current conditions.

The weight of tradition is certainly important in personnel matters. Rational employers do not calculate marginal costs and benefits prior to every hiring decision. Firms often rely on tried and tested ways of publicising their requirements through Jobcentres and the Careers Service or by word of mouth, and seek known types of recruit – young or old, experienced or novices, males, females or either, with or without qualifications – until customary methods cease to work, for whatever reasons. Firms see no need to review and change their ways unless and until recruitment, training, turnover or labour relations becomes a 'problem'.

At the time of our survey, 68 per cent of the firms reported no recruitment or training problems whatsoever. They could see that many young and older would-be workers faced problems stemming from the inadequate supply of jobs. They could appreciate governments' difficulties in tackling unemployment and, in the meantime, catering for the young and older unemployed. But recruitment and training were not problems for most companies. Some explained that their only difficulty, if the term applied, was the scope for choice. Press adverts were producing shoals of applications to process. Choosing the best had become more difficult. High unemployment, therefore, was prompting firms to consolidate, to draw in rather than to widen their nets.

The minority of firms where meeting labour requirements was a problem reported three main types of difficulty. Some were short of ready-trained skilled workers, but few were responding by expanding their volume of training. The managements did not always regard training as a solution, certainly to Monday's problems. They were scouring the country, and offering more attractive salaries or job titles. In some manufacturing firms a shortage of skilled labour had become a perpetual problem with which the managements felt they could possibly cope, but could not solve. A handful of firms claimed that 'generous' social security entitlements were making it difficult to hold unskilled labour. It is noteworthy that none of these firms complained of adult males' reluctance to take low-paid jobs. A more common grievance was that women with husbands on supplementary benefit were in situations where working 'on the cards' did not pay.

The third type of problem was a shortage of well-qualified school-leavers. Young people with five O-levels or better were still in strong demand in each of the three local labour markets that we investigated. Many employers had found their supplies running dry as more and more well-qualified 16-year-olds elected to remain in education. Many firms felt that they had been forced to raise entry standards and to seek A-levels or degrees rather than O-levels, and to recruit 18- or 21-year-olds instead of the bright, well-qualified 16-year-olds they would have preferred to train in the companies' ways.

Custom and practice can definitely help to explain why gender divisions persist. Unemployment may make the weight of tradition heavier than otherwise. However, in our view, tradition is rarely a complete explanation. When personnel problems had arisen, the firms had questioned and changed some traditions, but usually within prevailing conceptions of men's and women's work. Few firms that were short of skilled men were training women. Only a handful of companies with difficulties in attracting enough well-qualified male school-leavers were joining 'girls into engineering' and similar campaigns. Few were even beginning to think of women as potential skilled workers and managers. As explained below, many had absolutely no intention of 'wasting' their training capacity on too many females, however bright and well qualified. Firms complained when women, but not adult men, were unwilling to work for poverty wages. Such attitudes may be traditional. But so were many former practices that had been reviewed and changed alongside the occupational restructuring that was occurring in the 1980s.

Females' qualifications and aspirations

As previously mentioned, employers' favourite explanation of why men and women occupy different jobs is that the sexes rarely apply for each other's positions. Managements blame workers for the segmentation of firms' labour forces. Employers report that girls are simply 'not interested' in apprentice training for careers in engineering and construction. When males are promoted while females stay put, employers return to the argument that women are 'not interested' – that they will not take advantage of day release, attend evening classes, sit exams and train for long-term rewards.

The crusade for equal opportunities has obviously taken these arguments seriously. Hence the campaigns and demonstration projects to coax more girls into science and engineering, and to encourage them to contemplate careers in what was once men's work. A necessary step in any movement towards equality in employment must clearly be to bring boys and girls to the labour market with similar qualifications and aspirations, and there is still a considerable way to go. In secondary schools there are few signs of more boys and girls taking each other's traditional subjects. Girls are still somehow deflected from physics, chemistry and technical courses. Homes, schools and the media continue to interact with biology to produce masculine and feminine school-leavers instead of just individuals with different abilities and preferences. But would girls be given equal opportunities even if they had the same aspirations, and possessed the same qualifications, as boys?

Employers cannot shift all the responsibility for girls' inferior employment prospects. In schools, girls are not short of ambition or ability. They pass as many O-levels as boys, and are more likely to stay on. In occupations where some are now being given the opportunity, including local government, banking and insurance, more girls are studying for post-entry professional qualifications, competing for and beginning to squeeze males' career prospects (Crompton and Jones 1984). Girls and boys may be advised to study different subjects, act accordingly and develop different aspirations because all concerned realise that, once in the labour market, the sexes will face different opportunities. Labour supply adapts to demand, and vice versa.

Employers' interests

We realise that male and female school-leavers possess somewhat different qualifications and ambitions. However, we also know that firms would be able to recruit and train more females for higher-paid jobs, if employers wanted to make the effort. We are fully aware that tradition is on the side of gender divisions, but we also know that employers could erode this tradition, as they have done with so many others, if they believed that doing so would serve their own interests.

Self-interested employers would be irrational to discriminate between males and females purely on grounds of sex. Employers' self-interest, even their survival, can depend on hiring and training whoever will be most productive and profitable. Market forces would not allow firms to discriminate if labour supply was not pre-structured by gender, but the most relevant structures are not boys' and girls' aspirations and qualifications.

The firms that we investigated preferred to train boys because men were expected to pursue uninterrupted careers. The employers knew that, in most households, males' careers still take precedence. They knew that mothers remain more likely than fathers to withdraw from the labour market. It is still usually the male's occupation, if any, that determines where a family lives, and while these priorities persist employers who believe that maximum returns from training depend on the workers remaining in their companies will continue, quite rationally, to prefer training and then promoting men rather than women.

The domestic division of labour, reinforced by income tax and social security regulations, also means that adult women can be tempted into the labour market for lower rates of pay. While this situation persists, employers' self-interest demands the use of women as cheap labour. Most employers know why men never or rarely apply for women's jobs. They realise that women's wages will not tempt males with dependants. Employers do not blame or criticise unemployed men who do not apply. Men are not expected to work for women's wages. Some employers admitted that the occasional male applicant was always rejected or dissuaded. The managements knew that males, especially if married with dependants, would soon grow dissatisfied, leave for other jobs or decide that social security offered equivalent living standards and, possibly, greater security.

Technological and occupational changes

At the time of our research, changes in technology and in the structure of Britain's economy were redistributing the workforce between business sectors, and between occupational grades within sectors. These changes were affecting men and women, but in very different ways, because the local labour markets that we studied, and individual firms' workforces, remained deeply segmented for the reasons outlined above. Each sex's enclaves were changing in size, shape and location, and one net effect was a sharp growth in women's share of employment.

The shift towards service sector employment has operated, and will probably continue to work, to women's advantage. Most business sectors where employment in Britain is now stable or expanding employ above-average proportions of females. The sharpest contractions are in manufacturing industries with mainly male workforces. Within firms in most sectors, the proportions of blue-collar jobs are in long-term decline. In some respects, this trend also operates to women's advantage. The sectors where blue-collar jobs are most resilient include clothing, leather goods and hairdressing, which have more women than men in their manual grades. The preponderance of (low-paid) women in these sectors could be one reason why employers see little advantage in replacing labour with technology.

The long-term trend towards a higher proportion of women in the working population seems likely to continue. However, in the firms that we studied there were no signs of women taking over the top jobs. The only occupational grades where net increases in employment were in process, and likely to continue, were technical, management and professional, where most employees were men. Male workers, therefore, had the most to gain from occupational shifts towards these levels.

Despite occupying a growing proportion of all jobs, within the firms that we studied the relative quality of women's employment was deteriorating rather than improving. Many firms were creating clearer divisions between core and peripheral workforces. Managements interpreted these developments as an aspect of rationalisation – becoming more efficient, leaner and adaptable. Economic conditions were favouring firms that were capable of rapid changes in size and shape to exploit new technologies and markets. Core workers were usually qualified, skilled, well paid, as secure as their companies and male. Peripheral workers were typically unskilled, low-paid and female.

The firms in our sample, especially in distribution, hotels and catering, sport and recreation, and the financial sector, were making greater use of part-time staff (see Clark 1982). They realised that part-timers could reduce total wage costs and make it unnecessary to carry surplus staff at slack times, while all hands could be mustered when trade peaked. There was also a trend towards hiring temporary full- and part-time staff in offices, shops and non-skilled factory jobs. In the years of full employment, when firms faced labour shortages, so-called 'soulful' corporations had vested interests in encouraging even unskilled staff to develop company loyalty. Labour market conditions in the 1980s have encouraged different practices (Craig *et al.* 1983). Non-skilled labour has become abundant. At the time of our fieldwork, in each of the local labour markets, employers were discovering that unskilled labour could be hired and fired alongside workflows. Greater use of temporary and casual grades was not confined to back-street businesses. The same trend was evident in local government, the health services and even universities. One consequence was that entrants to the labour market, young people and also married women were facing a series of new screens. Their initial employment was most likely to be temporary. Permanent jobs were often reserved for temporary staff who had proved their worth. Needless to say, many temporary employees were truly temporary; they were not allowed to settle for long enough to earn promotion. Quantitatively, women's employment prospects were better than ever in the firms that we studied, but in qualitative terms their positions were not improving. Their segments of the workforce remained second-class, more so than ever if anything. There were no signs of role reversal in the labour market, but women's greater share of all jobs could still have broader social repercussions.

Up to now, male workers in manufacturing have been treated as the core members of the manual working class. This treatment is becoming unrealistic. The current trends are towards a higher proportion of manual workers in service sectors where labour forces tend to be female, part-time and often temporary. This trend has implications for trade unions, for politics and for the family.

A type of role reversal frequently predicted, though there is still no evidence of it actually occurring, is in the domestic division of labour. It has been envisaged that more jobs for women, and fewer for men, will result in more female bread-winners and more house-husbands. The relevant changes in the occupational structure could, but we doubt whether they actually will, inspire such a revolution. Employment in the technical, professional and management grades, jobs commanded mainly by men, is expanding. Current occupational trends are unlikely to force more domestic role reversals in middle-class households. Changes in the proportions of manual jobs for men and women are likely to create more situations where working-class wives have the better chances of employment. In some households this may lead to male dependants being supported by working-class wives. However, a more likely outcome, given the structure of Britain's tax and social security systems, coupled with the types of jobs for which women are eligible, is a clearer division between manual households where both partners work and others where neither is employed (see also Pahl 1984).

Prospects for equality

An implication of our evidence and analysis is that current efforts to promote sex equality are unbalanced, which will be why they are proving ineffective. Efforts are being made to bring boys and girls to the labour market on more equal terms. There are campaigns to persuade more girls to study mathematics and science, to interest more in engineering and to persuade those with the ability to take three A-levels and then compete for university places. The YTS is now offering initial training and further education to girls who enter the labour market at 16 and 17. These measures are not yet bringing males and females to the outset of their occupational careers as equal competitors, but even if they did, according to our evidence, the result would not be equal opportunities, because labour demand is not neutral. Changes in boys' and girls' aspirations and qualifications will not automatically reshape employers' preferences.

There are current campaigns to educate employers away from sex discrimination, to overcome inertia, to persuade managers to question traditional personnel practices, patriarchal values and assumptions and to make them aware of 'the problem' and then change their ways in their own enlightened self-interest (Bennett and Carter 1983). These campaigns have little impact because, as we have explained, traditional personnel practices still accord with many enlightened employers' interests and will continue to do so without changes in the domestic division of labour, income tax or social security regulations.

Governments have delivered equal pay and opportunity laws. They can give women further assistance by equal treatment in taxation and social security. However, changes in the domestic division of labour will probably have to be pioneered at the grass roots. Without these changes, women will continue to compete in the labour market with one hand tied by domestic priorities, and employers will continue to prefer male recruits in jobs with training and prospects of promotion. Firms will continue to see women primarily as a source of cheap, flexible, often temporary unskilled labour. Faced with inequalities in employment, women will continue to seek economic security and status in marriage and family life. This reinforcing circle remains intact (Cavendish 1982; Hunt 1980; Pollert 1981). It seems destined to outlast the careers of most school-leavers in the 1980s. Gender divisions in employment have yet to begin to crumble. Even so, our conclusions are not wholly pessimistic. The remaining obstacles can be identified, and they are not intractable.

Note

1 The research on which this chapter is based was financed by the Department of Employment, but the views expressed are solely the authors'.

9: The changing labour market: growth of part-time employment and labour market segmentation in Britain

Olive Robinson

Introduction

A 1983 Organisation for Economic Co-operation and Development (OECD) report found that 'the rapid expansion of part-time employment in virtually all Member countries over the past two decades is one of the most significant structural shifts occurring in the OECD labour market'. While expressing caution in making inter-country comparisons of the size and structure of part-time employment because of the great variety in definitions of part-time work and in methods of data collection, 'it was clear that over the recent decade full-time employment was actually declining in a number of countries but part-time employment was continuing to expand in all countries' (OECD 1983: 43–5).

Reviewing the incidence of part-time employment in the European Community, the present writer observed in 1979 that recognition of the permanent character of part-time labour was reflected in the pragmatic development of labour market legislation which enhanced the rights of part-time workers under national employment protection laws. Nevertheless there was a patent need for intensification of employment policies which would integrate the part-time and full-time elements of the labour force if the opportunities for discrimination inherent in the prevalence of labour markets separated by the number of hours worked were to be removed (Robinson 1979: 299–314). This conclusion was endorsed by the European Commission's proposal for a Council Directive on voluntary part-time work which sought 'to guarantee part-time workers the same rights as full-timers with due regard to the special nature of part-time employment'. The draft Directive issued in December 1981, and remaining unadopted seven years later, was prompted by the view that

> while its advantages are not in question, the growth of part-time work has nevertheless raised certain problems. In particular, part-time workers are often the subject of discriminatory treatment by comparison with full-time workers in relation to their legal status and their employment and working conditions, and are also at a disadvantage in terms of attitudes to their place in the labour market. This in turn has consequences for labour market policies, since it has led to a form of segmentation within the labour market which runs contrary to the policy objectives in all Member States to develop an integrated and transparent market with the aim of overcoming mismatches and other imbalances.
>
> (Commission of the European Communities 1981: 1)

The change in employment structure resulting from the growth in part-time employment is most pronounced in Britain. Five million of the employees in employment work part-time, constituting 24 per cent of the total, and the upward trend has not just been in progress for the past decade, but may be traced with little interruption back to 1951. Between 1951 and 1981 there was a fall in the number of full-time employees of 2.3 million (1.9 male and 0.4 female), while the number of part-timers rose by 3.7 million (0.7 male and 3.0 female). Women account for over 80 per cent of part-time employees, and their employment on a part-time basis has been the sole source of employment increase over a thirty-year period. The latest employment estimates indicate that these trends are continuing in the 1980s, confirming that the growth in work provision for employees is being achieved through the creation of part-time jobs (Table 9.1; Robinson, in NIESR 1986: 47).

It is not surprising in view of the close association of part-time employment with female labour force participation that attention is directed to the labour market treatment of part-time workers. It will be argued in this chapter that the circumstances in which part-time workers are deployed in both manufacturing and service industries in Britain are the outcome of the process of labour market segmentation which is exacerbating the inferior treatment of female employees. The ability of employers to implement policies which have increased the rate of female labour force participation at a time of historically high levels of unemployment cannot be understood solely in the context of external labour market influences. Nor do explanations of occupational segregation of men's and women's employment add greatly to our understanding of the implications of growing female part-time

Table 9.1 Growth of part-time employment in Great Britain, 1951–86 (employees in employment, all industries, thousands)

	MALE				FEMALE				ALL
	Full-time	Part-time	All	%*	Full-time	Part-time	All	%*	
1951[a]	13,438	45	13,483	0.3	5,752	754	6,506	11.6	19,989
1961[a]	13,852	174	14,026	1.2	5,351	1,892	7,243	26.1	21,269
1971[b]	12,840	584	13,424	4.4	5,467	2,757	8,224	33.5	21,648
1981[b]	11,511	718	12,229	5.9	5,304	3,781	9,085	41.6	21,314
1981[c]	—	—	12,164	—	5,260	3,813	9,073	42.0	21,237
1986[d] (June)	10,789	854	11,643	7.3	5,321	4,141	9,462	43.8	21,105

Sources: [a] Census of Population, 1951, Great Britain: one per cent sample, table 11.2; 1961 and Wales: industry tables, part 1, table 2; Scotland: occupation, industry and workplace, part II, industry table 2; 1971, Great Britain: economic activity table, part IV, tables 26 and 34.
[b] Employment Gazette, August 1973: census of employment June 1971; December 1983: census of employment September 1981; August 1984: historical supplement no. 1; March 1985: 117.
[c] Employment Gazette, March 1985: revised estimates.
[d] Employment Gazette, October 1987: historical supplement no. 2.
* Part-time as percentage of total male/female employment.

employment, particularly when it is concluded, as in Hakim for example, that 'while part-time working may be important in certain respects, its impact on the pattern of job segregation is almost non-existent' (Hakim 1979: 31). The creation of part-time rather than full-time jobs, it will be shown, is a consequence of developments in the patterns of employers' labour requirements which do not respond automatically to changes in the supply of labour. The ways in which employers use part-time labour may therefore be regarded as expressions of labour market segmentation, a process identified as an inevitable component of technological development, industrial restructuring and cost control in the face of increasing competition in a number of industries (cf. Nolan 1983: 309–10).

The argument that increasing part-time employment segments the labour market to the detriment of women working part-time relative to both women and men in full-time employment is based on extensive empirical investigation of the influences which generate part-time jobs in Britain, undertaken over the period 1979–84. The findings of this research, which focused on employers' use of part-time labour, indicate the decisive role played by labour market demand in determining the nature and extent of part-time employment. It will be seen in particular that the engagement of part-time workers is the result of significant changes in the utilisation of labour, changes which manifest the adoption of more cost-effective employment policies and which must be regarded as developments unlikely to be reversed (Robinson and Wallace 1984b; 1984c).

This approach to the examination of the reasons for the phenomenal growth of part-time employment in Britain differs from that of earlier studies. Explanations for the major change in labour force composition which has occurred in Western European countries and in the United States in recent decades have been sought principally through examination of the circumstances surrounding female labour supply. In a period of tight labour markets the availability of large numbers of married women ready to work during hours which are compatible with the discharge of their domestic responsibilities presented a plausible explanation for the introduction of part-time work schedules by employers, and underpinned the view that part-time workers constituted a 'marginal' labour supply. But the simultaneous growth of female part-time employment and unemployment of both men and women during the 1970s and 1980s casts doubt on the view that the expansion and prevalence of part-time employment should be regarded primarily as a response by employers to fluctuations in labour supply. When people working part-time represent the sole form of employment growth, as has been the case in Britain for three decades, it seems reasonable to infer that the change in employment structure stems as much (if not more) from forces originating on the demand side of labour markets as from the socio-economic aspirations which shape the work-hours preferences of married women (cf. Beechey and Perkins 1987: 37; Blanchflower and Corry 1987: 56, 60).

Part-time employment – the concept

Part-time employment is work for fewer hours than those worked by full-time employees. It is usually defined as 'regular, voluntary work carried out during working hours distinctly shorter than normal'. In Britain there is no statutory definition of either full-time or part-time work. Except for just under 3 million workers within the scope of Wages Councils and the Agricultural Wages Boards, hours of work are determined unilaterally or through collective bargaining. The Department of Employment defines part-time employment (except in the case of teachers) as work for not more than 30 hours per week, excluding main meal-breaks and overtime. The definition has existed for at least fifty years, and its relationship to normal full-time weekly hours has altered with the long-term reduction in the length of the full-time working week. Identification of part-time workers by the application of an hours cut-off criterion means of course that workers employed for 30 or fewer hours per week are classified as part-time although they may regard themselves as full-time, while those employed for more than thirty hours are defined arbitrarily as full-time, even though they and their employers may consider the work to be part-time. Reductions in full-time hours from a standard of 40 hours during the past ten years have narrowed the gap between the upper limit of 30 hours defining part-time employment and normal hours of full-time work, which in 1986 ranged from 30 to over 44 per week; some 11 per cent of men and 28 per cent of women classed as full-time employees normally worked for no more than 36 hours. It has to be stressed, however, that over the past decade the working hours of female part-time employees have been reduced by a greater amount than those of either male or female full-time workers. The percentage of female employees with hours not exceeding 8 to 16 per week rose in each industrial and occupational classification of female part-time employment reported by the New Earnings Survey (NES), reflecting an increase in the number of jobs with limited labour requirements and reductions in the hours of existing jobs. Reductions in normal part-time working hours reinforce the evidence of growth in part-time employment measured by the numbers employed for not more than 30 hours per week. The downward trend in the length of the female part-time working week would almost certainly be shown to be greater but for the exclusion from the NES sample of employees whose gross weekly earnings fall below the thresholds for Pay-As-You-Earn and National Insurance contributions (Table 9.2).

Table 9.2 Distribution of normal basic hours of adult women in part-time employment, covered by the new earnings survey, 1975 and 1986

	Nos. in analysis	Percentage with normal basic hours in range:							Mean basic hrs worked
		not over 8	8–16	16–21	21–24	24–26	26–28	29–30	
Manual occupations									
1975	8,715	3.8	16.1	32.0	15.4	11.6	8.1	13.1	21.4
1986	9,950	11.2	28.4	27.2	9.9	8.5	5.3	9.5	18.9
Non-manual occupations									
1975	6,975	3.9	14.3	38.1	14.4	9.4	7.3	12.6	21.4
1986	10,618	7.6	24.0	34.8	11.7	7.7	4.5	9.6	20.0

Sources: Department of Employment New Earnings Surveys, 1975 and 1986: part F, table 183.

Part-time and full-time employment – the principal differences

The features which distinguish part-time from full-time jobs are familiar. Part-time employment is concentrated in the services sector of the economy, is largely female and is relatively low-paid. In June 1986 almost 90 per cent of total part-time employment of 5 million was in services. The trend towards higher levels of employment in service industries in Britain is evident from the 1920s and has been intensified by the decline in manufacturing employment during the 1970s. The transfer of labour resources is apparent from the loss of 2.8 million jobs in manufacturing, 93 per cent of which were those of full-time employees, compared with the increase of 2.8 million in service industries, 65 per cent of which were part-time (Table 9.3).

Female part-timers, the majority married women, account for 83 per cent of all part-time workers, and for 44 per cent of female employees. They work largely in service activities; the rise in their numbers from 2.8 to 4.1 million between 1971 and 1986 occurred wholly within service industries, compared with a reduction of 176,000 in manufacturing; 49 per cent of all females employed in the service sector are part-timers. Approximately two-thirds of the increase was in the private sector, in the distributive trades, banking, insurance and finance, catering and leisure industries. (The use of part-time female labour in manufacturing, it should be noted, is not insignificant despite the comparatively small numbers involved. In relative terms the part-time proportion of female employment in all manufacturing industries in 1986 stood at 19.8 per cent, marginally below the 1971 ratio.)

The final distinctive aspect of part-time employment, its relatively low pay, is of long standing. From evidence pieced together by the 1963 and 1973 International Labour Organisation international surveys it was concluded that part-timers did not generally enjoy the same conditions of employment as full-timers in relation to pay and other employee benefits. Ten years later little change in the position was recorded in the OECD report which drew on more adequate data than were available earlier, and the most recent studies provide few signs of improvement (De Neubourg 1985: 559–76; Hurstfield 1987: 47–56).

For Britain evidence from the 1980 Women and Employment survey showed that part-time workers participated in the labour market on terms very different from those obtained by men and by women without families (Ballard 1984: 416). Earnings statistics reveal that part-timers' earnings fell typically at the lower end of earnings structures. Analysis of NES data since 1971 indicates that the hourly earnings of females in part-time employment have deteriorated relatively to those of both men and women working a full-time week in the same industries and occupations. Increased levels of part-time employment have been the chief source of growth in those service industries which are the lowest

Table 9.3 Employees in employment in Great Britain, 1971 and 1986 (thousands)

	MALES			FEMALES			ALL
	Full-time	Part-time	Total	Full-time	Part-time	Total	
1971 (June)							
All industries and services	12,840	584	13,424	5,467	2,757	8,224	21,648
Manufacturing industries	5,483	73	5,556	1,875	480	2,355	7,911
Service industries	5,280	472	5,752	3,411	2,198	5,609	11,361
1986 (June)							
All industries	10,789	854	11,643	5,321	4,141	9,462	21,105
Manufacturing industries	3,572	52	3,624	1,209	304	1,513	5,137
Service industries	5,730	755	6,485	3,934	3,741	7,675	14,160

Sources: *Employment Gazette*, August 1973: census of employment 1971; October 1987: historical supplement no. 2.

paid, largely lacking in collective bargaining arrangements and within scope of Wages Councils. The five councils covering the distributive and hotel and catering trades account for some 81 per cent of the 2.7 million employees protected by the legislation (until 1986, when the coverage was reduced by the restriction of Wages Council orders to the setting of minimum basic rates of pay to workers aged twenty-one or over). In the private sector, female part-time employment in the distributive trades grew entirely at the expense of female full-time employment between 1971 and 1986; over the same period almost 80 per cent of employment growth in the hotel and catering trades resulted from additions to the female part-time labour force (Craig and Wilkinson 1985: 10; Robinson and Wallace 1983; 1984a).

More generally, female part-time employment was the only source of extra labour in manual occupations, in which hourly earnings for all employees are lower than in non-manual occupations. In both groups the differential between female full-time and part-time hourly earnings has widened since 1975 (for manual occupations this deterioration has been continuous since 1947) (Robinson and Wallace 1981: 149–71). A 1984 survey of the annual wage round reported that it was 'largely inviolate' but that part-time workers were among the substantial minority who did not receive annual or periodic pay increases (Daniel 1984: 83). At occupational levels earnings relativities have moved in favour of full-timers in catering and other services, in which over 80 per cent of manual part-timers were employed in 1986, and in clerical and selling work, the occupations in which the majority of non-manual part-timers are to be found (Table 9.4).

Employers' use of part-time labour

As stated in the introduction to this chapter, the writer's concern with investigation of the forces which influence demand for part-time employees directs attention to employers' utilisation of labour. How employers in a number of industries in Britain with a significant part-time component in their employment structures deploy part-time workers has been examined at establishment and organisation levels, the points at which employment policies are implemented. The ways in which part-timers are actually used are illustrated in the hours of work and occupational and pay patterns prevalent in the period 1980–4, when the bulk of the empirical research was conducted.

In the food manufacturing industry, in establishments where from 33 to 87 per cent of the female labour force in manual occupations worked part-time, production was maintained over 15- to 16-hour days by employing full-time day workers and separate shifts a.m., p.m. and evening workers on production and packing jobs. The timing of work schedule eliminates loss of output due to meal-breaks, thus maximising

Table 9.4 Median hourly earnings of full-time and part-time employees by occupation, 1975 and 1986

Occupations	MALE Full-time pence/hour	FEMALE Full-time pence/hour	FEMALE Part-time pence/hour	FEMALE Part-time as % male f/t earnings	FEMALE Part-time as % female f/t earnings
1975					
Clerical	122.6	91.6	81.7	66.6	89.2
Selling	123.8	64.8	62.4	50.0	96.3
Catering, etc.	98.4	79.4	76.5	77.7	96.3
All non-manual	158.1	95.2	79.5	50.2	83.5
All manual	118.0	79.6	76.4	64.7	96.0
All occups.	128.0	89.2	76.9	60.1	86.2
1986					
Clerical	402.7	325.1	274.2	68.1	84.1
Selling	414.8	238.4	216.5	52.2	90.8
Catering, etc.	300.8	247.6	220.6	73.3	89.1
All non-manual	567.1	349.1	273.6	48.2	78.4
All manual	373.1	259.1	223.3	59.8	86.2
All occups.	433.0	324.0	240.4	55.5	74.2

the use of capital equipment by adding approximately one to two hours to daily production time without incurring extra costs from premium rates of pay for overtime or the rotating shifts worked by full-timers. In tobacco manufacturing a factory operating a 4.5-day week employed part-time alongside full-time labour to ensure continuity of production during the lunch break from Monday to Thursday. The afternoon shifts worked for 16.5 hours every four days, giving an untypically short part-time working week for manufacturing industry; at other factories of the same company part-timers worked on 5 days for 17.5 to 25 hours per week. In engineering firms part-time hours are adjusted in response to fluctuations in product demand; during slack periods weekly hours can be shortened, minimising the need for dismissals and enabling management to retain experienced labour and reduce the costs of recruitment and training when demand rises. Part-timers' hours have been altered to maintain output over an unchanged working day at plants where the length of the full-time working week was reduced in 1981–2 from 40 to 37.5 hours; 30 per cent of the part-time workers' weekly hours were reduced from 25 to 20, and those of another 5 per cent from 25 to 22.5 hours.

In non-manufacturing industries employers had for several years used part-time labour in the course of expanding the provision of services to include weekend and late evening operations, whilst reducing the working week of full-time employees to five days. Levels of part-time employment in the female labour force ranged from 12 per cent in transport catering to over 80 per cent among clerical staff in credit banking, and to more than 90 per cent in manual occupations in local authorities, hospitals, pubs and clubs. Part-time labour is used more flexibly than in manufacturing establishments to meet fluctuations in daily and weekly trading. In branch banking part-time clerks were employed by the day or half-day each week, on alternate weeks, and for month-end and other seasonal duties. Sales assistants in retail distribution worked on Saturday only, on Saturdays and Mondays and at peak trading times throughout a six-day week. Those who worked on Saturdays only were employed for 7.5 hours, those working for two days for 15.5 hours, with almost 30 per cent at particular stores working for fewer than 8 hours per week, and some 20 per cent for less than 16 hours. By replacing one full-time sales assistant with two or three part-timers, employers can save as much as 8 work-hours per week. It is deployment of labour in this manner that accounts for the decrease from 21.6 hours of almost 3 hours in the average basic part-time working week in retailing since 1975, an industry where the proportion of female sales assistants working part-time has risen from 50 to over 60 per cent in the last ten years.

In the hotel and catering trades, where two-thirds of the labour force are female and 73 per cent part-time, the long-term downward trend in part-time hours was widely reflected. Although in much of the industry part-time employment is regarded as work of less than 40 hours per week, 25 to 35 per cent of women in the principal occupations of counterhands and kitchenhands worked for fewer than 16 hours, and a further 25 per cent for 16 to 21 hours. Weekly hours of fewer than 16 were worked by catering staff at airports, motorway service stations, railways and hospitals, at times not adequately covered by the schedules of full-time workers employed on rotating shift systems geared to 24-hour and seven-day service.

Public sector use of part-time staff is exhibited clearly in local authority and health service employment. In local authority education departments at least 10 per cent of clerical workers had weekly hours of fewer than 16, and 50 per cent of the part-timers engaged to work during term time only, in the lowest-graded non-manual occupation of ancillary assistant, worked for no more than 16 hours per week. The school meals service was staffed predominantly by women on weekly contracts of 5.5 to 12.5 hours, and some 80 per cent of school cleaners were employed for under 21 hours per week. In hospitals all domestic assistants employed on similar contracts were female part-timers. Part-time nurses none the less tended generally to be engaged for longer hours, on regular night or weekend work, with increasing numbers of both qualified and auxiliary nurses working from 16 to 21 hours, enabling management to cope with the reduction from 40 to 37.5 hours in the full-time nurse's working week implemented in 1980–1.

The complex and changing patterns of hours worked by part-timers show that employers are not indifferent to the hiring of full-time or part-time workers, since the jobs for which they are recruited do not call for a normal full-time week. In manufacturing companies operating in stable or expanding markets, part-time labour is used to maintain continuous production or to raise output through the introduction of shift systems which avoid or minimise the payment of premium rates to employees. Organisations in contracting and increasingly competitive markets make use of part-time employment to reduce wage costs by reducing total hours of work. In service industries the deployment of part-time labour gives managers greater freedom to match their labour demand with changing patterns in operational or customer requirements, and has simplified the implementation of a five-day week for full-time employees when hours of business are extended to six days. The seven-day opening of shops and derestriction of licensing hours in the hotel and catering and leisure services can be similarly facilitated. By relating working hours more closely to labour needs employers contain wage costs, and at the same time provide part-time jobs with a wide variety of working hours. The diversity in working schedules serves to increase the numbers of women available to work for less than a normal full-time week, often at unconventional hours.

The patterns of employers' labour requirements are thus the main reason for the employment of part-time labour; part-time jobs exist in their own right and are not regarded as fractions of full-time jobs. Part-time workers are not engaged as substitutes for full-time employees in short supply. The only notable exception is nursing, where there are high rates of labour turnover among full-time qualified nurses. In organisations with significant levels of part-time employment, managers had waiting lists of women seeking full-time jobs and of part-time employees wishing to transfer to full-time work. While there are employers who say that the increased size of the labour force generates additional recruitment, training and administration costs, they do not attempt to reduce them by substituting full-time for part-time labour. Furthermore, in companies which have undergone long-term reductions in overall levels of employment, the relative size of the female part-time labour force has not been adversely affected.

Occupational grading of staff more favourable to full-time than to part-time employees was found to be normal practice, even in companies and organisations where terms and conditions of employment were collectively negotiated. This is so for a number of reasons, including preferential treatment of full-time workers in promotion policies, and the employment of part-timers on work requiring lower skills. In banking, female part-time staff were excluded from the more highly skilled clerical positions, and in retailing they were employed almost entirely in the lowest-graded occupation of sales assistant. The highest concentration of part-timers in low grades was found in service industry establishments wanting labour for short daily periods; in the case of credit banking, for example, 98 per cent of female part-timers were in the lowest grades, as were 99 per cent of those in the school meals service.

Irrespective of their weekly hours of employment, women were engaged on similar types of work encompassed by a narrow band of grades. Men were employed in a wider range of jobs, and did not always fill posts in the lower grades occupied by the majority of female full-time and part-time workers in the same employment. The grading of the lowest-paid jobs held by men frequently exceeded that of the majority of posts occupied by women in the same employment. Occupational segregation is due to external factors, women having fewer opportunities to obtain qualifications to enable them to apply for the more highly skilled posts; but men are also promoted more often than women to positions in which formal qualifications are not required. Occupational grading differentials between women in full-time and part-time employment are much narrower than those between men and women, and should be regarded as a major factor contributing to segregation of male and female employment.

The degree of concentration of female part-time employees in the lowest-graded occupations is the principal reason for hourly rates of pay below those of men and women in full-time employment. Apart from isolated examples in banking, clothing manufacture and insurance, employers did not discriminate directly against female part-time employees in respect of basic rates of pay. In manufacturing establishments and in retail distribution there were many examples of female part-timers benefiting from the implementation of equal pay as their hourly rates had before 1975 been below those of their full-time counterparts. Closer scrutiny of pay structures, however, reveals that earnings differentials originating in occupational grading schemes were extended by the application of wage payment systems which provide equal treatment for men and women in respect of basic rates of pay. Intervals between wage and salary rates, for instance, grow progressively larger for the more highly graded jobs from which the majority of women were excluded. Wage payment systems also allowed for the payment of additional earnings, notably from overtime and shift premiums which are received predominantly by men and to a much lesser extent by women in full-time employment. Men were therefore able to earn more than women in full-time or part-time employment engaged on work classified in the same occupational grade with the same basic rates of pay. In both private and public sector organisations where superannuation schemes are in operation, low-grade occupations were usually not covered. If part-timers are not ineligible for membership because of grading, superannuation is frequently tied to a minimum number of weekly hours, often exceeding half the normal full-time hours, minima which are achieved by only a fraction of part-time employees. The potential cost of including all part-timers in occupational pension schemes was one of the principal reasons given by large employers for opposing the European Commission's draft Directive on voluntary part-time work (House of Lords 1982: 37–8).

Labour market legislation and part-time employment

The terms and conditions of employment of part-time workers in Britain are influenced by the Redundancy Payments Act 1965, the Equal Pay and Sex Discrimination Acts 1975, the Employment Protection (Consolidation) Act 1978 and the legislation governing the National Insurance scheme. The position of women working part-time under legislation designed to prevent discrimination on grounds of sex is of obvious importance when almost half of the employed female labour force is now part-time. Although the operation of grading structures produces the lowest rates of pay for occupations held by the vast majority of women in part-time employment, there was little or no evidence of the existence of differentials between basic rates of pay to encourage employers to engage part-time rather than full-time labour in a given job. (The comparatively few full-timers in the low-graded jobs were paid the same hourly rates as part-timers working in the same establishment.) But from reports of claims for equal pay heard by industrial tribunals it is apparent that the payment of lower basic rates to female part-timers than to men engaged in the same kind of work continued for some years after the implementation of the Equal Pay Act. A judgement of the Employment Appeal Tribunal (EAT) in July 1981 ruled it unlawful to pay women at lower rates than men solely on the grounds that they are employed for less than the normal full-time week. The EAT judgement in this case provided additional clarification by distinguishing direct discrimination between men and women on the grounds of their sex from indirect discrimination in cases where one class of employee consists wholly or mainly of women, a situation which would almost certainly apply in cases involving part-time work. The judgement stated further that indirect discrimination may be intentional, as a means of concealing an employer's intentions to discriminate on grounds of sex, or it may be unintentional if the objective is to serve some different purpose. An employer may justify the payment of lower rates to part-time employees if, in the words of the EAT judgement, 'he can show that the difference is necessary to achieve some commercial benefit, other than to obtain cheap female labour' (*Jenkins v. Kingsgate*, 1981).

Discrimination against female part-time employees in the implementation of procedures for selecting staff for redundancy can arise particularly in manufacturing where at establishment level selection for dismissal on the basis of the 'last in, first out' principle may be applied to full-time workers only. Following decisions of the EAT and of the Industrial Tribunals (Scotland), the use of such procedures is contrary to the provisions of the Sex Discrimination Act unless the employer shows justification on grounds other than sex. A woman's claim may also fail if she declines an opportunity to accept full-time employment as an alternative to dismissal, in which case she may forfeit her right to claim compensation under provisions of the Redundancy Payments Act. These decisions must raise doubts regarding the validity of collective agreements on redundancy selection procedures which give less favourable treatment to female part-time employees than to men, but which are not illegal unless implemented in a discriminatory fashion (*Clarke and Powell* v. *Eley (IMI) Kynock*, 1982, *Dick* v. *University of Dundee*, 1982; cf. Walby 1986: 227).

As the provisions of the Sex Discrimination Act make no reference to the length of working week in the determination of discrimination, women are able to pursue claims for equal treatment with men in selection for redundancy dismissal irrespective of their working hours. This represents an advance from their entitlement to claim against unfair dismissal under the Employment Act 1980 only if they work for at least

16 hours per week, or 8 hours for those with five years' continuous employment with the same employer. Female part-time employees in a mixed labour force thus have an advantage in procedures to be followed in redundancy selection over part-timers who are part of a wholly female labour force, although the length of working week remains a factor in determining the remedies available in a successful claim of this nature. If a woman's working hours exceed the threshold stipulated by the employment protection legislation a tribunal is empowered to order either compensation or reinstatement; if her hours are below the threshold the remedy is limited to compensation.

The legal status of women in part-time employment has undoubtedly been enhanced by the concept of indirect discrimination, without which cases brought before industrial tribunals could fail simply by virtue of women working less than full-time hours. Yet the extent to which the majority of women in part-time employment will benefit from recent EAT judgements remains uncertain. Empirical research findings discussed above show that direct discrimination makes little if any contribution to differentials between men's and women's earnings, since with minor exceptions their basic rates of pay are the same for a given job or occupational grade. It is the use of pay components additional to basic or minimum rates which creates earnings differentials which are less readily classified as discriminatory under the provisions of existing legislation. Furthermore, the same judgements which ruled as unlawful policies of indirect discrimination against female part-timers, in respect of hourly rates of pay and of selection for dismissal on grounds of redundancy, also allow employers a defence of justification if the inferior treatment of part-timers achieves economic or other objectives. A defence along these lines may therefore circumvent the intentions of judgements designed to reduce if not to eliminate the possibility of indirect discrimination against women in part-time employment. The 1986 Bilka case from West Germany (*Bilka-Kaufhaus* v. *Weber Von Hartz*) has, however, clarified the criteria for justifying indirect discrimination. In this case the European Court of Justice held that the exclusion of part-time workers from an occupational pension scheme contravenes Article 119 of the Treaty of Rome if the exclusion affects significantly more women than men, unless the employer can show that the exclusion is based on 'objectively justified factors unrelated to any discrimination on grounds of sex' (Byre 1987: 61).

A consequence of the expansion of part-time employment is that the working week of a growing proportion of women is below the threshold for entitlement to employee rights, including maternity benefits, redundancy payments, guarantee payments during short-time working and the right to claim against unfair dismissal, unless discrimination on grounds of sex is also involved. A working week of at least 16 hours, or 8 hours for a person with five years' continuous employment with the same employer, is a necessary qualification for these benefits (in the 1986 White Paper, *Building Businesses . . . Not Barriers*, it is proposed by government to raise the weekly thresholds from 16 to 20, and 8 to 12 hours). While it has been seen that in manufacturing and in banking female part-timers are commonly employed for more than 16 hours per week, significant numbers work considerably fewer hours in service industry establishments, both public and private. In education, catering and other occupations in which continuous employment cannot be provided, the position of large numbers of women engaged on a part-time basis appeared to be strengthened by the 1983 judgement of the House of Lords that breaks in employment may not necessarily affect the continuity of employment required in claims against unfair dismissal (*Ford* v. *Warwickshire County Council*, 1983). None the less, the 1987 judgement in the case of a part-time teacher claiming unfair dismissal and/or redundancy held that employees cannot aggregate the hours worked under separate contracts with the same employer in order to reach qualifying hours for statutory employment rights (*Lewis v. Surrey County Council*, 1987).

The National Insurance scheme regulations have since 1975 required both employee and employer to contribute on an earnings-related basis above a prescribed monthly threshold, raised annually in April from £11.00 in 1975 to £38.00 in 1986. The conjunction of low hourly rates of pay with a short working week in service industries frequently yields gross weekly earnings which are below the levels at which National Insurance contributions are mandatory. Reductions in the length of the part-time working week therefore reduce employers' statutory liabilities and indirect wage costs. At the same time increasing numbers of part-timers are placed outside the scope of legislation providing social welfare and employee benefits in a manner which could be regarded as discriminatory against women.

The changes in the National Insurance rates introduced in 1985 preserve the threshold principle, but through the adoption of a graduated payments scale reduce weekly contributions liability over an earnings range which in 1986–7 extended for employees from £38 to £95 and to £140 for employers. The 1986 NES shows that for adult women working part-time in non-manual occupations the median hourly earnings were £2.74 and in manual occupations £2.23. The majority of employers of part-time workers with earnings above £38 per week would appear to be paying them less than £95 (using the 30-hour cut-off), and were therefore carrying proportionately lower National Insurance charges than under previous regulations. They also benefit additionally from differences in the rate of change in part-time hourly earnings and the insurance threshold levels. Using the median hourly earnings of female part-time workers in catering, cleaning, etc. occupations as an example, these rose from 76.5 pence per hour in 1975 to 220.6 pence in 1986, a rise of 180 per cent, whilst the insurance thresholds rose by 245 per cent; the part-time working week which yields earnings below the threshold has been increased from 14 to 17 hours.

Conclusion

The results of empirical examination of the utilisation of part-time labour in Britain at the point of employment confirm the characteristics of part-time employees identified from macro-level statistical data. They are predominantly female, work mainly in service sector industries and are generally engaged in unskilled, low-graded and low-paid occupations. The employment of part-time labour produces cost advantages for both manufacturing and service sector employers. These arise from less rigid schedules of working hours, the widespread association of part-time jobs with relatively low hourly rates of pay and the general exclusion of part-time employees from eligibility for fringe benefits attached to full-time employment. The advantages inherent in the employment of part-time labour are clearly evident once attention is focused on employers' use of part-time workers. In both manufacturing and service industries, by adjusting labour force composition and part-time working hours to operational requirements which are not geared to established patterns of a full-time week, employers are able to minimise the costs of dealing with fluctuations in demand for products and services which can be anticipated but not controlled. In the services sector in which 32 per cent of the employed labour force works part-time, and which accounts for almost 90 per cent of part-time employment in Britain, the deployment of part-time labour allows managers to monitor wage costs more rigorously by matching labour inputs to their increasingly uneven manpower needs; with such flexibility they are less likely to hire labour in excess of requirements when workers can be engaged virtually by the hour, though on a permanent basis. At firm, organisation or establishment levels, the points at which employment decisions are taken, policies which result in the growth of the part-time labour force reflect the responses of employers (whether in the private or public sector) to pressures to reduce and contain operating costs in an increasingly competitive or constrained environment.

Consideration of the circumstances in which part-time employment has grown in Britain affords little ground for detracting from the European Commission's assessment of the labour market implications of the growth of the part-time labour force, quoted at the beginning of the chapter. Indeed, part-time employment is sustaining if not increasing the occupational segregation of male and female employment which pervades Britain's employment structure, and may be seen as part of the process of labour market segmentation resulting in the employment of women in industries and occupations characterised by a minimum of skills, low pay, few opportunities for training or promotion and little job security (cf. Beechey and Perkins 1987: 37; Blanchflower and Corry 1987: 58; NEDO 1986: 85). It is demarcation along these lines which is amply demonstrated in Hakim's (1979) study of occupational segregation since 1901; the conclusion that part-time working does not affect the pattern of job segregation is based on analysis of changes in occupational distribution irrespective of hours worked, on the grounds that the conversion of part-time numbers to a full-time equivalent would have only a marginal effect on the measurement of occupational segregation. In a statistical sense this is undoubtedly correct. But calculations which express the size and composition of the labour force in terms of whole units tend to obscure the essential role of part-time labour in the expansion of female employment. Findings of the Census of Employment show that increased levels of female part-time employment have been the principal source of growth in industries and services which have historically provided many of the lowest-paid jobs, reinforcing the association of part-time work with the secondary employment sector characteristic adumbrated in the dual labour market model (cf. Dex 1987: 88; Schoer 1987: 88–90).

The intensification of occupational segregation to the detriment of women in employment provides strong reasons for questioning the impact of either the Equal Pay Act or the Sex Discrimination Act in removing discrimination against women in part-time employment. As far as pay is concerned the high degree of concentration of women in the lowest-graded jobs must limit the implementation of equal pay mainly to low-paid occupations in which few men are employed. The amendment to the Equal Pay Act introduced in January 1984 allows industrial tribunals greater scope to use job evaluation in determining claims brought by women whose jobs are not of a like or broadly similar nature to those of men. However, there seems little prospect that a greater application of evaluation or other methods of job classification will alter substantially the grading or the relative earnings attached to occupations held by the majority of women in part-time employment. The empirical studies showed that where the grading of part-timers' jobs resulted from formal job evaluation, the schemes were generally unisex and jointly negotiated and embodied collectively agreed appeals procedures. On the general feasibility of part-time employees making successful equal value claims the outlook is not sanguine. No claims have yet been raised by part-time workers under the Equal Pay (Amendment) Regulations 1983, while the Leverton case (heard by the Court of Appeal in January 1988) involved dismissal of the applicant's case for bringing an equal value claim on the ground (among others) that her weekly hours of work as a nursery nurse were 32.5 compared with the 37 hours worked by her male comparators doing work ranging from care-taker/supervisor to clerical and administrative duties (*Leverton v. Clwyd County Council*, 1986).

Similarly, it is not to be expected that the adoption of the proposals contained in the European Commission's draft Directive on voluntary part-time work, the only legislation designed specifically to improve the terms and conditions of employment of part-time employees, would reduce significantly the direct or indirect discrimination between part-time and full-time workers with respect to rates of pay, earnings or entitlement to employee rights and benefits. With regard to pay, implementation of the Directive would be confined largely to removing pay differentials between categories of female employees. Overtime payments to part-timers could be affected, as premium rates were not normally paid for hours below the full-time week or day. But as earnings components other than basic rates are of comparatively little importance in women's gross earnings a requirement to remunerate full-time and part-time employees on an equal basis would have less impact on direct wage costs in most industries with significant numbers of female part-timers than was experienced following the implementation of the Equal Pay Act. In respect to employee benefits it is unlikely that the inclusion of part-time employees, in occupational pension schemes for example, would advantage the majority, as in service industries in particular, superannuation is not widespread. It is perhaps ironic that the UK government's opposition to the draft Directive was based on the argument that it would 'impose additional costs and destroy jobs' (*Employment Gazette*, 1985 vol. 93, no. 3: 128).

Finally, while employers' uneven labour requirements provide an obvious incentive for the increasing utilisation of female part-time labour, most evident in the expanding services sector, it should be recognised that in the private sector service industries the upward trend of female part-time labour has for some years been supported by a number of influences. These include operational changes involving concentration of ownership and control, creation of larger units, extension of trading hours and innovations in the preparation and presentation of goods and services, influences notable in banking, retail distribution, hotels and catering, and the rapidly growing leisure industries. The consequent de-skilling of jobs has also reduced the numbers employed in specialist occupations and eased the problems of adjusting labour inputs to fluctuating trading levels. In labour-intensive industries the ability to curb wage costs through the employment of part-time labour represents an important factor in determining the pace at which such developments take place. In the public sector in the provision of health and education services, for example, the rising costs of investment in medical and educational technology exert a parallel impetus to increasing managerial control over wage costs.

In manufacturing industries the empirical evidence showed that female part-timers were employed in establishments operating at different levels of technological development. They were deployed to regulate output in response to varying product demands in firms using both labour- and capital-intensive methods of production, and their employment on work involving repetitive tasks was regarded as a means of raising productivity above the levels attainable from full-time workers. At establishments using the more capital-intensive methods of production, higher labour productivity is essential to the achievement of adequate returns on capital investment. However, it remains to be seen whether the advantages inherent in using part-time rather than full-time labour will hasten or retard the adoption of new technology which could further reduce labour requirements in manufacturing as well as in service industries.

The pursuit of labour cost economies through greater utilisation of female part-time labour assumes an increasing significance as 'the imperative of competitiveness' extends its compass directly within the private sector, and indirectly in the public sector through the imposition of cash limits and subcontracting of activities to private employers. Increased labour costs resulting from the application of non-discriminatory basic wage rates provided employers with an additional incentive to economise by reducing the number of hours worked, thereby accelerating the rate at which part-time jobs are created. It may indeed be argued that the process of labour market segmentation, effected through labour market operations though originating as a necessary consequence of technological development and organisational restructuring, has been intensified rather than impeded by the implementation of the Equal Pay and Sex Discrimination Acts. A persistent demand for labour to fill part-time jobs must raise levels of female labour force participation in work for which earnings fall below those acceptable to the vast majority of full-time male workers. Growth in female employment opportunities will thus continue to derive from the creation of part-time jobs, arresting rather than advancing the development of 'an integrated and transparent' labour market in Britain.

10: Current trade union attempts to remove occupational segregation in the employment of women

Valerie Ellis

Introduction

Occupational segregation and the associated problems of sex stereotyping in education and training and the domestic division of labour lie at the root of the inequality of women. This has become increasingly obvious as the ratio of average hourly earnings of women in work rose from 63.1 per cent in 1970 to the high point of 75.5 per cent of men's earnings achieved in 1977 and then receded to 73 per cent in 1979 and 73.6 per cent in 1987. Despite the Equal Pay Act, the long-awaited amendment allowing claims for equal pay for work of equal value and the Sex Discrimination Acts, which have removed some of the most glaring forms of direct discrimination but have been less successful in tackling indirect discrimination, the fundamental problems of inequality remain.

The sexual division of labour in the home conditions the role expectations of women and young girls and severely limits the working roles of wives and mothers. The lack of child care and other social support outside the home entrenches this position. The economic role of women has with a few exceptions been that of a 'reserve labour force' to be called upon when needed and dispatched to domesticity thereafter. The high level of unemployment, with the pressure for married women to retreat to the home to make way for the young and male 'bread-winner' unemployed, combines with the active promotion and growing proportion of peripheral casual and part-time employment opportunities in the service industries to keep women predominantly in the low-paid, unstable, 'secondary labour market'.

The participation of women in trade unions and the impact of union policies, both positive and negative, on the distribution of women in the labour force, which are the subject of this chapter, interact. The vigour with which trade unions pursue or, at the very least, do not impede the improvement of opportunities for women will to some extent depend on the amount of effective pressure which women themselves bring to bear through trade union action at the workplace and the influence they can exert within the power structure of individual unions, the Trade Union Congress (TUC) and other formal or informal inter-union groupings.

A study in 1981 which surveyed the existing evidence on women in trade unions from trade union and other sources indicated that women were heavily under-represented in the trade union power structure and that the position worsened at the more senior levels (Ellis 1981). Indeed, the position of women in trade unions was a mirror image of their segregated position in the labour market. The barriers to participation at senior levels in trade unions were very similar to those in the labour market and workplace. The survey concluded that the position had not changed significantly since 1955, when the TUC conducted a survey which

> indicated that women were active in unions to a considerable extent, but that this was confined largely to the local field. Women were frequently busy as shop stewards, collectors and on branch committees. They were more rarely to be found at district level and were very scarce on the national executive committees except where special provision was made in the rules for representation by women.
>
> (TUC 1955: 90)

Trade unions and positive action

Since the mid-1970s, however, there has been growing activity on women's issues in both the TUC and its constituent affiliated unions, particularly in defining the problems and raising awareness. The impact of such activity has depended not simply on the trade unions themselves, except in areas under their direct control, but on their ability to achieve changes in the legislative framework and to change employer practices. Often, as we shall see later, trade unions have acted jointly with or negotiated with employers both in identifying problems and in providing solutions, but as a recent study pointed out this is not always publicly acknowledged (Trade Union Research Unit 1987: 16).

The following analysis of what trade unions have done and are doing to remove occupational segregation and promote equality both at the workplace and in the unions will focus on the TUC and examples from unions but does not attempt to be comprehensive.

In 1977 the TUC held a special conference on equal pay to consider the experiences of various unions under the Equal Pay Act and drawing attention to its deficiencies. Although campaigns for the reform of the Equal Pay Act continued, the emphasis switched towards occupational segregation as the major underlying factor preventing the achievement of full equal pay and opportunities. At the 1978 Women's TUC several resolutions were passed and action was demanded on such issues as unemployment among women, training and apprenticeship, and the special problems of part-time workers. The 1980 TUC carried a composite resolution which noted with concern that very little progress had been made towards equality for women at work and that there was a need for new strategies to establish genuine equality of opportunity. The resolution called upon the TUC General Council to draw up, in consultation with individual unions, detailed proposals for positive action which could form the basis of future negotiations between unions and management.

In November 1980 a special conference of affiliated unions was called by the TUC to discuss positive action policies and review the experience of Sweden and the USA in affirmative action. The results of that conference together with proposals from the Women's Advisory Committee and the 1981 women's conference formed the basis of proposals put to the 1981 Congress and published as *Equal Opportunities: Positive Action Programmes*. The document recognised that

> the main impediment to equality for women – what is termed job segregation – is not being tackled and may well be getting worse. As long as women remain concentrated in the low paid industries, whose pay settlements continue to be lower than those in the male dominated sectors, the gap will not close. The Equal Pay Act does not provide for comparisons to be made with a man unless there is a man doing the same job. And where the Equal Pay Act fails women, the Sex Discrimination Act often cannot protect them.
>
> (TUC 1982: 3)

The document listed steps to be taken in collective bargaining and employment and in legislation and public policy. On collective bargaining and employment, it laid out certain general procedures:

> Unions should press an employer to commit the company publicly to being an Equal Opportunities Employer with a positive equal opportunities policy. An equal opportunities clause such as the TUC Equal Opportunities Clause should be inserted in all collective agreements.
>
> The policy statement should be backed up by an equal opportunity programme detailing the steps required to implement the aims.

The basis for the equal opportunity programme should be a joint management and union analysis of the existing workforce by sex and occupation.

Once the pattern of job segregation has been established unions should negotiate targets and timetables with the employer for the implementation of measures to counter the cumulative effect of job segregation and encourage women into non-traditional jobs with the appropriate training.

(ibid)

The TUC also recognised, however, that if its campaign was to be effective and credible trade unions would need to put their own house in order. The positive action document therefore also contained a TUC 'Charter for Equality for Women within Trade Unions' (see Figure 10.1) which had been issued in 1979. Many unions have followed a similar strategy of dealing simultaneously with equality in unions as well as in the workplace. We begin the detailed study of the role of trade unions in removing occupation and segregation, therefore, by addressing the question of the position of women within trade unions.

Equality for women in trade unions

In general, women have been the main growth area for trade unions in recent years. This partly reflects a growth in the number of women in the labour market but also a greater organisational effort by the unions themselves. For example, in the UK women's union membership increased by 41 per cent between 1970 and 1980. But the degree of organisation still lags behind men. Thus, while in the UK 41.2 per cent of the workforce are women, only 34 per cent union members are women and among part-time workers the degree of organisation is much worse. Whereas 51 per cent of full-time employees belong to a union, only 28 per cent of part-time workers do (Trade Union Research Unit 1986: 14–17).

The growth of women in trade unions is not, however, reflected fully in the decision-making structure of the unions. The evidence shows that at every level of the union women tend to be under-represented but that they are much better represented at workplace level than at more senior levels. A primary factor which often prevents women participating at all is domestic commitments. Women find it difficult enough to combine work and domestic commitments; to add a third, union activity is often impossible. This problem increases as one moves away from the workplace to district, regional and national levels, where activity outside normal working hours and often at a long distance from home is involved.

A TUC CHARTER

EQUALITY FOR WOMEN WITHIN TRADE UNIONS

1 The National Executive Committee of the union should publicly declare to all its members the commitment of the union to involving women members in the activities of the union at all levels.

2 The structure of the union should be examined to see whether it prevents women from reaching the decision-making bodies.

3 Where there are large women's memberships but no women on the decision-making bodies special provision should be made to ensure that womens views are represented, either through the creation of additional seats or by co-option.

4 The National Executive Committee of each union should consider the desirability of setting up advisory committees within its constitutional machinery to ensure that the special interests of its women members are protected.

5 Similar committees at regional, divisional, and district level could also assist by encouraging the active involvement of women in the general activities of the union.

6 Efforts should be made to include in collective agreements provision for time off without loss of pay to attend branch meetings during working hours where that is practicable.

7 Where it is not practicable to hold meetings during working hours every effort should be made to provide child-care facilities for use by either parent.

8 Child-care facilities, for use by either parent, should be provided at all district, divisional and regional meetings and particularly at the union's annual conference, and for training courses organised by the union.

9 Although it may be open to any members of either sex to go to union training courses, special encouragement should be given to women to attend.

10 The content of journals and other union publications should be presented in non-sexist terms.

Figure 10.1   TUC charter on equality for women in trade unions, 1979.

Without malice or design, but also without concern, men have shaped trade union life to suit those who have no childcare or other domestic responsibilities and on an expectation that every trade union activist has endless evening hours to devote to union work. . . .

To be on the union executive, you need to prepare yourself at weekend schools, on residential training courses and as a delegate to week-long congresses at the seaside resorts.

(Gill and Whitty 1983: 329–30)

For part-time workers the problems of domestic commitments are even worse. It is often such commitments which have led them to seek part-time work in the first place. There are also greater pressures from employers, who are reluctant to allow time off for trade union duties because they represent a proportionately greater slice of working time because they are often employed precisely to meet peak loads and cannot obtain time off during such periods. Discontinuity of employment arising from child rearing and other domestic commitments also means that women can be at a disadvantage. Even where there are no formal rules on seniority to qualify for officerships there are informal barriers. 'Trade union activists start being a shop steward or staff representative in their twenties and build up experience, expertise and support when women are having children' (Gill and Whitty 1983: 329). The TUC Charter on Equality in Trade Unions was designed to help overcome many of these obstacles to active participation of women and to provide for special representation for women at senior decision-making levels in the meantime.

The TUC recognised that the publication of its charter was only a first step and that progress would need to be monitored. In June 1983, therefore, a questionnaire was sent to all affiliated unions, and in March, 1984 a report was produced (TUC 1984). The survey produced forty-nine responses from unions containing 9 million workers, of whom 3 million were women. An Equal Opportunities Commission survey on women and trade unions was published in 1983 (EOC 1983) with a similar response rate and which covered some of the same ground.

Seventeen unions in the TUC survey had undertaken an examination of their internal structures to see whether they prevented women from reaching decision-making bodies, and five reported that this was currently under review. According to both surveys, in most unions women were still under-represented, particularly at national-level conferences and executives and among lay and full-time officials, although the situation was improving. A small number of unions reserved seats on their executive committee for women, although one or two unions which used to practise this system disbanded it as being discriminatory. Half the replies to the TUC survey indicated that they had women's or equal opportunities officers, mostly at national level but increasingly also at local level. Most unions responding to the TUC survey, although much less in the EOC survey, had established women's advisory or equal opportunities committees at different levels within the union. There were indications that such provisions had improved the position of women within those unions. Most of the national-level committees were directly accountable to the decision-making body of the union. Few of the unions had special women's conferences, and the efficacy of these varied considerably. A large number of unions surveyed provided special training for women. These ranged from women-only schools or courses, at both national and local level, to one-day conferences which were purely related to women's issues. In some unions women were also given preferential access to mixed training facilities. One point which the TUC report highlighted was the usefulness of literature or pamphlets geared towards women's issues as an incentive to fuller participation. Ten unions approached in the EOC survey also provided special encouragement to women members to take office via special publicity measures.

The TUC survey noted that most branch meetings were still held outside working hours and that ability to attend branch meetings was a problem, particularly in the current political climate. But even if unions had done nothing else to encourage women to participate they had usually taken initiatives to provide child-care facilities at conferences and schools, and take-up of child-care facilities at union functions had increased steadily.

The TUC report concluded that although some progress had been made since 1979 the examination of the overall structure of the union was in many cases cursory; and, despite some spectacular individual breakthroughs, there were still too few women officials. The report ended with further recommendations re-emphasising and expanding upon the original charter. Further monitoring of the situation took place in 1985, and a report was presented to the 1986 Women's TUC. This showed more progress in all the areas since 1983, including further research commissioned to identify the main barriers to women taking part on equal terms in trade union activities. Nevertheless, there was still a long way to go.

The TUC surveys of 1983 and 1985 do not contain detailed figures from individual unions of the distribution of women at various levels in the union hierarchy. Figures taken from elsewhere, however, show that although there has been some real improvement in the representation of women the position is still far from satisfactory (see Table 10.1).

Some unions still do not collect figures on how many women they have in membership. At the 1987 Women's TUC the National Union of Journalists urged the TUC to insist on such figures and to monitor the role and status of women, such information being 'essential to enable

Table 10.1 Representation of women in trade unions, 1986–7 (1979–80)

Union	Total 1986 membership (thousands)	Women as % of total membership (1980)[b]	Women as % on national executive	Women as % on TUC delegation 1986 (1979)[c]	Women as % of full-time officials (1980)[b]	Women's or similar committees Yes	No
TGWU	1,434	16 (16)	5 (0)	9 (3.6)	2 (1)	x	
AEU	857	10	0	4 (0)	0.4	x	
GMBATU	817	30 (34)	3 (0)	6 (5.4)	4 (5.3)	x	
NALGO	759	52 (50)	38 (20)	34 (18)	13 (6.7)	x	
NUPE	660	68 (67)	42 (30.7)	26 (21.9)	8 (4.7)	x	
USDAW	382	61	19	31 (31.7)	13	x	
ASTMS	323	26 (17)	12 (8.3)	19 (4)	10 (9.5)	x	
NUT	254	73 (66)	21 (9.1)	37 (24.3)	7 (15.5)	x	
UCATT	249	1	0	0 (0)	0	x	
COHSE	225	80	14	20 (22.2)	18	x	
TASS	241	11	4	18 (10.5)	4	x	
UCW	196	40	14	0 (17.6)	25	x	
BIFU	158	53 (49)	12 (11.1)	27 (11.5)	22 (14.6)	x	
CPSA	148	71	29	43 (20)	26	x	
APEX	86	54 (51)	31 (7)	36 (23.1)	5 (3.6)	x	
IPCS[a]	90	9 (8)	(25)	39 (15)	30 (33)	x	
SCPS	85	20–30	19	29 (15)	33	x	
NUTGW	77	91 (92)	27 (33.3)	77 (56.3)	14 (19.1)		x
IRSF	55	60	22	8 (8.3)	37		x
CSU	30	44	20	14 (10)	10		x

Sources: Table for 1986–7 taken from EOC 1986. 58.
[a] Figures for IPCS from the author.
[b] Figures for 1980 from Coote and Kellner 1980.
[c] Figures for 1979 from TUC report, 1979.

individual unions, and the movement generally, to introduce measures to achieve adequate representation at all levels and promote positive action measures for these groups of workers'.

The Women's TUC of both 1986 and, particularly, 1987 indicated a high degree of dissatisfaction with progress in achieving equal rights within unions and outside. It therefore carried a motion at the 1987 conference which recognised that

> women in the trade union movement have a vital role to play in the regeneration of the economy and the advancement of employment rights. To strengthen the whole movement many more women need to be encouraged and enabled to participate in trade union activity and to feel that trade unions are committed to their particular concerns. The provision of adequate resources for equal opportunities work in the movement is essential to this.
>
> Conference expresses its serious concern at the limited resources made available within trade unions to support this work, and recognises that failure to provide sufficient resources seriously undermines the credibility of trade unions' commitment to women.
>
> (TUC 1987a: 16)

It called for more resources and for a Women's Department to be established within the TUC. At the full TUC in September 1987 a commitment was made to establishing an Equal Rights Department which would give a high priority to women's issues.

Job segregation – setting the bargaining agenda

One union which has particularly focused on the need to concentrate much greater effort on improving the position of women (and low-paid workers in general) is the General, Municipal, Boilermakers and Allied Trades Union (GMB). It has produced, as part of its campaign, the most detailed trade union analysis to date of sex bias in the labour market, based on a survey of agreements covering 100,000 of its own members predominantly in manual grades, and analysis of government statistics. In the introduction to the document the GMB says:

> the labour market, as currently structured and operated, rewards working women far less than men. This is due to four factors:
> • Women are in lower-graded jobs than men.
> • Women receive fewer bonus and shift payments.
> • Men work longer hours.
> • There is systematic undervaluing of the jobs that women do.
> . . . sex bias costs women workers £15 billion a year. This single fact

underlines the urgency of adopting a new strategy in bargaining with employers to get the issue of sex bias properly on to the negotiating agenda.

(GMB 1987: 2)

The study found that shorter hours (mostly part-time working) accounted for 65 per cent of the difference in gross earnings between men and women. But even when the effect of different hours was allowed for, women workers still had less hourly earnings than men, and 73 per cent of that difference was accounted for by job segregation, with the remaining 27 per cent accounted for by differences in bonus and shift pay, etc. (GMB 1987: 4–6). The GMB concluded that there were thirteen key issues related to the elimination of sex bias which must be included as an entry on the bargaining agenda, including job evaluation, training, maternity and child care, and, above all, job segregation.

Above all, agreements must ensure that women are not concentrated in the lowest-graded jobs. GMB negotiators must raise with employers the question of initial recruitment policies. In addition, the issue of promotion policies must also be raised. . . . These should involve positive programmes of action with regard to the training of women members to fit them for the higher-graded positions.

(GMB 1987: 21)

The study concludes with a programme for action which is to be a standing item on the negotiating agendas of all negotiators until achieved, with progress monitored by the national offices and the National Equal Rights Advisory Committee. It refers to the interdependence of equality in the workplace and equality in the union.

The success of this programme can only be measured by the extent to which our women membership achieve higher wages and better conditions. It goes without saying that the programme can only be successful if the level of participation of women in the GMB rises as has already been planned. The demands of women for access to the levels of power in our society, and for the improvement in their economic and social conditions, will continue. For the GMB to identify with and fight for these demands and to open its own structures and to encourage its own women members will immensely strengthen and develop the GMB as a progressive organisation in our society.

(GMB 1987: 23–4)

The Confederation of Health Service Employees (COHSE), which established a National Equal Opportunities Committee in 1987, has also been giving a high priority to equal opportunities and carried out its own survey of the employment of women in the National Health Service (NHS). These detailed statistics confirmed that women tended to be concentrated or segregated into particular kinds of jobs (e.g. nursing, clerical, cleaning, catering and laundry) whereas they were virtually absent from others, e.g. works professional (3 per cent), ambulance (11 per cent). Moreover they were concentrated into the lowest grades of the most badly paid groups, e.g. women made up 84 per cent of all staff in the bottom three administrative and clerical grades (COHSE 1986: 6–9). This study was partly the result of and also an additional catalyst to a growing commitment to deal with the problems of low pay and job segregation by COHSE. In 1986 COHSE, together with its negotiating partners, GMB, the National Union of Public Employees (NUPE) (which had also been studying the problems of its women members: see below) and the Transport and General Workers' Union (TGWU), produced a major pay claim which demanded among other things

a comprehensive review of the values placed on different jobs in the light of the 'Equal Pay for Work of Equal Rights' regulations. The existing grading structure fails to reflect changing social values, particularly in relation to the worth of jobs traditionally done by women. 67% of auxiliary staff are women. Of the 38% of the total workforce who work part-time, 97% are women. They are disproportionately highly represented in the lowest grades and poorly represented in the highest grades.

(NHS Ancillary Whitley Council Trade Union Side 1986: 14)

Similar studies of job segregation have also been made by other unions. For example, in education studies by the National Union of Teachers (NUT) and National Association of Teachers in Further and Higher Education (NATFHE) show a definite pattern of job segregation. Thus in schoolteaching, 78 per cent of women but only 49 per cent of men were on the lowest two teaching scales; 10 per cent of men but only 4 per cent of women were head teachers. In further education, 50 per cent of women lecturers were in L1 posts and almost 80 per cent in L1 and L2 combined; whereas only 32.4 per cent of men were in L1 posts, and 67 per cent in L1 and L2 combined (Kane 1982: 16).

In 1981 the Banking, Insurance and Finance Union (BIFU) studied the position of women in banking and found that despite a previous report on equal opportunities they were still concentrated in the low-grade, lower-paid jobs. For example, in the Midland Bank in 1974 only 7.1 per cent of female staff but 39.4 per cent of male staff were above Grade IV. In 1979 the percentage of women in these grades had increased by only 8 per cent, and the Midland Bank was better than most of the other clearing banks. The study showed that while policies may not be so blatantly sexist as in the past there was still evidence of a 'two-tier' recruitment policy – employers often relaxing their entry qualification standards to admit entrants, predominantly women, who will have little career prospects. Access to promotion depended largely on management discretion, and evidence indicates that women take two years longer to reach those grades; so not only is women's promotion rarer, it takes more time and effort to achieve. Similarly, training lay within managerial discretion, and 'one of the very common complaints is that the work experience given to female trainees is merely designed to fit in with the planned variety of tasks offered to male trainees' (BIFU: 1981).

BIFU urged its representatives to ensure that their employer agreed to an equal opportunities policy and programme, to investigate and monitor the situation and to implement relevant policies. Examples of action taken include joint action with the Midland Bank where BIFU and the Association of Technical and Managerial Staffs (ASTMS) take part in regular joint meetings with the company's equal opportunities unit. At such meetings recruitment, transfers and training statistics are provided, and the equality programme is regularly monitored.

BIFU has also taken unilateral action to improve opportunities. For example, it has initiated training courses in 'bridging skills' to help more secretarial and clerical women out of those areas into major non-traditional career routes such as computing and sales. Both BIFU and the NUT have held assertiveness-training and confidence-building courses for women to help them improve their career progression (Labour Research Department 1987: 12).

In the Civil Service, a Joint Review Group, consisting of management and union representatives, was established in January 1980 'to review the development of employment opportunities for women in the non-industrial civil service since the Kemp-Jones report of 1971 and to make recommendations'. The report of the group showed that although women represented 48 per cent of the total non-industrial Civil Service they were concentrated in particular occupations and in the lower grades; the position has chaged very little since 1975 (Management and Personnel Office: 1982).

The Joint Review Group made a wide range of recommendations to improve career development for women. These included equal opportunities training for all those involved in selection and promotion boards and in annual reporting; the inclusion of women on such boards wherever possible; further research on the extent and reasons for lower promotion rates and promotability markings for women; more flexible training arrangements to take account of domestic responsibilities; special women-only developmental courses to build confidence; and reinstatement in their former grade wherever possible for women who have broken their career in the Civil Service for domestic reasons. Action on these recommendations was agreed, and implementation and its effectiveness are monitored jointly.

In 1979 a study of women in local government showed that they were concentrated in certain occupations and in the lower grades of the hierarchy (Local Government Operational Research Unit 1982). In response, the major union involved in the study, the National and Local Government Officers' Association (NALGO), in its pamphlets on *Positive Action for Women Workers* and *How Equal Are Your Opportunities?*, stressed the importance of equal opportunties policies, programmes and training for those involved in selection and promotion. NALGO also identified internal advertising as important, together with flexible training provision and assertiveness training for women. Best practice as operated in some of the local authorities for use in collective bargaining on the issues was also publicised (NALGO 1984).

In addition to tackling the problems of low valuation of women's jobs and the promotion of equal opportunities for earnings and career advancement, unions have also addressed directly the fundamental issues underlying occupational segregation. Broadly they can be grouped into two main areas: the barriers, both attitudinal and institutional, to wider career choice and development; and the discontinuities and restrictions on employment engendered by the need to combine work and domestic responsibilities. We take these issues in turn.

Occupational choice

The world of work, particularly the technological occupations, is regarded as a 'man's world'. The traditional view is that women are best suited for jobs that either are an extension of their roles in the family or are repetitive and boring. Those women who do enter non-traditional occupations often find themselves isolated as a minority in a male-dominated and male-defined situation.

The TUC statement on positive action programmes makes a number of recommendations in the education and training field which are directed not only to the unions directly involved in education but to all trade unionists whether parents, school governors, councillors or in other representative capacities. The recommendations cover better career opportunities for women teachers, the promotion of equal access to all education and training opportunities, special courses to enable women and girls to make good the deficiencies of the past and to train for new technologies, changes in school curricula and equal opportunity training and awareness for all those involved in education and training.

The teaching unions have been very active in examining the problems of sex stereotyping and the role of education and training in promoting equal opportunities, and the TUC has made representations to various institutions concerned with education and training. It has pressed for greater equality of opportunity for girls on the Youth Training Scheme (YTS) programme, and a review group on the YTS on which the TUC was represented has recommended offering more public support for employers who adopt positive opportunities policies; giving greater prominence to Manpower Services Commission (MSC) materials concerned with widening opportunities for women; making clear the sanctions which might follow from illegal discrimination; and the value of co-opting women on to Area Manpower Boards. The TUC also ensured that the 1983–7 MSC Corporate Plan made specific reference to the development of women-only courses and bridging courses. Attempts have also been made to raise the proportion of women training at skill centres by better publicity and the provision of child-care facilities. This pressure has had some impact: for example, in 1987 the MSC published the YTS Equal Opportunities Code. Nevertheless, MSC reports show that women's training is still largely confined to traditional areas, and there is still a major problem of sex stereotyping.

The role of the media in propagating sexist images of women has also been tackled. Thus a report on 'Images of Inequality' was presented to the 1984 Women's TUC and covered the portrayal of women in the media and advertising. It followed a resolution passed at the 1982 Congress which called on Congress to campaign actively against the portrayal of degrading images of women among trade unions, the media and those who worked in or represented media organisations. The document concluded with a set of action points for trade unionists and others, and the TUC made representations to the media and the advertising industry. These representations had some, although limited, success. The media unions themselves continue to campaign hard on the issue, and the NUJ produced guidelines for promoting equality through journalism entitled 'Images of Women' which gives practical advice on avoiding sexist stereotypes and language. It also produced an *Equality Style Guide*.

Recruitment of women into non-traditional areas

Cases of direct discrimination by unions to prevent women entering non-traditional occupations are now rare. Ironically the Society of Graphical and Allied Trades (SOGAT '82), which elected a woman General Secretary in 1985 and has given strong and effective support to the campaign for equal opportunities, was found guilty of sex discrimination because of the practices of its male-dominated London Central Branch who effectively controlled entry into the higher-paid, higher-status work, leaving the London Women's Branch with the lower-status work. Having been unable to merge the two branches, senior members of SOGAT themselves prompted the EOC to make an inquiry. Eventually in November 1986 the situation was resolved, with the Central Branch and Women's Branch being amalgamated and their respective seniority lists combined. This met the requirements of the non-discrimination notice issued by the EOC in September 1986 (EOC 1987a: 16).

It has been much more difficult, however, to persuade union members that work rules which are universal, and therefore apparently fair, may be indirectly discriminatory. Seniority or length of service in employment or in the grade often form the primary criteria which unions prefer to see applied in a wide range of personnel policies such as redundancy, promotion, job rotation, job progression and many other aspects of pay and conditions. Since women as a group tend to have shorter service overall and a greater degree of discontinuity in employment, they tend to suffer from the use of the seniority criterion.

Other examples include apprenticeship rules which, although they apply equally to all, have aspects which may make it more difficult for women to complete them, particularly the insistence on entry in the teens and a long period of apprenticeship. The resistance of some craft unions or certain of their districts to 'dilution' of their trade by the training of semi-skilled workers or mature entrants also has an indirectly discriminatory effect. For example, the Technical and Supervisory Section (TASS) of the Engineering Workers' Union has pointed out how women in the drawing office found it virtually impossible to move out of the ancillary 'tracer' category into the more skilled drawing office jobs: 'Most draughtsmen were recruited from the shop floor, from craft or technical apprenticeships. These avenues of promotion were not open to women and few tracers have ever had the opportunity to become draughtswomen' (TASS n.d.: 19). TASS therefore committed itself to securing fair treatment for tracer members. In the Civil Service similar action has been taken by the Institution of Professional Civil Servants (IPCS) to resolve problems both through the Joint Review Group and by ensuring through negotiation that the qualifications and experience for promotion into the mainstream professional and technology grades no longer disadvantage women who have not come through the traditional apprenticeship and work-experience route.

In the construction industry, which has so far been almost wholly a male preserve, the Union of Construction Allied Trades and Technicians (UCATT) established an Employment of Women Working Party in 1982 to examine ways of improving opportunities for girls and women in construction work and to consider methods of improving participation in the union by women members. The working party's research demonstrated the high degree of job segregation in construction. UCATT issued a policy statement on encouraging women to enter construction at all levels and spelt out the need for shop stewards and other officials at branch and regional level to ensure that action was taken. It issued its own leaflet encouraging girls to enter craft training schemes and co-operated with the Construction Industry Training Board in encouraging women and girls to train and enter the industry. In 1987 the General Secretary of UCATT was quoted as saying, 'The female membership of UCATT has increased by nearly 50 per cent in three years' (Labour Research Department 1987: 12).

The Fire Brigades Union (FBU) appointed an Equal Opportunities Policies Committee following a critical conference resolution in 1985. The committee carried out a detailed study showing that only 35 out of 57,400 firefighters were women (FBU 1987: 3). Women were concentrated in control-room jobs, and their only national executive committee member was from that area. It produced an Equal Opportunities Declaration for negotiation with local authorities and recommended that a much greater effort be made by the union to increase and integrate women into the full range of fire service work.

The EOC and the Engineering Council designated 1984 Women into Science and Engineering (WISE) year, and several individual unions and the TUC took further initiatives to encourage women into those occupations. As part of its contribution to WISE year, the TUC and the Confederation of Shipbuilding and Engineering Unions (CSEU) organised a conference in November 1984 which was attended by ninety delegates from unions in science, engineering and teaching. The aim of the conference was to discuss in depth how the engineering industry, the educational system, training schemes and the trade unions could increase the flow of women into engineering and science and to ensure that they filled jobs at all levels instead of being concentrated in the routine jobs at the base of the job hierarchy. Several points were raised for both immediate action and long-term consideration by trade unions. In particular it was noted that the attitudes of male trade unionists to the entry of women into thier 'male preserves' needed to be tackled. Unions could assist by providing special support for girls and women in the industry, particularly those in male-dominated areas of work – including assertiveness training and general consciousness raising among all members to overcome the obstacles faced by a 'woman in a man's world'.

Two further resolutions on the subject were passed at the 1985 Women's TUC to ensure that the issue was kept at the forefront. In December 1985 the TUC issued guidance to trade unions (TUC 1985b) highlighting the actions which unions should take, covering the removal of sex stereotyping and the widening of choice in education and to increase the intake of women into scientific and engineering occupations.

In 1987 at the Women's TUC concern was still being expressed on this issue, although it was acknowledged that some progress had been made, for example increased entry into the skilled manual trades. However, this was primarily happening through special MSC schemes and skill centres. 'Conference is concerned that girls of school-leaving age are still not entering industries such as construction and engineering in any great numbers via the traditional traineeship/apprenticeship method of entry' (TUC 1987a: 23). The Women's TUC therefore called for more girls to enter apprenticeships and for further special 'link' and conversion mechanisms to help short-circuit the continued problem of sex stereotyping in schools and to facilitate entry into non-traditional occupations.

Work/domestic interface

Much detailed work has been done on the impact of the domestic division of labour on women's paid employment outside the home. The break in career, however short, due to child rearing, and the need to find work compatible with that function, is a major factor both in the choice of job or career in the first place, and in the availablity and type of jobs filled after re-entry to the labour force.

A major survey in 1984 showed that a substantial minority of women experience downward occupational mobility on re-entry into the labour market after childbearing. The longer the career break the more likely the woman was to re-enter at a lower level. This was particularly the case if she returned to part-time working. Forty-five per cent of women in the survey experienced downward mobility on re-entering in a part-time capacity (Martin and Roberts 1984: 208).

The position is neatly captured in the Joint Review Group's report on the Civil Service, which described the position of women in employment thus:

> the structure and organisation of employment has been designed by men to an essentially masculine working and career pattern, and takes no account of women's needs. In particular, it gives no recognition to the role of women in childrearing and home-making – and this applies with even more force to the growing number of one-parent families where the roles of breadwinner and home-maker cannot be divided.
>
> The disadvantage that women experience in competing in a 'man's world' is of two kinds. More obviously women are expected to take the prime responsibility for the care of children and aged relatives and the maintenance of the home. Therefore, it is the women's working life that is constrained by the need to look after children after school and during school holidays and to respond to illness or other domestic crisis. None the less, 50% of all women with dependent children now have paid employment and 25% of women with a child under five. Little account is taken of this by employers in the organisation of work except where they may be seeking a tap of sources of labour not otherwise available.

The responsibility of providing substitute parental care in most cases rests with the mother, with comparatively little support from either the employer or central or local government.

(Management and Personnel Office 1982: 2–3)

The analysis of action by unions to tackle the problems arising from the work/domestic interface falls into two broad areas: the campaign for improved maternity and paternity provision and recognition of domestic responsibilities, and the development of alternative working patterns.

Assistance for working parents

In 1976 the TUC General Council established a working party on child care, composed of representatives of unions with members working in the field of day care and education for children under five and of unions representing large numbers of women workers. Its recommendations when it reported in 1977 marked a revolution in attitude compared to the immediate post-war period when the unions acquiesced in the closure of day nurseries established during the war. The report's main recommendation was: 'A comprehensive and universal service of care and education for children from 0 to 5 must be made available by the state. A national programme for pre-school services must be drawn up by the government jointly with the unions' (TUC 1977: 112). However, this was regarded as a long-term goal, and various interim recommendations for the reform of existing facilities were also specified. The working party report was accepted by Congress in 1978 and later embodied in the TUC 'Charter on Facilities for Under-Fives', updated and reissued in 1987.

Despite the effort devoted to the pursuit of nursery provision by both the unions directly involved in education and nursery care, such as the NUT and the National Union of Public Employees (NUPE), and by other unions, progress has been small. The amount of local authority nursery provision is declining because of public expenditure cuts, and although some local and other public authorities have provided workplace nurseries (NALGO 1984: 12–13) they are more than matched by closures such as that of the only Civil Service nursery at Llanishen. In the private sector the recession has resulted in many nursery closures, and in both public and private sectors the level of unemployment and the corresponding ease of recruitment has removed any incentive the employers might have for establishing or maintaining nursery facilities. More effort, therefore, has had to be put into fighting nursery closures than in to securing their opening.

In 1980 the Women's TUC carried a resolution on maternity and paternity leave, calling upon the General Council to update and reissue details of current best practice in this area to assist unions in their negotiations. Following a survey of union achievements in this sphere the TUC published a booklet, *Collective Bargaining Agreements,* which set out current statutory parental rights, current collective agreements improving on the statutory provision, European practice and future considerations for negotiation. Many unions, such as NALGO, published their own guides and negotiating objectives.

As with nursery provision, unions have had to be on the defensive, campaigning with pressure groups such as the Maternity Alliance against adverse changes in statutory provision. In its revised *Guide to Maternity Rights* in 1987 the TUC covers recent changes in legislation and argues that unions should press employers to improve upon statutory maternity and paternity rights. A further TUC guide is to be produced on best practice in negotiated agreement.

In March 1985 the TUC brought together the whole area of women's opportunities and the social infrastructure required to support it in a discussion document *TUC Policies and the Family*, designed as an alternative to the Conservative government's philosophy of privatised self-help and a return to 'Victorian values'. The report opened with a rejection of the traditional image of the family, which it describes as 'the male, white breadwinner providing for the mother at home looking after 2.4 children – a totally inaccurate and indeed misleading picture of many families in modern Britain' (TUC 1985a: 2). The document appeared to mark the death of the 'male bread-winner'/women working for 'pin money' image which had dogged the campaign for equal opportunities both within and outside the trade union movement. The objective was the sharing of both domestic responsibilities and work opportunities between the sexes, and detailed recommendations for trade union negotiators were made. A similar change in attitude is reflected in the TUC and many individual unions on the question of alternative working patterns.

Restructuring working patterns

Traditionally many trade unions have opposed part-time working as a form of 'cheap labour' competing with those in full-time jobs. They now recognise that, particularly in the absence of full-time child-care facilities, part-time working and job-sharing are in some cases a preferred mode of working, particularly for people who wish to be able to combine work and domestic responsibilities. The emphasis has therefore shifted to spreading part-time opportunities throughout the job hierarchy rather than being concentrated in a part-time 'ghetto' and to ensuring that pay and conditions of work match, pro rata, those of full-timers.

This was reflected most vividly in the opening paragraph to the TUC General Council's statement on part-time working issued in September 1987:

> The TUC believes in freedom of choice for all workers to choose a work pattern that suits them, whether they are full-time workers, part-time workers or workers that at present have no job at all, a freedom of choice that takes account of their needs. That is why the TUC is opposed to part-time workers being treated like second-class citizens by unscrupulous employers. That is why the TUC believes trade unions must ensure part-time workers are not treated as second-class union members.
>
> (TUC 1987b: 2)

The statement provided a detailed analysis of the incidence of part-time working, noting a steady trend since the 1950s but also recognising it as part of a concerted strategy encouraged by the government to increase 'flexibility' in the use of labour. While opposing the adverse consequences of flexibility, it argued that there was a need to pay greater attention to the aspirations of part-time workers:

> One of the major challenges facing the trade union movement is the need to organise part-time workers – to extend to them the benefits that trade unions can offer. . . .
>
> All need to demonstrate an acute sensitivity to the special concerns of part-time workers and a commitment to securing equal status for them . . .
>
> (TUC 1987b: 11)

and to negotiating for part-time workers:

> Unions also need to ensure that their collective bargaining strategies reflect the interests of part-time workers. . . . essentially collective bargaining should seek to tackle the discrimination faced by many part-time workers in terms of their rates of pay, rights at work, and access to better paid, more secure employment.
>
> (TUC 1987b: 12)

The paper then sets out a long check-list of action for unions to welcome part-timers into membership and to review existing collective agreements to ensure that their interests are covered.

Several individual unions have taken up the challenge of organising and campaigning for part-time workers. For example, NUPE, which has for a long time organised part-timers, published a report, *A Fair Deal for Part-Time Workers*, which highlighted their problems and framed a ten-point charter demanding pro-rata conditions for part-timers and a higher priority for them on the bargaining agenda. Similarly, the Union of Shop, Distributive and Allied Workers (USDAW) has developed a charter for part-timers following research on part-time working initiated by its women's committee.

Efforts are also being made to open up the whole job hierarchy to more flexible patterns of working and, in particular, to develop opportunities for part-time work and job-sharing in the more senior grades. This was one of the major recommendations of the Joint Review Group in the Civil Service, and some progress has been made in facilitating job-sharing and part-time working outside traditional areas of part-time work.

A similar change has taken place on 'homeworking', where a desire to ban it altogether has gradually been replaced by an alternative view that, while not wishing to encourage homeworking, there is a recognition that in some situations there is little alternative, and that with new technology it is likely to grow rather than diminish. In its latest statement on homeworking the TUC says:

> Homeworking as a feature of employment in this country is growing. As such it must be regulated to the same extent as other types of employment. This is vital if the situation of homeworkers is to be improved and the effects of unfair competition on on-site workers reduced.
>
> Homeworkers more than ever need protection: through legislation and through trade unions membership.
>
> (TUC 1985a: 25)

The statement then sets out detailed policies which need to be pursued both in terms of effective trade union organisation and collective bargaining and through TUC pressure to make protective legislation more effective in that area.

Conclusion

This chapter has charted in very broad outline the progress which trade unions in the UK have made in first of all recognising the problem of job segregation and then trying to do something about it. Although it has not been detailed here, the pattern is repeated in trade unions and trade union federations in Europe and elsewhere. The policy statement guidelines and action programmes set out here can be found with variations in the European Trade Union Congress, the International Confederation of Free Trade Unions and international secretariats such as the Public Services International. Why has this happened and how effective has the action been?

There has been some recent progress in improving the position of women within trade unions, as Table 10.1 demonstrates. Special provisions for women are being made in many unions, and more women are therefore in powerful decision-making positions. But they are still under-represented, and it will take a long time for all the barriers to be broken down and for the special measures to become redundant. The growing number of women active in the unions reinforces the internal pressure to achieve equality in both the union and the workplace.

Of much greater influence than the internal pressure from women, however, is the changing composition of the labour market. The growing proportion of women in the labour force and the decline in the traditional male-dominated industries with a high density of union membership has forced unions to begin to come to terms with the need to organise women and hence to deal with their demands. The changes in the nature of the labour force represented by the growth of part-time working, the concept of the 'flexible firm', the pace of technological change and the discontinuities in employment which that has brought means that many of the problems traditionally associated with 'women's work' will affect men too. Unions will need to address the problems of continuing education, retraining, equal pro-rata terms and conditions for different working patterns and the structuring of those working patterns to meet human as well as technological needs. The traditional full-time, lifetime career in a large organisation is likely to be as dead for men in the future as it often is for women today. The unions have to attract and welcome women members to survive. As the General Secretary of the TUC said to the TUC Women's Conference in 1987, 'For a union movement that has been historically male, craft and activist oriented, concentrated in large manufacturing industries, this suggests a minor revolution.'

This minor revolution has begun, and union bargaining agendas are more influenced by 'women's needs' than they used to be. The will, on the trade union side, is now stronger, and many policies are in place, but the climate in which positive action has been attempted in recent years could hardly have been less favourable. The high level of unemployment and the corresponding weakness of the trade unions' bargaining position, enormous public expenditure cuts, privatisation and the attempt to roll back the frontiers of employment protection legislation impede even modest progress in removing occupational segregation and achieving equal opportunities for women. Nevertheless, there has been some progress in some areas, particularly those related to career progression which cost little money and are attractive to the employer in terms of making effective use of women's talents. Part-time working and job-sharing are becoming more acceptable in certain areas outside the normal part-time 'ghettos', and working patterns can be adjusted to suit employees as well as the employer. The Civil Service, local government and banking can provide examples. Moreover, some deals have recently been made, for example in local government and the health service, which have begun to tackle grading structures and the problems of job segregation and low pay.

11: Occupational segregation and women's politics

Jane Mark-Lawson

Introduction

Women occupy a gender-specific position in the workplace, gender being one of the main structural features that circumscribe the filling by persons of occupational places. It is axiomatic that the way in which gender, and indeed other systems of social differentiation, affects the allocation of places in the occupational structure will have wider social effects. Occupational segregation is one of the sites on which wider social inequalities, inequalities of gender, or ethnicity and of age, are both produced and reproduced. Various authors have pointed to the interrelations between the maintenance of forms of occupational segregation at work and other significant sites on which inequalities are reproduced. In the case of patriarchal relations, for instance, the household, violence and the state have been identified as significant. Other authors have tried to identify the historical development and generation of segregation by gender (Hartmann 1979b; Mark-Lawson and Witz 1988; Seccombe 1986). This chapter examines some aspects of the effects of occupational segregation by gender on wider social relations. In particular it is concerned with the relationship between forms of occupational segregation, on the one hand, and political behaviour and service provision, on the other.

The chapter approaches these issues through an empirical examination of two different localities in the inter-war period. The two localities exhibited very different forms of occupational segregation by gender. Moreover, in one of the localities rapid economic restructuring in the period saw overt disputes between male workers, female workers and employers over the form such segregation should take. The chapter looks, firstly, at women's politics in the two towns, then briefly describes variations in service provision and in household relations and goes on to examine the different forms of occupational segregation by gender in the two localities – differences in the position of both male and female workers and the political responses these gave rise to.

The evidence presented here suggests that local gender politics both affects the wider local political environment and, at the same time, feeds back into forms of occupational segregation and gender workplace politics. For segregation is itself partially constituted through gender politics at local and national levels. This has been adequately demonstrated in terms of workplace politics, particularly in terms of the role of trade unions and of professional bodies in setting the boundaries of the gendering of occupations. It has been less frequently considered in terms of the other forms of political behaviour.

In its attempt to elucidate the mechanisms which lie behind the political participation of women, this chapter begins from the analytic assumption that women will have a tendency to organise to pursue particular sets of material interests. These interests, reflecting differences between men's and women's gendered material position in both the workplace and the household, will be different from the interests of male workers. For the purposes of analysis the relevant sets of interests are defined as the transfer of responsibility for service provision from the household, the private market, mutual and charitable institutions to the state (see Mark-Lawson, Savage and Warde 1985). Data from the two localities is used to examine the structural features which either encouraged or inhibited the political organisation of women in those areas in pursuit of 'statist' solutions to the provision of services – maternity and child welfare services, housing, health, etc.

It is probably uncontentious to assert that links exist between political behaviour and the workplace situation of political actors. In the case of *women's* political organisation, however, this link has been treated either as non-existent or as circumscribed by domestic circumstances. Recent work on women and politics has, however, attempted to show that such a link exists for women in exactly the same way as it does for men. Such work is rich and varied in the empirical instances covered and the conceptual approaches used, but three main propositions emerge as relatively taken-for-granted assumptions: firstly, that political activity among women is a relatively new phenomenon; secondly, that once women become politically active they behave (in terms of party and workplace politics) in the same way as men; and, thirdly, that women's political participation is directly linked to their increased economic participation (Lovenduski 1986; Lovenduski and Hills 1981; Purcell 1979; Randall 1982; Siltanen and Stanworth 1984). Such arguments, however, tend to overlook the complexity of the institutional sites in which women find themselves. Women's experience in the workplace differs from men's in a number of ways, in terms of processes and occupations, in terms of the types of authority relations under which they labour and in terms of their position within trade unions, for instance. Moreover, even where women *are* in the same structural position in the workplace as men (and this chapter will show that this was the case in some localities in the inter-war period), their position in other institutions, such as the family, was still proscribed by gender.

The two localities

The two towns chosen for analysis, Nelson in north-east Lancashire and Luton in Bedfordshire, were of similar size in 1921: Luton MB had a population of *c* 57,000 and Nelson Metropolitan Borough (MB) *c* 40,000. Both localities had a high women's economic activity rate, considerably higher than the rate nationally. In 1931 the rate for Luton was 45.2 per cent and that for Nelson 57.2 per cent compared to a rate of 29.7 per cent in England and Wales. As a result of the dual income structure of many working-class households, both towns had relatively high levels of household income (although high rents in Luton ate into household budgets). The two towns experienced the process of economic restructuring characterising the inter-war period in different ways. In Luton the economic base, which began to change after 1900, saw a number of 'new' industries attracted to the area as well as a very rapid growth of vehicle production and engineering locally. Unemployment in Luton was low throughout the period, and the population of the town grew rapidly, reaching *c* 97,000 by 1939. Nelson remained basically an occupational community – a one-industry, one-process town based on cotton weaving. Economic decline in Nelson in this period reflected that of the cotton industry as a whole, although the fact that Nelson produced fine cloth for the home and West European market meant it suffered less than other cotton towns. (As a major exporter, the cotton industry, along with other staple export industries in the period, suffered from adverse market conditions: Aldcroft 1970; Constantine 1980; Cronin 1984.) Unemployment was relatively high in Nelson in the early 1930s, and by 1951 population had fallen to *c* 34,000.

Political outcomes: services for women in Luton and Nelson

Let us begin by looking at the *effects* that women's political organisation had in the two localities: at local political *outcomes* in terms of the types of welfare services provided locally for women. This section is premissed on a view that where women have a 'voice' in local politics this will be observable in terms of the provision of services which benefit them. I concentrate here on maternity and child welfare services (M&CW) for three reasons: firstly, because this was an indisputably gender-related service; secondly, because most national and local women's organisations in this period were pressing for extensions of such services in the face of a (politically embarrassing) rising maternal mortality rate (Lewis 1980); thirdly, because levels of spending on this

Table 11.1   Approximate per capita (women between 15–44 years of age) net expenditure on maternity and child welfare services in Luton, Nelson, Lancaster and Preston, 1924–5 and 1935–6)

	Luton	*Nelson*	*Lancaster*	*Preston*
1924–5	3½d	5s 11d	7d	8d
1935–6	1s 10 d	8s 2d	4s 1d	5s 6d

Source: Mark-Lawson, Savage and Warde 1985: 200, table 11.1; and Borough of Luton, *Epitome of Accounts*, years ending 1925 and 1936.

service varied enormously between localities (Lee 1986; Mark-Lawson 1987).

Table 11.1 shows differences in spending on M&CW services in four localities in the mid-1920s and mid-1930s. Nelson was by far the most generous at both dates, while Luton was the meanest. This reflects the fact that Nelson had a very good M&CW service both compared to Luton and to England and Wales generally. These services, in common with other services such as housing, were maintained in Nelson throughout the period in spite of attempts by the Ministry of Health to force Nelson to cut back on its spending. In Nelson municipal services were regarded as a preferred form of provision for all ratepayers. Municipal services were the best that could be provided, and a notion of optimum rather than minimum levels of service prevailed. This view was not associated with any one particular party. Indeed, in the 1920s, when relative levels of spending on services were higher in Nelson than elsewhere, the local council was made up of equal numbers of councillors from each of the main political parties. Labour did not take control of the council until 1927.

In Luton, by contrast, M&CW was seen as best provided via the voluntary sector, as indeed were other services. Municipal M&CW was regarded as a matter for the Poor Law Guardians since only the very poor would use such a service. In 1924 the work of the volunteers was praised in local council in terms which made it quite clear that one kind of woman *staffed* the centres and quite another type *used* them.

> The importance of these centres and the beneficient work they do for mothers and expectant mothers who are in straightened circumstances cannot be emphasised too much . . . the centres have been the means of bringing comfort to many poor women and their children.
> (*Luton News and Bedfordshire Advertiser* (*LNBA*), 27 November 1924)

Such deferential relations of provision engendered an approach which tended to blame maternity problems on 'poor' mothers (with the term 'poor' used in two senses here).

In Luton women were apparently unsuccessful in pressing the council for extentions of services which might have been seen as in their interests. Indeed, the needs of women were juxtaposed with those of 'ratepayers' (in spite of the fact that a high proportion of ratepayers were women). All forms of municipal services in Luton were regarded by the local council as a last resort only to be used by 'the poor'. Other types of provision were seen as preferable – the household, the market on which services could be bought, mutual forms of provision such as friendly societies' slate clubs, etc. or alternatively charitable or voluntary forms of provision. With the very rapid growth of Luton in the period these attitudes became increasingly untenable, and by the late 1930s Luton faced a crisis in terms of its service provision, a crisis that remained unacknowledged in the period.

Women's political organisation in the two towns

If it were the case that women's political mobilisation was unproblematically linked to their economic participation, given that the two towns had a similarly high female economic activity rate, we might expect to find women organising and having local political effects in similar ways in the two towns. This was far from the case.

Nelson provides an example of an area in which women, far from being politically marginal, played a full part in local formal politics. They dominated the town and the voters list by sheer force of numbers even in 1921 before the extension of the franchise to women under thirty. All local political parties were eager to attract 'the woman's vote', seen as qualitatively different from the man's vote. All political parties had some form of institutional organisation of women, and there were a number of other local political organisations either concerned with specifically women's issues (such as the local National Union of Women's Suffrage Societies and, later, the National Union of Societies for Equal Citizenship) or attracting a large female membership (such as the League of Nations and the Independent Labour Party (ILP)). The Women's Co-operative Guild was, unlike other areas, not only active but also broadly 'political', with lectures on both formal political subjects and 'women only' subjects such as 'hygiene' or birth control. Nelson also had a large women's peace lobby, both during the First World War and afterwards. In 1934 a local labour activist and feminist, Selina Cooper, organised a 'No More War' conference in Nelson and in the same year she visited Germany to investigate the plight of female political prisoners there. Indeed, Nelson produced a surprising (given its size and location) number of women active in national and international women's politics (see

Liddington 1984; Mark-Lawson 1987). Liddington and Norris (1978) have demonstrated the pivotal position of Nelson in the Lancashire campaign for women's suffrage in the pre-war period.

Most significant for the argument presented here is the strength of women within *local* political processes. There was a large, and at some points dominant, female contingent in the local ILP, which was highly influential within the local Labour Party (membership of the ILP and the Nelson women's peace movement, as you might expect, overlapped). The organisational base for the ILP was the individual and the household rather than the workplace, and it is perhaps not surprising that it drew in so many women nationally and locally. More unusual was the influence of women within the local labour movement through trade unionism. In the 1920s in Nelson, in spite of the small size of units in the town, weaving was a closed shop with 100 per cent trade union membership (Fowler and Fowler 1984). The local Weavers' Association dominated the local Labour Party, and in 1931 women weavers outnumbered men by 7,669 to 6,895. This set of circumstances gave women a more considerable political voice than they had elsewhere, certainly than they had in Luton. It did not, however, give them political power. Positions of power within both the Weavers' Association and the Labour Party were held by men, with a few notable exceptions (Liddington 1984).

As Howell (1983) has shown, the configuration of labour movement politics in Nelson was distinct. Independent Labour politics normally flourished where trade union politics was weak, in Yorkshire in particular as opposed to the more conservative trade union politics of Lancashire towns. Nelson had the workplace politics of a Lancashire town and the party politics of a Yorkshire town. Women were very much 'present' in political life in Nelson: in terms of local political parties and workplace politics, in terms of feminist politics and in terms of national and international political organisations. That presence was, on the whole, articulated through the institutions of the labour movement, although all political parties espoused the cause of women, and all political parties pursued state welfare ends (see, for a fuller account of this process, Mark-Lawson 1987; Mark-Lawson, Savage and Warde 1985).

Luton presents a very different picture. In spite of the involvement of women in paid work, there was little organisation or activity of women either in party or in workplace politics. The labour movement, which in Nelson provided a conduit through which women's demands could be routed, was characterised in Luton by a hostility to women's workplace politics, a hostility that spilled over from the union movement to other sections of the labour movement. This hostility could hardly have encouraged women to see the Labour Party as a viable means of forwarding their issues. There was a branch of the Women's Co-operative Guild locally but it does not appear to have been very active.

Its meetings are not reported in the local press, nor was it represented in resolutions or petitions to the local council even during debates over such gender-specific issues as maternity and child welfare in the town. A Women's Labour Association was formed in 1918, and while at certain points in the 1920s this was one of the most stable elements of the Luton Labour Party, it was not regarded with favour by the more dominant trade union sections. The lack of women's representation within formal politics, I would argue, was one of the reasons why the Luton Labour Party, and indeed all other political parties in the area, failed to prioritise state service provision as a political issue locally.

If what could broadly be described as 'socialist feminism', strongly present in Nelson, was absent in Luton, there were formal institutions in which women were organised. Groups such as the Luton Women's Council (which consisted mainly of social workers and church workers), the Luton and District Board of the St Albans and Chelmsford Diocesan Union for Preventive, Rescue and Penitentiary Work, the Bedford County Union of the National British Women's Total Abstinence Union and the Luton Women's Liberal Association are the kinds of body within which women's organisation was located in Luton. Such groups at various points did argue for more women councillors, more women in public life, women Justices of the Peace, equal pay and women police. Thoroughly middle-class and eminently respectable, such women made few demands of the local council in terms of the extension of service provision. Indeed, many of them were personally involved in local charitable provision.

Local political issues in which working-class women did get involved were regarded as outside the pale of constitutional politics locally. There was a rent strike in Luton as in other areas during the war and this was led by women. Women were prominent in a short-lived Luton Food Vigilance Committee in 1918, a body which pressed the council to implement its powers to provide school meals and for a wider Labour Party policy on food. At a meeting in 1918 Labour leaders were criticised for failure to organise both the food and the workshop question. This meeting was denounced as 'Bolshevist' by the local paper, and the local Labour Party refused to recognise the organisation. Similarly, women supported an organisation called Comrades of the Great War, which put up a number of candidates in the 1919 local elections and pressed for extensions of services, particularly housing and services to help war widows.

Women were also present in large numbers at a peace celebration in July 1919 which turned into a full-scale riot lasting two days. The town hall and municipal offices were burnt down, and £200,000 of damage was sustained in the town. The treatment of ex-servicemen and war widows locally, the housing shortage and high rents seem to have been the issues which sparked this off, although the immediate cause was the refusal of the council to allow the Comrades of the Great War to use a local park for a memorial service. On the first night of rioting the town hall and municipal offices were burnt down by a large mob 'armed with bricks, hammers and other weapons'. A piano warehouse beside the burning town hall was broken into 'and the instruments dragged into the street. To the tune of "Keep the Home Fires Burning" the wilder elements of the huge gathering danced and sang, some even mounting a grand piano for the purpose' (*LNBA,* 24 July 1919). During a further demonstration two days later 'the angry mob which included many women, pulled down a brick wall . . . and used the bricks as missiles' (ibid.).

Women in Luton were not politically quiescent. They defended themselves publicly against attacks by organised male workers and participated in a variety of political events in the town. They were, however, denied access to constitutional political routes of protest and organisation. In Nelson, by contrast, women were well organised and constituted a considerable political presence in the locality. Here the strength of women in the locality allowed service issues to be constructed as desirable by all political parties.

The next section will go on to examine the sets of wider gender relations on which the political organisation of women in the two towns rested. These were constituted via a number of different sites, including importantly the workplace and the household. At the same time, the form taken by women's political organisation affected the wider political environment of the towns. In Nelson the strong presence of women in political life inhered in their position in both the workplace and the household, and at the same time that presence set 'statist' strategies on the agenda for all political parties. In Luton women's political organisation was pre-empted by the patriarchal strategies of male workers, both in the workplace itself and in the labour movement. These differences were importantly constructed through variations in occupational segregation in the two towns and through forms of workplace control. This issue is approached via an examination of the economic structure and in particular the position of women in the workplace in Luton and Nelson.

Occupational structure and gender segregation in the workplace

The dominance of cotton weaving in Nelson is reflected in both the homogeneous occupational structure and the high women's economic activity rate. In 1931, 61 per cent of those in work in the town were employed by the cotton industry, and weaving and associated processes in Nelson employed roughly similar numbers of men and women: 6,895 men and 7,669 women, representing 49.1 per cent of economically active men and 77.1 per cent of women. The significance of this in terms of work for women lies in the fact that, while in other cotton towns (such as Preston, which had a similar women's activity rate: 52.7 per cent in 1931) weaving was women's work, in Nelson conditions in the workplace were more egalitarian. The striking feature that differentiates Nelson from other localities is the pattern of *male* employment. In Nelson there was no alternative industry outside cotton for men, the only other substantial sector being commerce (9 per cent) and general labouring (9 per cent). By contrast, in Preston in 1931 only 10 per cent of men worked in cotton (Mark-Lawson, Savage and Warde 1985: 211).

Three consequences follow from this. Firstly, in Nelson, unlike other areas, weaving could not be treated as 'women's work', a fact illustrated by levels of wages for men and women in the town which was roughly similar. Mrs Abbot, Chair of the Open Door Council, visited Nelson in 1930 and told the *Nelson Leader* (29 March 1930) of 'the interest with which she had seen men and women cotton operatives working side by side with equal rights'. Women weavers in Nelson were probably among the highest-paid women workers in the country and both men and women earned about 48s a week in 1922.

Secondly, and following from this, both the reality and the ideology of a 'family wage' (a male wage high enough to maintain a dependent wife and children) were absent in Nelson. In 1922 wages in Nelson were (on average) as follows:

Colliery surface workers – 39s for a week of six shifts.
Labourer at a waste works – 49s per week.
Labourer at a paper works – 47s 6d per week.
Four-loom weaver – 48s per week.
Foundry worker – 43s 6d per week.

(*Nelson Leader,* 8 September 1922).

A local councillor, presenting these figures to a council meeting, pointed out that 'in the case of weavers both the husband and the wife generally went to work so there was twice 48s coming in' (*NL* 8 September 1922). The fact that many households were not based on a family wage gave rise to problems in the face of unemployment during the period because Ministry of Labour regulations were firmly based on the notion of the bread-winning male. The Nelson Employment Committee was at pains to point this fact out and to argue that married women should not be denied unemployment benefit in the area, since family survival was based on dual-income households.

Thirdly, the particular gender division of labour in the workplace in Nelson meant that patriarchal aspects of control must have been less marked than elsewhere. Mike Savage has demonstrated that in Preston, where most weavers were women, the few men being youths expecting promotion, the control exerted by the overlooker (who was always male) was vested in his 'maleness'. Male overlookers controlled the labour of female weavers, and the sexual division of labour in weaving was linked to the authority structure of the mill. Patriarchal forms of control were 'imported' from the family and the neighbourhood into the workplace (Savage 1985, 1987). The condition of being male was as vital to becoming an overlooker in Nelson as elsewhere. However, in Nelson both men and women were subject to the same (male) control:

> Even though most *women* did roughly the same work in both Nelson and Preston, their work experiences were distinctly different, because in Nelson men and women worked alongside each other and earned similar wages . . . Thus the conditions under which men and women sold their labour power were similar in Nelson.
>
> (Mark-Lawson, Savage and Warde 1985: 212)

In Luton segregation by gender was marked both within and between sectors. As Table 11.2 shows, 59 per cent of women but only 13 per cent of men were employed in hat-making, while few women worked in engineering in the inter-war period. Hat manufacture was the major employment sector in Luton from about 1870 up until the Second World War, with production based in very small workshops and carried out by an army of outworkers. The trade was dominated by small 'makers-up', usually men who blocked hats in domestic workshops and sold to middlemen. Dony (1942) describes the work of the makers-up in the late nineteenth century; their houses

> being specially adapted for the work, those built at the time often having sculleries at least twice or three times as large as is usual in working-class homes. In these the blocking and stiffening was done, while the scullery was an equally large upper room where the sewers worked. The sewers were usually the wife of the maker-up and a number of his relatives with a considerable proportion of young girls. The larger factories did not take apprentices and the smaller establishments provided the only way of learning the trade.
>
> (Dony 1942: 104–5)

The small size of units persisted in the inter-war period. In 1927 there were over 400 hat manufacturers in Luton, and the reports of the Factory Inspectors for the 1920s show 51.5 per cent of businesses employing less than ten workers (*LNBA* 21 July 1927; Pinder 1970: 149).

Hat-making was seen as a particularly suitable occupation for women. Out workers, according to the *Hatters Gazette*, 'are generally good hands who, either through getting married and having a home to keep, or from some other domestic tie, such as an invalid relative, do not wish to work in a factory doing forty hours' (2 September 1918). Conditions of work were 'sweated' in the sense that, during the season, hours were long and unpredictable. However, earnings were relatively good, higher

Table 11.2   Industrial distribution of workers in major employment sectors in Luton, 1931

	Males	*Females*
Total population	32,806	35,717
Total pop. aged 14 and over	25,904	29,042
Unoccupied and retired	1,579	15,914
Out of work	1,833	321
Total in industries	22,492	12,807
VI Manufacture of metals (mainly engineering)	6,759	378
Wiring and contracting	2,369	132
Vehicle construction	2,308	152
Other metal industries	1,546	259
IX Manuf. of clothing	4,313	7,950
Hats and caps: straw	3,168	6,716
XIII Building	1,690	17
XVI Transport and communication	1,028	18
XVII Commerce and finance	3,727	1,173
XIX Professions	414	272
XXI Personal service	675	1,429

Source: Census 1931: industry tables, table 2.

than any other clothing group (*Report of the Board of Trade Enquiry into Hours and Earnings of Labour, Vol II, The Clothing Trades*; Dony 1942: 135). The *Daily Express* in 1926 described Luton as a 'Town Made Rich By Shingling'. 'Women earn while men do the housework,' the headline announced. But the seasonal nature of the work must be taken into account. Wages of £2 5s per week could be earned in the season, but such earnings were confined to certain times of the year (*LNBA*, 26 April 1928; 21 March 1929).

For the purposes of the present argument, hat-making in Luton exhibits three significant features. Firstly, the unit of organisation in the smaller workshops which dominated the trade was the family. Hat-making workshops were both family homes and places of work, and in the season hundreds of women and girls would come in from the surrounding countryside and lodge with hat-making families to provide the necessary extra labour. Consequently, in the workplace women experienced the same patriarchal relations as they did in the home.

Secondly, in the larger factories and workshops the industry exhibited a high degree of gender segregation of tasks, as Table 11.3 shows. The absence of an apprenticeship system for the occupations filled by women, who learned the trade from older workers, meant there was no 'skilled' work for women, reflected in Trade Board rates of pay which included no category of skilled female work (*Hatters Gazette*, 15 March 1920). Skilled male workers supervised and controlled the work of women in the hat industry.

Thirdly, labour in hat-making was flexibly organised around a definition of women first and foremost as domestic workers. Hours were flexible, and, although there was a high women's economic activity rate, both the major sectors assumed that a woman's place was first and foremost in the home. Hat work via its flexibility and engineering via the concept of the family wage.

Table 11.3   Occupational segregation in the Luton hat industry: breakdown of occupational category XIII, makers of textile goods and articles of dress, Luton MB, 1931

	Males		Females	
	number	per cent	number	per cent
Milliners	35	1	3,693	47
Hat sewers, finishers or trimmers	411	13	3,178	41
Hat formers, plankers, stiffeners	1,634	52	154	2

Source: Census 1931: occupational tables.

The size of units and the nature of organisation in hat manufacture mitigated against trade unionism. In the early 1920s, 300 hat workers joined the Workers' Union (later the Transport and General Workers), but this was very short-lived. The National Federation of Women Workers also had limited success in recruiting hat workers although it periodically sent organisers and speakers to the town. By the late 1930s in the straw hat industry less than 1 per cent of workers were in trade unions. That this was a feature of the locality rather than the sector is demonstrated by the success of trade unionism among felt hat workers in the North.

Most women workers, as Table 11.3 shows, were concentrated in hat work. By contrast, the other significant industries locally, engineering and vehicle production, afforded few opportunities to women. I want briefly to consider the segmented nature of the Luton labour market and the mechanisms through which that segmentation was maintained via an examination of the restructuring of the Luton economy which took place between 1900 and 1928. Again the position of women within that process is of particular interest.

The process of restructuring in Luton dates from around 1900 when the newly formed Luton New Industries Committee began an attempt to diversify the basis of the Luton economy by attracting new industry, specifically male-employing industry, to the town. In a special supplement in *Engineering* the virtues of locating in Luton were extolled. Cheap land, cheap electricity, an absence of trade unionism in ten of the eleven local engineering shops and low male wages were described as the main advantages. High household income allowed the payment of low male wages. As the booklet explained (in terms which incidentally demonstrate the advantages to employers of widespread paid work for women):

> Mechanics have to consider not only their personal labour remuneration, but the opportunities for their sons and daughters finding profitable employment. . . . Luton has advantages which equal, and may even in some respects excel, those of the Lancashire towns, for the straw-hat and bonnet-making industry offers a field for women's industry without disadvantages. In plaiting, in [machining], or in finishing, pleasant work is obtainable, at wages which average nearly 30s in some few cases. It is clean, healthy and in some departments even artistic labour . . . and thus it happens that the head of the family can afford to labour at 18s to 20s a week when he has three daughters each earning 15s to 20s.
>
> (Keens 1900: 10–11)

The New Industries Committee was extremely successful. Between 1900 and 1914 Luton attracted a number of companies unrelated to the hat trade: in chemicals, engineering, vehicle production and food processing. The awarding of government contracts during the First World War strengthened local firms, and in the mid-1920s, once the immediate post-war slump was over, new industries started arriving again. By 1930, among a diversity of 'new' industries, Luton housed the British sites of three important multinational companies: one American (General Motors) and two Swedish (Skefko and Electrolux).

Ironically, certain features of the local labour market were to prove unexpectedly problematic for employers. According to Holden (1983), the indigenous labour force proved unreliable and resistant to the adoption of new workplace practices. Hat workers, used to a free and easy form of work discipline, were unorganised and did not adapt well from the traditional small units of production to the demands of mass production and the assembly line. Moreover, workers previously attached to hat work tended to leave engineering jobs when the hat season started. Used to a seasonal pattern and an annual cycle of household income, ex-Luton hat workers, whose behaviour appeared irrational to the larger engineering employers, in fact pursued an

entirely rational household strategy. In 1929 a letter to the local paper
from Vauxhall's production manager claimed:

> the experience of Vauxhall Motors Ltd in employing out-of-work
> hat trade operatives is very unfortunate inasmuch as the hat trade
> busy season commences at their busiest time, so that any such
> operatives that may have been engaged earlier in the season and
> trained to their work, leave them just when they have most need of
> their services.
>
> (*LNBA*, 14 November 1929)

Electrolux and Skefko had the same problem with their unskilled female
assembly workers, finding that the higher wages in hat work meant their
employees left when the season started. As Holden puts it:

> Besides the high seasonal wages the hat trade proved attractive to
> women because of the flexibility of working hours and conditions.
> They could work at home if they so wished on many operations,
> thus enabling women with small children and other dependants to
> work. In addition they were not subjected to the regimentation of
> work which was the norm on assembly lines in the new industry
> factories.
>
> (Holden 1983: 253)

A significant feature of economic restructuring in Luton is the
antagonistic gender relations it created in the workplace. Such
antagonism was not, of course, confined to Luton; it existed in a number
of occupations and localities in the immediate post-war period and the
1920s. As Braybon has shown, the wartime experience did little to
improve the position of women workers (Braybon 1981). The
arguments used in Luton to try to restore the pre-war position were not
that women should not be in work at all but that they should not be in
'men's' work. In other areas, where trade unions had made dilution
agreements with employers during the war, women were easily
dislodged from the workplace (Braybon 1981), but in Luton the low
levels of trade unionism in the town allowed controversies to rage over
the 'gendering' of tasks. A lack of trade union solidarity meant that
employers found it easier to continue to use the cheaper labour of
women after the war.

A 1919 newspaper survey of local industry showed that many of the
firms employing women during the war intended to continue the
practice. Some of the new employers, such as Trident Manufacturing,
had a chiefly female staff (*LNBA*, 13 February 1919). Skefko had
replaced many men with women during the war, while another firm,
which had switched products during the war, 'solely employed female
labour and divided the various processes in such a way that output was
increased' and claimed they would continue to do so (*LNBA*, 30 January

1919). Even in hat work the traditional division of labour had been challenged. One of the larger hat manufacturers said:

> Girls have replaced many of the men. Not all are satisfactory, probably two out of every four. How are we going to move those two . . .? I am quite certain that firms will never go back to the old happy-go-lucky days when there was no organisation or system in regard to hours of labour and the extent of the work a man should turn out.
>
> (*LNBA*, 24 April 1919)

Not surprisingly the response to such statements was rapid organisation on the part of male workers and a spate of hostile comments about women in the workplace in the local papers. A letter from 'a discharged soldier' in engineering to the local paper described how

> with the help of a union the married women with husbands had been discharged . . . but . . . there are six girls in the department . . . ex servants and straw hatters and there's been plenty of vacancies for both . . . so there's no excuse.
>
> (*LNBA*, 25 March 1920)

Women workers defended themselves against such charges although they could do little to prevent their eventual expulsion from engineering. Such women were particularly incensed when a Labour councillor suggested that to relieve unemployment all those in work should give 1s per week towards a fund for the unemployed. 'This is not fair,' one woman wrote; 'The girls have been turned out of the engineering shops by the men and now they are going to make them help keep them.'

Gender workplace politics and forms of segregation in Luton in the 1920s can be characterised as negotiable and hostile as attempts were made to shift the boundaries of the previous gender division of labour. In Luton this hostility was not expressed as a view that women should not be economically active, rather that women should not be in 'men's' work.

The local Labour Party reflected the strengths and strategies of local trade unionism. As we have seen, the major employment sector for women was not unionised. Hence the majority of women workers in the town had no voice in the labour movement. The Labour Party itself was weak and suffered from an all-pervasive factionalism. There were splits between old-style Lib/Lab craft unions and a newer and more radical style of unionism from the Amalgamated Society of Engineers (ASE) which grew rapidly between 1917–21 but thereafter collapsed under the aggressive anti-unionism of the largest employer, Vauxhall Motors.

Neither of these factions were in the least sympathetic to women. Indeed, as we have seen, the growth of the ASE was partly premissed on hostility to women in the workplace. By the mid-1920s, with the decline of the ASE, dissent centred on a split between the ILP (which contained many white-collar workers including women) and the craft unions. A leading member of the local Labour Party (the parliamentary candidate in 1919) epitomises this hostility in a letter to the local paper:

> Since the war the ILP has attracted to itself a body of pacifists, prigs, Puritans, prohibitionists and Pharisees . . . It has been said of them that to smoke would make them sick, to drink they are physically incapable, so they come into the Labour Movement for their excitement.
>
>   (Letter from Willet Ball, *LNBA*, 4 April 1926)

Another Labour Party worker attacked the ILP for 'Pacificism, attacks on the churches, vegetarianism, birth control and "stunts" of this nature' (*LNBA*, 3 March 1927). The Labour Party in Luton was opposed to the extension of welfare services, as indeed was the dominant Liberal party; consequently, formal politics in Luton lacked any conduit through which women's demands could be routed.

The discussion so far has shown that a high women's economic activity rate is not a sufficient condition of women's political activity. However, it could be the case that the type of work performed by women explains the difference between Luton and Nelson. Women in cotton weaving might have been politically active while women in hat manufacture were not. But other work suggests that not all women cotton weavers were similarly involved in political activity. In Preston, where women were engaged in cotton weaving in almost the same proportions as in Nelson, they were almost totally absent from local politics (Mark-Lawson, Savage and Warde 1985). The difference between Nelson and both other cotton towns and Luton was in gender divisions in the workplace and forms of occupational segregation.

There is also evidence, although this is more schematic, that the position of women in households also varied between the two localities (Mark-Lawson 1987). I would suggest that household structure and household relations interact with, although they cannot be reduced to, economic structure. The two spheres exist in a symbiotic relationship mediated by the structuration of local labour markets. In Nelson, where a homogeneous labour market existed, where there was little segregation by gender and where male wages were relatively low and female wages relatively high, household structure must have tended towards the more egalitarian mode identified by Gittins (1982). By contrast, in Luton women's work was segregated by gender and was seasonal with a great many homeworkers. The much proclaimed advantage of hat work for women was precisely that it did not present any challenge to a patriarchal domestic division of labour because its flexibility allowed women to juggle domestic tasks and paid work.

Conclusion

In Luton women's political organisation was pre-empted by the patriarchal strategies of male workers, both in the workplace itself and in the labour movement. As a consequence, women in Luton remained largely absent from formal political life both in terms of the tenor of local politics – women are rarely referred to as voters or as ratepayers – and in terms of the issues pursued. Yet, as in Nelson, women made up a significant part of the local workforce. Participation in paid work, in this case, was not a sufficient factor to allow women to engage in the formal political arena. Indeed, much of the workplace politics in Luton was concerned with keeping women off certain processes and out of certain occupations. There were women in the Luton branch of the ILP, and rampant hostility between the industrial branch of the labour movement and the ILP was partly expressed as gender hostility. Luton women, though, were not 'quiescent' in any sense. They could, and did, take part in particular types of protest – although these were rarely channelled through formal political procedures. In Nelson, by contrast, the strong presence of women in political life inhered in their position in both the workplace and the household. At the same time, that presence changed the nature of the local political environment, setting 'statist' strategies on the agenda for all political parties.

I have argued for the significance of the gender relations under which women labour in inhibiting or encouraging women's political activity. These relations derive from forms of occupational segregation and control of work. Women, I would suggest, cannot exhibit the same forms of political behaviour as men. The restrictive effects of patriarchal control and occupational segregation by gender are confined to women workers, and the conditions which prevent women from organising, both in the workplace and in the arena of party politics, are gender specific. Moreover, as I have shown, women's political activity matters, in the sense that its presence or absence acts on, and affects the formation of, local political environments. Gender politics locally, which both inheres in and reproduces local patriarchal relations and forms of occupational segregation, affects the strategies, the tenor and the outcome of local political processes.

Bibliography

Aldcroft, D. H. (1970) *The Inter-War Economy: Britain 1919–1939.* London, Batsford.

Aldrich, H., Jones, T. and McEvoy, D, (1984) 'Ethnic advantage and minority business development', in R. Ward and R. Jenkins (eds.), *Ethnic Communities in Business.* Cambridge, Cambridge University Press.

Alexander, S. and Taylor, B. (1982) 'In defence of patriarchy', in M. Evans (ed.), *The Woman Question.* London, Fontana.

Allen, S. and Wolkowitz, C. (1987) *Homeworking: Myths and Realities.* Basingstoke, Macmillan.

Alliance Against Sexual Coercion (1981) *Sexual Harassment Handbook,* Boston, Mass.

Amos, V. and Parmar, P. (1984) 'Challenging imperial feminism'. *Feminist Review,* 17, 3–20.

Amsden, A. H. (ed.) (1980) *The Economics of Women and Work.* Harmondsworth, Penguin.

Anwar, M. (1979) *The Myth of Return.* London, Heinemann.

Armstrong, J. (1982) *Leicester Outwork Campaign: Action Research with the Hidden Army.* Leicester, Leicester Outwork Campaign.

Atkinson, J. (1986) *Changing Working Patterns: How Companies Achieve Flexibility to Meet New Needs.* London Institute of Manpower Studies, National Economic Development Office.

Attwood, Margaret and Hatton, Frances (1983) 'Getting on: gender differences in career development, a case study in the hairdressing industry', in Gamarnikow *et al.,* op. cit.

Ballard, B. (1984) 'Evidence from the Women and Employment Survey 1980, women part-time workers'. *Employment Gazette,* 92, 409–16.

Banking, Insurance and Finance Union (1981) *Equality for Women – Proposals for Positive Action,* London, BIFU.

Barker, D. L. and Allen, S. (eds.) (1976) *Dependence and Exploitation in Work and Marriage.* London, Longmans.

Barron, R. D. and Norris, G. M. (1976) 'Sexual divisions and the dual labour market', in Barker and Allen, op. cit.

Beechey, V. (1978) 'Women and production: a critical analysis of some sociological theories of women's work', in Annette Kuhn and Ann Marie Wolpe (eds.), *Feminism and Materialism: Women and Modes of Production*. London, Routledge.

Beechey, V. (1979) 'On patriarchy'. *Feminist Review*, 3, 66–82.

Beechey, V. (1983) 'What's so special about women's employment?' *Feminist Review*, 15, 23–46.

Beechey, V. (1986) 'Women's employment in contemporary Britain', in Beechey and Whitelegg, op. cit.

Beechey, V. and Perkins, T. (1987) *A Matter of Hours: Women, Part-Time Work and the Labour Market*. Cambridge, Polity.

Beechey, V. and Whitelegg, E. (1986) *Women in Britain Today*. Milton Keynes, Open University Press.

Bennett, J. (n.d.) 'Medieval peasant marriage; an examination of marriage licence fines in the *Liber Gersumarum*'. Unpublished paper.

Bennett, Y. and Carter, D. (1983) *Day Release for Girls*. Manchester, Equal Opportunities Commission.

Bergmann, B. (1980) 'Occupational segregation, wages and profits when employers discriminate by race or sex', in Amsden, op. cit.

Bishton, D. (1982) *The Sweat Shop Report*. Birmingham, All Faiths for One Race.

Blanchflower, D. and Corry, B. (1987) *Part-Time Employment in Great Britain*. London, Department of Employment, Research paper 57.

Blaxall, M. and Reagan, B. (eds.) (1976) *Women and the Workplace: The Implications of Occupational Segregation*. Chicago, University of Chicago Press.

Boserup, E. (1971) *Women's Role in Economic Development*. London, Allen & Unwin.

Braverman, H. (1974) *Labor and Monopoly Capital: The Degradation of Work in the Twentieth Century*. New York, Monthly Review Press.

Braybon, G. (1981) *Women Workers in the First World War: The British Experience*. London, Croom Helm.

Brenner, J. and Ramas, M. (1984) 'Rethinking women's oppression'. *New Left Review*, March/April, 33–71.

Britton, E. (1977) *The Community of the Vill: A Study of the History of the Family and Village Life in Fourteenth-Century England*. Toronto, Macmillan.

Brown, C., (1984) *Black and White Britain: The Third PSI Survey*. London, Heinemann.

Building Businesses . . . Not Barriers (1986) Cmnd 9794. London, HMSO.

Byre, A. (1987) *Indirect Discrimination*. Manchester, Equal Opportunities Commission.

Cameron, A. (1985) 'Bread and roses revisited: women's culture and working-class activism in the Lawrence strike of 1912' in Milkman, op. cit.

Carby, H. (1982) 'White woman listen: black feminism and the boundaries of sisterhood', in Centre for Contemporary Cultural Studies, *The Empire Strikes Back: Race and Racism in '70s Britain*. London, Hutchinson.

Cavendish, R. (1982) *Women Workers on the Line*. London, Routledge.

Clark, A. (1982 [1919]) *Working Life of Women in the Seventeenth Century*. London, Frank Cass; reprinted 1982, London, Routledge.

Clark, G. (1982) 'Recent developments in working patterns'. *Employment Gazette*, 90, 284–8.

Clark and Powell v. *Eley (IMI) Kynock Ltd,* 1983. *Industrial Relations Law Reports,* 11, 11.

Cockburn, C. (1983) *Brothers: Male Dominance and Technological Change.* London, Pluto.

Cockburn, C. (1985) *Machinery of Dominance: Women, Men and Technical Know-How.* London, Pluto.

Cockburn, C. (1987) *Two-Track Training: Sex Inequalities and the Youth Training Scheme.* Basingstoke, Macmillan.

Collins, E. G. C. and Blodgett, T. B. (1981) 'Sexual harassment – some see it – some won't'. *Harvard Business Review,* 59, 2, 76–95.

Commission of the European Communities (1981) *Proposal for a Council Directive on Voluntary Part-Time Work,* Com. (81) 775 Final. Brussels, EEC.

Commission for Racial Equality (1975) *Immigration Control Procedures: Report of a Formal Investigation.* London, CRE.

Confederation of Health Service Employees (1986) 'Women and equal opportunities in the NHS: COHSE survey'. *COHSE Research Bulletin,* March.

Connell, R. W., Ashenden, D. J. Kessler, S. and Dowsett, G. W. (1982) *Making the Difference: Schools, Families and Social Division.* Sydney, Allen & Unwin.

Connelly, P. (1978) *Last Hired, First Fired: Women and the Canadian Workforce.* Toronto, Women's Press.

Constantine, S. (1980) *Unemployment in Britain Between the Wars.* London, Longman.

Cooper, C. and Davidson, M. (1982) *High Pressure: Working Lives of Women Managers.* London, Fontana.

Coote, A. and Kellner, P. (1980) 'Hear this, Brother: women workers and union power'. *New Statesman,* Report No. 1. London.

Corn, J. (1979) 'Making flying "thinkable": women pilots and the selling of aviation 1927–1940' *American Quarterly,* 6, 31, Fall.

Coyle, A. (1985) 'Going private: the implications of privatisation for women's work'. *Feminist Review,* 21 Winter, 5–24.

Craig, G. and Wilkinson, F. (1985) *Pay and Employment in Four Retail Trades.* London, Department of Employment, Research Paper 51.

Craig, C., Rubery, J., Tarling, R. and Wilkinson, F. (1983) 'How labour markets operate'. Paper presented at Social Science Research Council Labour Markets Workshop, Manchester.

Crompton, R. and Jones, G. (1984) *White-Collar Proletariat: Deskilling and Gender in Clerical Work.* Basingstoke, Macmillan.

Crompton, R. and Mann, M. (eds.) (1986) *Gender and Stratification.* Cambridge, Polity.

Crompton, R. and Sanderson, K. (1986) 'Credentials and careers: some implications of the increase in professional qualifications among women'. *Sociology,* 20, 1, 25–42.

Cronin, J. E. (1984) *Labour and Society in Britain 1918–1979.* London, Batsford.

Daniel, W. W. (1984) 'Who didn't get a pay increase last year?'. *Policy Studies Journal,* 5, 78–85.

Davies, M. (1975) 'Woman's place is at the typewriter: the feminisation of the clerical labor force', in R. C. Edwards, M. Reich and D. M. Gordon (eds.) *Labor Market Segmentation.* Lexington, Mass. Lexington Books.

De Neubourg, C. (1985) 'Part-time work: an international comparison' *International Labour Review*, Geneva, 124, 559–76.

Dex, S. (1983) 'The second generation: West Indian female school leavers', in Phizacklea, op. cit.

Dex. S. (1987) *Women's Occupational Mobility: A Lifetime Perspective*. Basingstoke, Macmillan.

Dick, v. *University of Dundee*, 1987. *The Industrial Tribunals (Scotland)*, 82, 1.

Doeringer, P. B. and Piore, M. J. (1971) *Internal Labor Markets and Manpower Analysis*. Lexington, Mass. Lexington Books.

Donnison, J. (1977) *Midwives and Medical Men*. London, Heinemann.

Dony, J. G. (1942) *A History of the Straw Hat Industry*. Luton, Gribbs, Bamforth.

Edwards, R. (1979) *Contested Terrain*. London, Heinemann.

Eisenstein, (ed.) (1979) *Capitalist Patriarchy and the Case for Socialist Feminism*. New York, Monthly Review Press.

Eisenstein, Z. (1981) *The Radical Future of Liberal Feminism*. New York, Longman.

Ellis, V. (1981) *The Role of Trade Unions in the promotion of Equal Opportunities*. London, Equal Opportunities Commission/Social Science Research Council.

Elson, D. and Pearson, R. (1981) 'Nimble fingers make cheap workers: an analysis of women's employment in Third World manufacturing'. *Feminist Review*, 7, Spring, 87–107.

Employment Gazette (1984) 'A survey of 17-year-olds who left school aged 16 with two or less O levels in urban areas', August.

England, P. (1982) 'The failure of human capital theory to explain occupational sex segregation', *Journal of Human Resources*, 17, Summer, 358–70.

England, P. (1984) 'Wage appreciation and depreciation: a test of neoclassical economic explanations of occupational sex segregation' *Social Forces*, 62, 726–49.

Equal Opportunities Commission (1983) *Women and Trade Unions – A Survey*. Manchester, EOC.

Equal Opportunities Commission (1983) *Women in Engineering*. Manchester, EOC.

Equal Opportunities Commission (1985) *Occupational Segregation by Sex*. Manchester, EOC, Research Bulletin 9.

Equal Opportunities Commission (1986) *Women and Men in Britain: A Statistical Profile*. London, HMSO.

Equal Opportunities Commission (1987a) *11th Annual Report 1986*. London, HMSO.

Equal Opportunities Commission (1987b) *Women and Men in Britain: A Statistical Profile*. London, HMSO.

Everitt, A. (1967) 'Farm labourers', in J. Thirsk (ed.), *The Agrarian History of England and Wales. Vol. IV, 1500–1640*. Cambridge, Cambridge University Press.

Farley, L. (1978) *Sexual Shakedown*, New York, McGraw-Hill.

Fawcett Society (1985) *The Class of '84*. London, Fawcett Society.

Fevre, R. (1982) *The Labour Process in Bradford*, Bradford, Transition to Work Project.

Fire Brigades Union (1987) *Equal Opportunities Policy*. London, FBU.

Ford v. *Warwickshire County Council*, 1983. *Industrial Relations Law Reports*, 12, 3.

Fowler, A. and Fowler, L. (1984) *The History of the Nelson Weavers' Association*. Nelson, Nelson, Burnley, Rossendale and District Textile Workers' Union.

Freidson, E. (1977) 'The future of professionalism', in M. Stacey and M. Reid (eds.), *Health and the Division of Labour*. London, Croom Helm.

Friedman, A. L. (1977) *Industry and Labour*. Basingstoke, Macmillan.

Fryer, P. (1984) *Staying Power*. London, Pluto.

Gaffikin, F. and Nickson, A. (n.d.) *Jobs Crisis and the Multinationals: The Case of the West Midlands*. Birmingham, Trade Union Resource Centre.

Gamarnikow, E., Morgan, D. Purvis, J., and Taylorson, D. (eds.) (1983) *Gender, Class and Work*, London, Heinemann.

Game, A. and Pringle, R. (1984) *Gender at Work*, London, Pluto.

General, Municipal, Boilermakers and Allied Trades Unions (1987) *Winning a Fair Deal for Women – A GMB Policy for Equality*. London, GMB.

Giddens, A. (1973) *The Class Structure of the Advanced Societies*. London, Hutchinson.

Gill, T. and Whitty, L. (1983) *Women's Rights in the Workplace*. Harmondsworth, Penguin.

Gilroy, P. (1982) 'Police and thieves', in Centre for Contemporary Cultural Studies, *The Empire Strikes Back*. London, Hutchinson.

Gittins, D. (1982) *Fair Sex: Family Size and Structure 1900–39*. London, Hutchinson.

Glucksman, M. (1986) 'In a class of their own? Women workers in the new industries in inter-war Britain'. *Feminist Review*, 24, 7–37.

Gordon, D. M., Edwards, R. and Reich, M. (1982) *Segmented Work, Divided Workers*. Cambridge, Cambridge University Press.

Gordon, P. (1984) *Deportations and Removals*. London, Runnymede Trust.

Gordon, P. (1985) *Policing Immigration: Britain's Immigration Controls*. London, Pluto.

Greater London Council (1986) *London Labour Plan*. London, GLC.

Greenwich Homeworkers Project (1987) *Annual Report*. Greenwich.

Gregory, J. (1987) *Sex, Race and the Law: Legislating for Equality*. London, Sage.

Greenbaum, J. (1976) 'Division of labor in the computer field'. *Monthly Review*, 28, 3, July–August.

Griffin, C. (1985) *Typical Girls?*. London, Routledge.

Gross, E. (1968) 'Plus ça change . . . The sexual structure of occupations over time'. *Social Problems*, 16, Fall.

Hacker, S. (1983) 'Mathematisation of engineering: limits on women and on the field', in Rothschild op. cit.

Hadjifotiou, N. (1983) *Women and Harassment at Work*. London, Pluto.

Hajnal J. (1965) 'European marriage patterns in perspective', in D. V. Glass and D. E. C. Eversley (eds.), *Population in History*. London, Arnold.

Hakim, C. (1979) *Occupational Segregation: A Comparative Study of the Degree and Pattern of the Differentiation between Men and Women's Work in Britain, the United States and Other Countries*. London, Department of Employment, Research Paper No. 9.

Hakim, C. (1981) 'Job segregation: trends in the 1970s' *Employment Gazette*, 89, 521–9.

Hakim, C. (1984) 'Homework and outwork: national estimates from two surveys'. *Employment Gazette*, 92, 7–12.

Hakim, C. (1987a) 'Homeworking in Britain: key findings from the national survey of home-based workers'. *Employment Gazette*, 95, 92–104.

Hakim, C. (1987b) 'Trends in the flexible workforce'. *Employment Gazette*, 95, 549–60.

Hall, R. (1985) *Ask Any Woman*. Bristol, Falling Wall Press.

Hanmer, J. and Saunders, S. (1984) *Well-Founded Fear*. London, Hutchinson.

Hartmann, H. (1976) 'Capitalism, patriarchy and job segregation by sex', in Blaxall and Reagan, op. cit.

Hartmann, H. (1979a) 'Capitalism, patriarchy and job segregation by sex', in Eisenstein, op. cit.

Hartmann, H. (1979b) 'The unhappy marriage of Marxism and feminism: towards a more progressive union'. *Capital and Class*, 8, 1–33.

Hartmann, H. (1981) 'The unhappy marriage of Marxism and feminism: towards a more progressive union', in Sargent, op. cit.

Hilton, R. H. (1975) *English Peasantry in the Later Middle Ages*. Oxford, Clarendon.

Holden, L. T. (1983) 'A history of Vauxhall Motors to 1950'. Unpublished MPhil thesis, Open University.

House of Lords (1982) Select Committee on the European Communities. *Voluntary Part-Time Work, Minutes of Evidence*. London, National Economic Development Office.

Howell, D. (1983) *British Workers and the Independent Labour Party 1888–1906*. Manchester, Manchester University Press.

Humphries, J. (1977) 'Class struggle and the persistence of the working-class family'. *Cambridge Journal of Economics*, 1, September, 241–58.

Hunt, P. (1980) *Gender and Class Consciousness*. London, Macmillan.

Hurstfield, J. (1987) *Part-Timers under Pressure, Paying the Price of Flexibility*. London, Low Pay Unit.

Jenkins v. *Kingsgate (Clothing Productions) Ltd*, 1981. *Industrial Relations Law Reports*, 10, 9.

Jex-Blake, S. (1886) *Medical Women: A Thesis and a History*. Edinburgh, Oliphant, Anderson & Ferrier.

Jonung, C. (1983) 'Patterns of occupational segregation by sex in the labour market', in Gunther Schnid (ed.), *Discrimination and Equalisation in the Labour Market: Employment Policies for Women in Selected Countries*. Berlin, International Institute for Management, Wissenschaftszentrum.

Joseph, G. (1981) 'The incompatible ménage à trois: Marxism, feminism and racism' in Sargent, op. cit.

Kahn-Hut, R., Kaplan Daniels, A. and Colvard, R. (eds.) (1982) *Women and Work: Problems and Perspectives*. New York, Oxford University Press.

Kane, M. (1982) 'A case for positive action'. *National Association of Teachers in Further and Higher Education Journal*, February.

Kanter, R. M. (1977) *Men and Women of the Corporation*. New York, Basic Books.

Keens, T. (1900) 'Luton as an industrial centre', Supplement in *The Engineer*.

Kerr, C. (1954) 'The Balkanisation of labour markets', in E. W. Baake (ed.),

Labour Mobility and Economic Opportunity. New York, Wiley/MIT Press.

Kessler, S. J. and McKenna, W. (1978) *Gender: An Ethnomethodological Approach*. New York, Wiley.

Kessler-Harris, A. (1987) '*Equal Opportunity Commission* v. *Sears, Roebuck and Company*: a personal account'. *Feminist Review*, 25, 46–69.

King, G. (1810) *Natural and Political Observations*. London.

Kraft, P. and Dubnoff, S. (1984) 'Software for women means a lower status'. *Computing*, February.

Kreckel, R. (1980) 'Unequal opportunity structure and labour market segmentation'. *Sociology*, 14.

Kussmaul, A. (1981) *Servants in Husbandry in Early Modern England*. Cambridge, Cambridge University Press.

Labour Research Department (1987) 'Are unions working for women?'. *Labour Research*, March.

Lander, J. (1986) 'Fighting dirty: cleaning workers, their conditions and their organisation'. *International Labour Reports*, November/December, 21–2.

Lapidus, G. W. (1976) 'Occupational segregation and public policy: a comparative analysis of American and Soviet patterns', in Blaxall and Reagan, op. cit.

Larkin, G. (1978) 'Medical dominance and control: radiographers in the division of labour'. *Sociological Review*, 26, 843–58.

Larkin, G. (1983) *Occupational Monopoly and Modern Medicine*. London, Tavistock.

Larson, M. (1977) *The Rise of Professionalism*. Berkeley, Calif., University of California Press.

Lee, R. (1986) 'Dual legitimation and uneven development: welfare expenditure in the inter-war city'. Paper delivered at the Urban Change Day School, Queen Mary College, London.

Leeds Trade Union and Community Resource and Information Centre (1983) *Sexual Harassment of Women at Work*. Leeds, TUCRIC.

Leverton v. *Clwyd County Council*, Employment Appeals Tribunal, June 1986.

Lewis, J. (1980) *The Politics of Motherhood: Child and Maternal Welfare in England, 1900–1939*. London, Croom Helm.

Lewis v. *Surrey County Council*, House of Lords, 1987.

Liddington, J. (1984) *The Life and Times of a Respectable Rebel: Selina Cooper, 1869–1949*. London, Virago.

Liddington, J. and Norris, J. (1978) *One Hand Tied behind Us: The Rise of the Women's Suffrage Movement*. London, Virago.

Liff, S. (1986) 'Technical change and occupational sex-typing', in D. Knights and H. Willmott (eds.), *Gender and the Labour Process*. Aldershot, Gower.

Local Government Operational Research Unit (1982) *Women in Local Government: The Neglected Resource*. London, LGORU.

Lovenduski, J. (1986) *Women and European Politics: Contemporary Feminism and Public Policy*. Brighton, Wheatsheaf.

Lovenduski, J. and Hills, J. (eds.) (1981) *The Politics of the Second Electorate: Women and Public Participation*. London, Routledge.

Loveridge, R. (1983) 'Sources of diversity in internal labour markets'. *Sociology*, 17, 44–62.

MacKinnon, C. (1978) *Sexual Harassment of Working Women*. New Haven, Conn., Yale University Press.

MacKintosh, M. (1977) 'Reproduction and patriarchy'. *Capital and Class*, 2, 119–27.

Management and Personnel Office (1982) *Equal Opportunities for Women in the Civil Service*. London, HMSO.

Manton, J. (1965) *Elizabeth Garrett Anderson*. London, Methuen.

Mark-Lawson, J. (1987) 'Women welfare and urban politics: comparative analysis of Luton Nelson 1917–1939'. Unpublished PhD thesis, University of Lancaster.

Mark-Lawson, J., Savage, M. and Warde, A. (1985) 'Gender and local politics: struggles over welfare policies, 1918–1939', in L. Murgatroyd *et al.*, *Localities, Class and Gender*. London, Pion.

Mark-Lawson, J. and Witz, A. (1988) 'From family labour to family wage? The case of women's labour in 19th century coalmining'. *Social History*, 13, 2.

Martin, J. and Roberts, C. (1984) *Women and Employment – Lifetime Perspective: Report of the 1980 DE/OPCS Women and Employment Survey*. London, HMSO.

Martin, S. (1981) 'Sexual harassment in the workplace: from occupational hazard to sex discrimination'. Paper delivered to the Law and Society Annual Meeting, Amherst, Mass.

Matthaei, J. A. (1982) *An Economic History of Women in America: Women's Work, the Sexual Division of Labour, and the Development of Capitalism*. Brighton, Harvester.

McDonough, R. and Harrison, R. (1978) 'Patriarchy and relations of production', in A. Kuhn and A. M. Wolpe (eds.), *Feminism and Materialism*. London, Routledge.

McGraw, Judith A. (1982) 'Women and the history of American technology'. *Signs*, Summer.

McIntosh, A. (1980) 'Women at work: a survey of employers'. *Employment Gazette*, 88, 1142–9.

Middleton, C. (1979) 'The sexual division of labour in feudal England'. *New Left Review*, 113–14, January–April. 147–68.

Miles, R. and Phizacklea, A. (1984) *White Man's Country*. London, Pluto.

Milkman, R. (ed.) (1985) *Women, Work and Protest: A Century of US Women's Labour History*. Boston, Routledge.

Milkman, R. (1987) *Gender at Work: The Dynamics of Job Segregation by Sex during World War II*. Chicago, University of Illinois Press.

Mincer, J. (1962) 'Labor force participation of married women: a study of labour supply', in National Bureau of Economic Research, *Aspects of Labor Economics*. Princeton, NJ, Princeton University Press.

Mincer, J. (1966) 'Labor force participation and unemployment: a review of recent evidence' in R. A. Gordon and M. Gordon (eds.), *Prosperity and Unemployment*. New York, Wiley.

Mitter, S. (1986) 'Industrial restructuring and manufacturing homework: immigrant women in the UK clothing industry'. *Capital and Class*, 27, Winter, 37–80.

Murphy, R. (1984) 'The structure of closure: a critique and development of the theories of Weber, Collins and Parkin'. *British Journal of Sociology*, 35, 547–67.

Murphy, R. (1986) 'Weberian closure theory: a contribution to the ongoing assessment'. *British Journal of Sociology*, 37, 21–41.

Myrdal, A. and Klein, V. (1970) *Women's Two Roles: Home and Work*. London, Routledge.

National Economic Development Office (1986) *Changing Working Patterns*. London, NEDO.

National Health Service Ancillary Whitley Council Trade Union Side (1986) *Claim for Improved Pay and Conditions of Service from 1 April 1986: Health Workers' Pay Time for Justice*. London.

National Institute of Economic and Social Research (1986) *Unemployment and Labour Market Policies*. Aldershot, Gower.

National and Local Government Officers' Association (1984) *How Equal Are Your Opportunities? Comparison of Local Improvements Won by NALGO*. London, NALGO.

Newnham, A. (1986) *Employment, Unemployment and Black People*. London, Runnymede Trust.

Nolan, P. (1983) 'The firm and labour market behaviour'. in G. S. Bain (ed.), *Industrial Relations*. Oxford, Blackwell.

Oppenheimer, V. K. (1969) *The Female Labour Force in the United States: Demographic and Economic Factors Governing its Growth and Changing Composition*. Berkeley, Calif., University of California Press.

Organisation for Economic Co-operation and Development (OECD) *Women and Employment: Policies for Equal Opportunities*. Paris, OECD.

OECD (1983) *Employment Outlook*. Paris, OECD.

Oschinsky, D. (1971) *Walter of Henley and Other Treatises on Estate Management and Accounting*. Oxford, Clarendon Press.

Pahl, R. (1984) *Divisions of Labour*. Oxford, Blackwell.

Pahl, R. (ed.) (1988) *On Work*. Oxford, Blackwell.

Parkin, F. (1974) 'Strategies of social closure in class formation', in F. Parkin (ed.), *The Social Analysis of Class Structures*. London, Tavistock.

Parkin, F. (1979) *Marxism and Class Theory: A Bourgeois Critique*. London, Tavistock.

Phillips, Anne and Taylor, Barbara (1980) 'Sex and skill: notes towards a feminist economics'. *Feminist Review*, 6, 79–88.

Phizacklea, A. (ed.) (1983a). *One Way Ticket: Migration and Female Labour*. London, Routledge.

Phizacklea, A. (1983b) 'In the front line', in Phizacklea, op. cit.

Phizacklea, A. (1988) 'Entrepreneurship, ethnicity and gender', in P. Bhacu and S. Westwood (eds.), *Enterprising Women*. London, Routledge.

Phizacklea, A. and Miles, R. (1987) 'Racism and British trade unions', in G. Lee and R. Loveridge (eds.), *The Manufacture of Disadvantage*. Milton Keynes, Open University Press.

Pinder, D. A. (1970) 'The Luton hat industry: aspects of the development of a localised trade'. Unpublished PhD thesis, University of Reading.

Polachek, S. (1976) 'Occupational segregation: an alternative hypothesis'. *Journal of Contemporary Business*, Winter, 1–12.

Polachek, S. (1981) 'Occupational self-selection: a human capital approach to sex differences in occupational structure'. *Review of Economics and Statistics*, February, 60–9.

Pollert, Anna (1981) *Girls, Wives, Factory Lives*. Basingstoke, Macmillan.

Postan, M. M. (1954) 'The famulus: the estate labourer in the twelfth and thirteenth centuries' *Economic History Review*, London, Supplements No. 2.

Purcell, K. (1979) 'Militancy and acquiescence among women workers', in S. Burman (ed.), *Fit Work for Women*. London, Croom Helm.

Randall, V. (1982) *Women and Politics*. London, Macmillan.

Read, S. (1982) *Sexual Harassment at Work*. Feltham, Hamlyn.

Reich, M., Gordon, D. M. and Edwards, R. C. (1973) 'A theory of labor market segmentation'. *American Economic Review*, 63, 2, 359–65.

Reskin, B. F. (1984) *Sex Segregation in the Workplace: Trends, Explanations, Remedies*. Washington, DC, National Research Council, National Academy Press.

Reskin, B. F. and Hartmann, H. I. (eds.) (1986) *Women's Work, Men's Work: Sex Segregation on the Job*. Washington, DC, National Research Council, National Academy Press.

Roberts, K., Dench, S. and Richardson, D. (1987) *The Changing Structure of Youth Labour Markets*. London, Department of Employment, Research Paper 59.

Roberts, M. (1979) 'Sickles and scythes'. *History Workshop Journal*, 7, Spring.

Roberts, M. (1985) 'Words they are women, and deeds they are men: images of work and gender in early modern England', in L. Charles and L. Duffin (eds.), *Women's Work in Pre-Industrial England*. London, Croom Helm.

Robinson, C. B. (ed.) (1857) *Rural Economy in Yorkshire in 1641*. Durham.

Robinson, O. (1979) 'Part-time employment in the European Community'. *International Labour Review*, Geneva, 118, 299–314.

Robinson, O. (1984) 'Part-time employment and industrial relations developments in the EEC'. *Industrial Relations Journal*, 15, 58–67.

Robinson, O. and Wallace, J. (1981) 'Relative pay and part-time employment in Great Britain', *Oxford Bulletin of Economics and Statistics*, 43, 149–71.

Robinson, O. and Wallace, J. (1983) 'Employment trends in the hotel and catering industry in Great Britain'. *Service Industries Journal*, 3, 260–79.

Robinson, O. and Wallace, J. (1984a) 'Earnings in the hotel and catering industry in Great Britain'. *Service Industries Journal*, 4, 143–60.

Robinson, O. and Wallace, J. (1984b) 'Growth and utilisation of part-time labour in Great Britain'. *Employment Gazette*, 391–7.

Robinson, O. and Wallace, J. (1984c) *Part-Time Employment and Sex Discrimination Legislation in Great Britain*. London, Department of Employment, Research Paper 43.

Rogers, J. E. T. (1986) *A History of Agriculture and Prices, 1259–1400*, Vols. I and II. oxford, Clarendon.

Rogers, J. E. T. (1984) *Six Centuries of Work and Wages*. London, Swann Sonnenschein.

Rothschild, Joan (ed.) (1983) *Machina ex Dea: Feminist Perspectives on Technology*. New York, Pergamon.

Rowbotham, S. (1982) 'The trouble with "patriarchy" ', in M. Evans (ed.),*The Woman Question*. London, Fontana.

Rubery, Jill (1980) 'Structured labour markets, worker organisation and low pay' in Amsden op. cit.

Rubery, J. and Tarling, R. (1982) 'Women in the recession'. *Socialist Economic Review*. London, Merlin Press.

Russell, D. E. H. (1973) *The Politics of Rape*. New York, Stein & Day.

Russell, D. E. H. (1982) *Rape in Marriage*. New York, Macmillan.

Russell, D. E. H. (1984) *Sexual Exploitation*. Beverly Hills, Calif., Sage.

Russell, J. C. (1948) *British Medieval Population*. Albuquerque, N. Mex. University of New Mexico Press.

Sacks, Michael Paul (1976) *Women's Work in Soviet Russia: Continuity in the Midst of Change*. New York, Praeger.

Sargent, L. (ed.) (1981) *Women and Revolution: The Unhappy Marriage of Marxism and Feminism*. London, Pluto.

Savage, M. (1985) 'Capitalist and patriarchal relations at work: Preston cotton weaving, 1890–1940',. in L. Murgatroyd *et al., Localities, Class and Gender*. London, Pion.

Savage, M. (1987) *The Dynamics of Working-Class Politics: The Labour Movement in Preston, 1890–1940*. Cambridge, Cambridge University Press.

Schur, E. (1984) *Labelling Women Deviant*. New York, Random House.

Scott, R. J. (1973) 'Women in the Stuart economy'. Unpublished M.Phil thesis, London University.

Seccombe, Wally (1986) 'Patriarchy stabilised: the construction of the male breadwinner wage norm in nineteenth century Britain' *Social History*, Vol. II, no. 1, Jan 1986, pp 53–76.

Seddon, V. (1983) 'Keeping women in their place', *Marxism Today*, July, 20–2.

Sedley, A. and Benn, M. (1982) *Sexual Harassment at Work*. London, National Council for Civil Liberties, Rights for Women Unit.

Select Committee on Midwives Registration (1892) vol XIV.

Shoer, K. (1987) 'Part-time employment: Britain and West Germany'. *Cambridge Journal of Economics*, ii, 83–94

Siltanen, J. and Stanworth, M. (eds.) (1984) *Women and the Public Sphere: A Critique of Sociology and Politics*. London, Hutchinson.

Silverman, Dierdre (1976–7) 'Sexual harassment: working women's dilemma'. *Quest*, vol. III, no 3, 15–24.

Sinclair, Elaine (n.d.) *Retraining Women Operators to Fill Technical Skill Shortages*. Sheffield, Manpower Services Commission.

Skold, Karen Beck (1980) 'The job he left behind: American women in the shipyards during World War II' in Berkin and Lovett, op. cit.

Smiles, Samuel (1968)[1862]) *Lives of the Engineers*, Vol. 1. Newton Abbot, David & Charles.

Smithyman, S. D. (1978) 'The undetected Rapist'. Unpublished doctoral dissertation, Claremont Graduate School, California.

Snell, K. D. M. (1985) *Annals of the Labouring Poor*. Cambridge, Cambridge University Press.

Stanko, E. A. (1985) *Intimate Intrusion*. London, Routledge.

Stanko, E. A. (1987) 'Typical violence, normal precaution: men, women, and interpersonal violence in England, Wales, Scotland and the USA', in J. Hanmer and M. Maynard (eds.), *Women, Violence and Social Control*. London, Macmillan.

Stansfeld, J. (1877) 'Medical women'. *Nineteenth Century*, 1, 888–901.

Stewart, A., Prandy, K. and Blackburn, R. M. (1980) *Social Stratification and Occupations*. London, Macmillan.

Stone, L. (1977) *The Family, Sex and Marriage in England, 1500–1800*. London, Weidenfeld.

Tawney, R. H. (1912) *The Agrarian Problem in the Sixteenth Century*, London, Longmans.

Technical and Supervisory Section of the Amalgamated Union of Engineering

Workers (n.d.) *Women's Rights and What We Are Doing to Get Them: A Trade Union in Action*. London, TASS.

Thorne, I. (1915) *Sketch of the Foundation and Development of the London School of Medicine for Women*. London, Women's Printing Society.

Trade Union Congress (TUC) (1955) *Women in the Trade Union Movement*. London, TUC.

TUC (1977) *The Under-Fives: Report of the TUC Working Party*. London, TUC.

TUC (1982) *Equal Opportunities. Positive Action Plan*. London, TUC.

TUC (1984) *Equality for Women within Trade Unions*. London, TUC.

TUC (1985a) Statement on 'Homeworking'.

TUC (1985b) *TUC Policies and the Family: Discussion Document*. March. London, TUC.

TUC (1985c) *Women into Science and Engineering*. Circular No. 103, December. London, TUC.

TUC (1987a) *Report of the 57th TUC Women's Conference*. March. London, TUC.

TUC (1987b) *General Council Statement – Part-Time Workers*. London, TUC.

Trade Union Research Unit (1986) *Women and Trade Unions: Trade Unions and Women*. Oxford, Ruskin College, Technical Note No. 100.

Trade Union Research Unit (1987) *Equality: Keeping the Pressure On*. Oxford, Ruskin College, Discussion Paper No. 37.

Treiman, D. J. (1979) *Job Evaluation: An Analytical Review*. Interim Report to the Equal Employment Opportunity Commission. National Academy of Sciences, Washington, DC, National Academy Press.

Treiman, D. J. and Hartmann, H. I. (eds.) (1981) *Women, Work and Wages: Equal Pay for Jobs of Equal Value*. Committee on Occupational Classification and Analysis, Assembly of Behavioural and Social Sciences, National Research Council. Washington, DC, National Academy Press.

Waddington, I. (1984) *The Medical Profession in the Industrial Revolution*. Dublin, Gill & Macmillan.

Walby, S. (1983) 'Patriarchal structures: the case of unemployment', in Garmarnikow *et al.*, op. cit.

Walby, S. (1986) *Patriarchy at Work: Patriarchal and Capitalist Relations in Employment*. Cambridge, Polity.

Walby, S. (1988) 'Flexibility and the changing sexual division of labour', in S. Wood (ed.), *The Degradation of Work?*. London, Hutchinson.

Ward, R. and Reeves, F. (1984) 'West Indian business in Britain' in R. Ward and R. Jenkins (eds) *Ethnic Communities in Business*. Cambridge, Cambridge Univerity Press.

Weir, A. and McIntosh, M. (1982) 'Towards a wages strategy for women', *Feminist Review*, 10, 5–20.

West Midlands Low Pay Unit (1984) *Below the Minimum*. Birmingham, Low Pay Unit.

Westwood, Sallie (1984) *All Day, Every Day*, London, Pluto.

Widom, C. and Maxfield, M. (1984) 'Sex roles and the victimisation of women: evidence from the British crime survey'. Paper presented to the American Society of Criminology Annual Meeting.

Willis, Paul (1977) *Learning to Labour*. Aldershot, Saxon House.

WING (Women Immigration and Nationality Group) (1985) *World's Apart*. London, Pluto.

Wise, S. and Stanley, L. (1987) *Georgie Porgie: Sexual Harassment in Everyday Life*. London, Pandora.

Wolverhampton Homeworkers Research Project (1984) *Report* (compiled by Kamlesh Rai and Kulvinder Dhew). Wolverhampton, Trades Council.

Young, I. (1981) 'Beyond the unhappy marriage: a critique of the dual systems theory', in Sargent op. cit.

Index